30119 028 587 23 8

WAC
9/19

Tom Bi  rse at University College Cork, Ireland. He spent a lot of time running round castles as a child, moved to Norway for a year in pursuit of the Vikings, and hasn't looked back since. He is the author of *Reading the Runes* (Routledge, 2017), and editor of *Translating Early Medieval Poetry* (Boydell, 2017) and *Reimagining the Vikings* (MIP, forthcoming) and runs the *World-Tree* teaching archive. He teaches courses on Norse myth, medieval literature and Old English language at UCC and occasionally takes time out to sail with the crew of a reconstructed Viking ship.

D1081506

THE
NORSE
MYTHS

STORIES OF THE NORSE GODS
AND HEROES VIVIDLY RETOLD

DR TOM BIRKETT

Quercus

First published in Great Britain in 2018 by Quercus
This paperback edition published in 2019 by

Quercus Editions Ltd
Carmelite House
50 Victoria Embankment
London EC4Y 0DZ

An Hachette UK company

Copyright © 2018 Tom Birkett

The moral right of Dr Tom Birkett to
be identified as the author of this work has been
asserted in accordance with the Copyright,
Designs and Patents Act, 1988.

All rights reserved. No part of this publication
may be reproduced or transmitted in any form
or by any means, electronic or mechanical,
including photocopy, recording, or any
information storage and retrieval system,
without permission in writing from the publisher.

A CIP catalogue record for this book is available
from the British Library

PB ISBN 978 1 78648 881 7
Ebook ISBN 978 1 78648 880 0

Every effort has been made to contact copyright holders.
However, the publishers will be glad to rectify in future
editions any inadvertent omissions brought to their attention.

Quercus Editions Ltd hereby exclude all liability to the extent
permitted by law for any errors or omissions in this book and for any loss,
damage or expense (whether direct or indirect) suffered by a
third party relying on any information contained in this book.

10 9 8 7 6 5 4 3 2 1

Typeset by Jouve (UK), Milton Keynes

Printed and bound in Great Britain by Clays Ltd, Elcograf S.p.A.

Papers used by Quercus are from well-managed forests and other responsible sources.

For Deb, Rob and Emily

LONDON BOROUGH OF SUTTON LIBRARY SERVICE (WAL)	
30119 028 587 23 8	
Askews & Holts	Sep-2019
293.13	

Contents

Introduction

This book is a retelling of one of the most extraordinary bodies of stories to survive from anywhere in the medieval world: a rich mythology that gave us Thor and one-eyed Odin, passionate Freyja and the battle-hungry valkyries, frost-giants, metalworking dwarves and mysterious elves; the looming presence of Ragnarok. It is largely thanks to the precocious literary culture of medieval Iceland that the Norse myths were recorded, and it is fortunate that so much material has come down to us, not only dealing with the Norse gods and goddesses, but also the legendary heroes and the Norse explorers who followed in their footsteps. Some of these sources take the form of poetry – at times allusive and strange, and assuming that the reader already knows the stories well – but there are also prose sagas dealing with the legendary past, and the comprehensive medieval 'guide-book' to the Norse gods written by the Icelander Snorri Sturluson, as well as supporting evidence in artwork, inscriptions and artefacts from the Viking Age. This is what has remained of a living, breathing world of stories that were passed on orally and shared in many different forms – through poetry, stories, performances and rituals that probably ranged from the elaborate to the banal and everyday. One of the hallmarks of a living mythology is the fact that its stories change and adapt, and even amongst the written sources from medieval Iceland the same myths are remembered and presented in quite different ways.

Retelling such a comprehensive collection of stories – complex, colourful and contradictory as they are – has been both a pleasure and a daunting task. It has been a great pleasure to revisit some of the myths that I first read as a child, and to look at them again as stories rather than as texts to study; it has been daunting to cover so much ground and to make some of the less accessible myths work for the page. The task is made more, not less, daunting by the many forms in which the Norse myths have been reworked before, from early translations of Eddic poems (which if anything made them stranger than the originals) to recent blockbuster versions of the myths like Marvel's *Thor* (which makes it hard to picture the Norse god without a six-pack and a cape). What this retelling aims to do is to present the myths in a coherent form, in language that doesn't make them too aloof or take away their dignity, and in a way that takes account of some of the vast amount of scholarship on Norse literature and culture. The version of the Norse myths and legends that follows is not a direct translation of any one source, nor is it a work of fiction based loosely on the myths: I've aimed to bring together, rather than embellish, what we know.

Norse myth is in one way easy to define: it is stories dealing with the Norse gods and goddesses. But the gods also feature in the accounts of heroes like Sigurd Dragon-Killer and Ragnar Shaggy-Pants, and abridged versions of these legendary narratives have also been included. This retelling also includes stories of historical figures from the Viking Age, some of whom worshipped the Norse gods or traced their descent back to Odin and Freyr. The explorations of the Norse sea and river travellers – who took their ships west as far as North America and east to the Caliphate – have been included partly to give a human context for the world of Norse belief, but also because they are, in the end, just great stories. Some of these tales of human endeavour, like Leif Erikson's discovery of Vinland, have become legends in themselves.

The version of the myths presented by the medieval Icelander Snorri Sturluson provides the material for most of the extended narratives about the gods, but Snorri doesn't cover everything – he doesn't record the myth of Odin's sacrifice, for example, and glosses over Freyr's dealings with a giantess. Snorri also wrote extensively about the early Scandinavian kings who also fall under the scope of this retelling, but it is necessary to turn to different sources (both from Iceland and elsewhere) to learn about other legendary heroes, as well as about the Norse exploration of the North Atlantic and the Viking adventures in the east. I've drawn on Eddic and Skaldic poetry, on legendary sagas, and on some more historical accounts when dealing with colourful figures from the Viking Age. It's impossible not to take a few liberties with the sources, but then again no source that's come down to us marks the beginning of the story, there's no one 'authentic' version, and myths are meant to be retold.

The book ends with a brief discussion of the survival of the sources for Norse myth and the many ways in which it has been used and reinterpreted in art, literature, politics and popular culture. That's one part of the story which is still being told, and in many ways it's as fascinating as the Norse myths themselves. There are suggestions for further reading at the end: both the sources themselves and some introductions to scholarship on this rich world.

It has been hard to know what to include, and what to leave for further exploration. But at least it is easy to know where to begin: with the creation myth, and the beginning of all things.

1

The Creation of the World

It was early in time when Ymir settled: there was neither sand, nor sea, nor cooling waves. Earth was not to be found, nor the skies above. The gap was yawning; there was no grass anywhere. ('The Prophecy of the Seeress', 3)

Ginnungagap

The gap was yawning.

There was nothing there, but there was a lot of nothing and it was waiting. How long had the gap been there? There was no way of knowing. Time didn't pass, because there was no way to mark it passing. There was no sun. There was no moon. There were no stars, no earth or sky or sea or sand, and there was no up and no down. The name of this place was Ginnungagap: and nothing and everything was there.

Rivers begin to run. They flow from somewhere else, from the icy realm of Niflheim, and they emerge in the darkness at the spring called Hvergelmir which is where all rivers come from. The spring is full of serpents which writhe and churn, and their poison mixes with the water to form the eleven rivers known as Elivagar. As these rivers drain into Ginnungagap, ice congeals on the water, and before long (or after forever – there's no way of counting) the void is frozen over. A poisonous drizzle hisses through the air and as it settles it turns to frost. Frost fills the emptiness.

Niflheim is as cold as coldness itself, but there's another place beyond the void called Muspelheim and it is as hot as fire. Sparks from Muspelheim warm the edge of Ginnungagap and as the ice melts a warm mist drifts towards the centre of the void. Where the ice and fire meet it is as temperate as a windless day in spring.

Life begins to rouse itself from the melt-water and the venom and the mists. The name of the first being is Ymir, and it is both man and woman and the ancestor of all giants in the world. The first couple, a giant and giantess, squeeze themselves out of Ymir's sweaty armpit as the great being sleeps. Then, both the giant's legs come together and in the sweat between them they spawn a son. This is how the long line of frost-giants begins.

Ymir would find it hard to survive in that misty nothingness, if it wasn't for Audhumla the cow and her milk. Audhumla has no grass to eat, but she licks the salt from the frost of Ginnungagap and that is how she keeps herself alive.

There's more.

Audhumla likes to lick one patch of frost in particular. She runs her tongue patiently across the rime and eventually a patch of hair appears. The next day a head emerges from the ground. And on the third day Audhumla licks the body of a man free from the frost. This beautiful man is named Buri. He is the first god. Buri has a son called Bor. Bor marries Bestla, the daughter of a giant called Bolthorn, and this will be the first of many marriages between gods and giant-women. Bor and Bestla have three boys together: their names are Odin and Vili and Ve, and they will make the world.

The Killing of Ymir

Odin and his brothers needed building materials. There wasn't much in Ginnungagap except for the mists and the rime-covered rocks, so the three brothers murdered the giant Ymir, broke its body into pieces, and used the giant's flesh and bones to make the world. Ymir bled so much that all of Ginnungagap was flooded, and all the giants drowned, except for Ymir's grandson Bergelmir and his wife, who rode out the deluge floating in a trough. The gods didn't let Ymir's blood go to waste: they used it to enclose the world with a great ocean, which is so huge that most people think that it is impossible to cross. Even after surrounding the world with water, they still had a few drops left over to fill the lakes and pools on land, and some of them are very deep indeed.

The gods made the earth with its hills and valleys from Ymir's flesh. They raised steep cliffs and mountains from its bones, and they used the giant's broken teeth to fill the sea-shores and the mountain passes with stones and grit. Odin and his brothers also found maggots twitching blindly in Ymir's corpse. The gods gave these creatures consciousness and wisdom and the love for crafting precious things and they became the dwarves. Dwarves still live in the rocks and under the mountains of the earth, deep in Ymir's flesh. Next, the gods lifted Ymir's skull into Ginnungagap to form the great dome of the sky. To hold up the skull, the gods set a dwarf at each corner: these four dwarves are named North, South, East and West, and they keep the sky from falling down.

At this time the heavens were empty – the sun did not know

where she had a hall; the stars did not know where their place was; the moon did not know his potential. But the gods set everything in order: they fetched sparks from the burning realm of Muspelheim and threw them high into Ginnungagap to create the stars. They fixed the planets' course and set the position of the sun and the moon in the sky. To measure out the years they appointed a new moon and called in the tides, and they gave names to night-time and her children, calling them morning and midday, afternoon and evening. From then on it was possible to tell the time of day and the passing of the seasons and the years.

The gods wasted nothing in their creation of the world – they threw Ymir's brains up into the sky to form the billowing clouds; they used the giant's bristling hair to make the trees, and they even put the eyelashes to use as a great wall to mark out and protect the world. This enclosure they called Midgard: our Middle Earth. It was a beautiful world they had created, from such a violent start.

The Creation of Night and Day

The surviving giants were banished outside Midgard to the mountains and the iron forests on the shores of the encircling sea. One descendant of Ymir made his home in the mountains, and his name was Narfi. He had a daughter called 'Night', who was dark like most of her family. She was married three times to three very different husbands. The first husband was called Naglfargi, and they had a son together who was named 'Prosperity'. Her second marriage was to Annar, and they had a daughter called 'Earth', who is sometimes called the 'Sister of Prosperity'. Night's third and final marriage was to Delling, the Shining One, and this was a far superior match for Night, as

Delling was not a giant but a descendant of the gods. Their son was a beautiful child, truly eye-catching and clearly belonging to his father's family: his parents called him 'Day'.

Little of this escaped Odin. Before the boy was fully grown, Odin came and abducted Night and Day from their home and gave them each a horse and a chariot to ride through the sky. The giantess Night rides ahead pulled by a horse called 'Frost Mane', and the foam from the horse's bit falls to earth each morning and is called the dew. Everyone has seen it, sprinkled on the grass in the early morning before the sun has warmed the fields. Day follows his mother on a chariot pulled by 'Shining Mane', and the brightness of the horse lights up the whole sky and the earth below. Mother and son follow each other on an endless journey through the heavens: always travelling at the same speed, under the careful eye of Odin.

The Golden Age

Midgard was made, the gods and giants had their appointed realms, and trees and grass carpeted the land of Ymir's flesh. Now that the world was protected from the giants, the gods turned their energies to the creation of the finer things in life. First they built great wooden temples high up above the plains. Next they timbered halls for shelter, and they set up workshops so that smiths could fashion tools and work precious metals into precious things. There was no limit to the gold found at that time across the world, and the gods furnished their halls with golden tables laid with golden plates and bowls. The forges rang with the bright sound of hammers, and the forests resounded with the tick-tock of axes felling trees. The gods met regularly on the plains of Idavoll to share in the wealth, pass laws and judgements, and to allot bright dwellings to the shining gods. But they weren't always busy with building and smithing and making precious things. They also had time to sit back and enjoy what they had created, to play a game of *tafl* in the meadows with beautiful golden gaming pieces. This was the Golden Age enjoyed by all the gods.

So there were days of leisure in that first age of the world, before the giant-women came. But there were still no people to enjoy the land or to share in the new wealth. One day, Odin and his brothers were walking along the seashore, and they came across two pieces of driftwood – one of ash and one of vine. The logs looked oddly like a man and woman. The brothers dragged the driftwood up the shore and puzzled over their lifelike appearance: were these crude likenesses the work of dwarves, who love to craft and to carve? The brothers decided that these curious lumps of wood should be given life: Odin approached first, and gave them breath; Vili gave them consciousness and the ability to move; and Ve gave them their complexions, their speech, their hearing and their sight. The three gods then offered the humans clothing to protect their living skin against the sun and the salt spray blowing off the sea, and they named the man Ask and the woman Embla. They were given a home in Midgard within the protecting wall, and from them all people are descended: right up to this day. The poets still call women 'bright birches of gold' and the men 'apple-trees of battle': humankind began as driftwood and men and women have a close affinity with trees. These things are not forgotten.

Two of the descendants of Ask and Embla were put to work by the gods early in the days of the world: Mundilfæri was a man who was blessed with two exceptionally beautiful children: a boy the proud father named Mani; and a radiant daughter he named

Sol. The gods were angered by the father's arrogance in naming his children after the real sun and moon, so they stole the beautiful brother and sister away and set them in the heavens to drive the horses that pull their namesakes through the sky. Sol is in charge of the chariot of the sun, and Mani is in charge of the chariot of the moon. The horses that pull the sun are called Arvak, who is awake early, and Alsvin, who rides very quickly across the sky, and they have runes engraved on their ears and their hooves. The sun's rays are as hot as a furnace, and to travel so close to it would be extremely uncomfortable, if it weren't for the bellows the gods fastened to the horses' shoulders – these bellows are called 'Iron-Cold', and they keep the horses cool. Odin also sent two children up to join the chariot of the moon: their names are Bil and Hjuki, and they had just been to collect water from a well when Odin caught up with them and snatched them away. They are still carrying the pole and bucket behind them as Mani rides his chariot across the night sky, and you may catch sight of them on the surface of the moon as it passes by.

Sol would love to stop once in a while to rest her horses, but every day, she races at full pelt across the sky, as if in fear for her life. And she has good reason to be afraid, because the loud wolf Skoll is running at her heels, and one day he will catch her, but it is not the time to speak of this. Another wolf called Hati runs in front of the sun and tries to catch the moon. This will also happen. Hati also goes by the name of 'Moon-Hound' and he will spray the heavens with blood from fallen men and swallow the moon in the violent days when the sun loses its brightness and the winds howl across the world. But it is too early in the years to tell this tale: the world is freshly made, and Ragnarok is just a rumour in the distance. Like thunder rolling in the mountains of far-off Jotunheim.

2

The Nine Worlds

I recall nine worlds, nine ogresses, the celebrated tree of fate beneath the ground. ('The Prophecy of the Seeress', 2)

At the centre of creation is Midgard. This is the world where humans live beneath the dripping boughs of Yggdrasil. But Midgard is not the only world. Some say there are nine in total, and they are home to gods and giants, elves and dwarves, the living and the dead.

Asgard

Towering above Midgard is the stronghold of the Æsir: it is known as Asgard. It is a rich land and many of its sanctuaries are made of gold and nothing else. Odin has his high seat, Hlidskjalf, in Asgard, and from this vantage point he can see out over all nine worlds. Asgard is protected by a great wall: the gods planned for it to make their home impregnable, but it is still unfinished. A rainbow bridge called Bifrost runs down from Asgard to the world of men. It can be crossed by the gods, but the red band in the rainbow is made of fire that would burn any human bold enough to cross it. The rainbow bridge will break at the end of the world, when the giants use it to storm the stronghold of the gods.

Valhalla

There are many fine halls in Asgard, from the shining Glitnir to the marshy home of Fensalir, but Valhalla is the most renowned as it is home to Odin and his troop of hand-picked warriors known as the Einherjar. This vast hall stands in the middle of the eternal plains of Idavoll: its rafters are made from spears and it is thatched with polished shields which catch the morning light. An eagle soars high above Valhalla, a grove of trees with red-gold leaves grows in the yard, and a great stag stands on the roof dripping water from its antlers which feeds the rivers in the worlds below. The hall has five hundred and forty doors and out of each door eight hundred warriors will rush to war at the end of the world. But there is only one way into Valhalla for the Einherjar: they must pass through the Slaughter-Gate, escorted from the field of battle by women who ride to earth whenever there is rumour of war. These goddesses of battle-fire and opened veins are better known as valkyries. They determine who dies when swords are drawn and who's allowed to live. Odin claims half of those who die heroic deaths to join him in Valhalla: the goddess Freyja claims the other half, and the valkyries bring these warriors to her own hall at Folkvang. Only warriors who have died heroically will find a place amongst the Einherjar, as the gods want companions who will not flee when Heimdall blows his horn and the skies darken at the approach of Ragnarok.

Every day the sun rises through the sky, chased by the swift wolf Skoll, and every day the Einherjar challenge each other to sword-play in the plains outside Valhalla, preparing for their final battle with the giants. They fight fiercely and many are cut down, but they always pick themselves up and return to Valhalla for their evening meal. A goat called Heidrun stands above the hall and mead pours from its udders into a great cauldron. The warriors are thirsty, but there is always enough mead for everyone to drink their fill after the fighting.

The valkyries who choose the warriors from amongst the dead also serve them at the tables in Valhalla and pass the full horn from one hero to another. For meat the Einherjar have a giant boar that is cooked and eaten in the evening. After its bones are picked bare it is revived like the fallen warriors, to be butchered on the following day. The Einherjar will spend their time fighting and feasting and building their strength until the Gjallarhorn is blown and Odin calls on them to march to war.

Vanaheim

The other tribe of gods, the Vanir, come from the realm called Vanaheim. Vanaheim is even harder for humankind to reach than Asgard and only the gods are certain of the way. The old god Njord was raised in Vanaheim and his children Freyr and Freyja are the most famous members of the Vanir tribe: they have power over the fields and the fertility of all creatures in the world, and they are greatly valued by the other gods. But the gods of Asgard and Vanaheim were not always on such good terms.

In the early days of the world, a woman came to Asgard from the Vanir tribe. Her name was Gold-Veig, and she was a prophetess. At that time the Æsir had a great desire for gold: they took

Gold-Veig and stabbed her with spears, and then threw her into the smelting fires of Asgard. But Gold-Veig emerged from the forge unharmed. Three times the Æsir tried to burn her, and three times she stepped out of the flames without a blemish. The gods had no choice but to let her go. She became famous across Midgard for her prophecies and for her great skills of enchantment. She was called the 'Bright One' by those women of the household who valued her witchcraft and made her offerings. Meanwhile, news reached Vanaheim of Gold-Veig's treatment by the Æsir, and the Vanir were not pleased.

The Æsir called an assembly to decide what to do about the threats coming from the Vanir tribe. The gods of Asgard could offer compensation, and share the tribute provided by humankind with the gods from Vanaheim, but this would mean giving up their control of sacrifice and worship in the world below. So they decided instead to take their weapons and march to war. Odin threw his spear over the advancing Æsir to seal the victory. But like Gold-Veig, the Vanir were surrounded by powerful enchantments and were impossible to kill. Neither side could gain the upper hand in the fighting and the only thing the war succeeded in doing was laying waste to Vanaheim and reducing the walls of Asgard to rubble. The two tribes would have to come to terms.

As part of the agreement, the Æsir agreed to share tribute with the Vanir gods and to exchange hostages to ensure that there would be no back-tracking on their vows. The gods sealed their pact by spitting in a jar and creating a spittle-man to remind them of the promises they'd made. Since that time there have been Vanir living in Asgard and worshipped alongside the Æsir.

Jotunheim

All the untamed regions of the world outside the protection of
Midgard are known as Utgard – the outer space – and it is here
that the giants have their realm of Jotunheim. It is a wild land of
mountains and dark forests, at the mercy of the elements and
the chaos of the unbound world. A river called Ifing separates
the land of giants from the realm of the gods. The river flows
quickly, and it is very hard to cross: if it were ever to freeze over,
the giants would soon be at the gates of Asgard and their assault
would make the war between the Æsir and the Vanir seem like a
game of *knattleikr* played with sticks and balls. Even though
Jotunheim is a dangerous and wild place, it is the source of many
things that the gods value most: the land of the giants is full of
precious objects, and the inhabitants of Jotunheim remember
what happened at the very beginning of the world. More precious still to the gods are the women of Jotunheim: a giantess
gives birth to powerful children. This is a one-way exchange:
very few giants in Jotunheim can claim to have married a goddess, though several have tried.

Jotunheim is also home to Mimir's Well, which takes its name
from the wise being, Mimir, who came to drink from its waters
every morning using the great Gjallarhorn as a cup. Mimir's
Well is a place where sacred knowledge can be obtained, though
always for a price. Odin went there once and exchanged one of
his eyes for a drink from the well: Mimir was not willing to
accept anything less. From then on, Odin was known as the
one-eyed god, but he also gained great wisdom, and considers it
a fair exchange. Some say that his eye is still floating in Mimir's
Well, and that he sees what other gods cannot.

The encircling sea borders Jotunheim, and it stretches off to

the horizon and much further still. A huge creature called Jormungand lives in the depths of this encircling sea, and it has
grown so large that it has wrapped itself around the world and
bites on its own tail. The serpent encloses Midgard in its coils,
and when it moves it makes the oceans churn and causes waves
to crash against the land.

The Worlds of Elves and Dwarves

Alfheim is the dwelling place of the bright elves, and it is located
high in the heavens where the light is clearest. The elves who live
in this wide, blue realm are more beautiful than the sun to look
at. It is said that the gods gave Alfheim to the infant Freyr as a
gift when he grew his first tooth. In contrast to the brightness of
Alfheim, Svartalfheim is a realm deep under the ground where
dwarves and dark elves live amongst the roots of the World-
Tree. Unlike their shining kin in the heavens, these creatures are
as pale as the rocks that they inhabit. It is here in their under-
ground realm that they work metal and precious stones, and
make objects that the gods are always keen to get their hands on.

Niflheim and Muspelheim

The oldest of the realms are Niflheim and Muspelheim: they
were present at the beginning and they will endure through the
upheaval at the end of the world. Niflheim is a land of mists and
ice that lies to the north; a cold, dark place and the source of all
rivers. Muspelheim is very different: it is a land of fire and sear-
ing heat, and it provided the gods with the sparks to make the
sun and stars. The heat of Muspelheim was needed to melt the
ice in Ginnungagap and to set all life in motion, but it is a hostile

land that will also play a role in the destruction of the world. Muspelheim is ruled over by the giant Surt, who carries a flaming sword, and the fire-giants that he leads will storm the stronghold of the gods at Ragnarok and burn everything in their path. In the blackened caverns and broken valleys of the world it is possible to look into Surt's realm and even to feel the heat that rises from Muspelheim. A great lava cave in Iceland is named Surtshellir and the land around its mouth is charred and broken.

Hel

Hel is the realm of death, and it lies far below the land of the living, accessed through valleys so deep and dark that it is impossible to see a thing. In this subterranean world, the monstrous woman known as Hel rules over the deceased: some say that her dominion over death gives her power over all nine worlds. She shares her name with the realm she oversees, and she claims the largest portion of the dead to share her boundless hall. Hel is populated by those who die of illness, accidents and creeping age. All of them are given lodgings by the goddess of death, and there will always be room in this vast realm for more. The road to Hel leads across the noisy river Gjoll to a single, soaring gate. The path is guarded by a blood-stained dog chained in Gnipa Cavern, and the way is littered with the shallow graves of trolls. Very few people pass that way out of choice. Odin and Hermod are two of the gods to have returned from a journey to Hel, both of them riding on the eight-legged Sleipnir, a horse who can pass between the lands of the living and the dead. Hel's miserable hall is called Eljudnir, the 'Rain-Lashed Place', and at its entrance is a stumbling block where many unsuspecting people fall. Her dish is called 'Hunger' and her knife 'Famine', her servants 'Lazy' and 'Idle', and her chamber is a sick-bed hung with drapes that glisten like feverish skin. Another hall in Hel is named 'Corpse Shore', and it lies far from the light of the sun with its only door pointing north. Serpent spines are used for wattle, and venom drips in from the leaking roof. Here oath-breakers and murderers and those who deceive a trusted wife are sent to wade across rivers full of knives as a wolf rips at their limbs. It is not a pleasant place.

The World-Tree and the Sacred Wells

The nine worlds could not exist without Yggdrasil, the World-Tree, growing at their centre and anchoring all things in place. Yggdrasil is an ash tree, but older, and larger, than any other. Like all trees, its branches reach up into the heavens and its roots run deep into the ground: in this way it connects the realms of gods and giants, humans and dwarves. One of its roots marks the way to Jotunheim and the home of the giants, and Mimir's Well lies at its tip. Another root runs all the way to the cold lands of Niflheim and hangs over the waters of Hvergelmir, the first spring in the world. The third of the World-Tree's supporting roots extends into Asgard, and it is here that the gods gather around the Well of Fate to make laws and pass judgements. These three wells sustain the tree as it rises high above Midgard and dew falls into the valleys from its leaves.

The World-Tree has the advantage that it never loses its leaves in winter, but it also suffers more than most trees do. Four stags run around its canopy eating the lushest of the leaves; the goat Heidrun stands on the roof of Valhalla and picks at its lower branches; and serpents gnaw at the tree's roots in the darkness. The dragon Nidhog is the most feared of the many creatures that live under the protection of that mighty tree. It rips at corpses beneath the roots of Yggdrasil and when it uncurls itself and flies up from the dark hills of Niflheim it is a bad sign for humankind.

At the very top of Yggdrasil sits an eagle with a wide view of the world, and it has knowledge of many things. A hawk named 'Wind-Weathered' perches between the eagle's eyes. The squirrel Ratatosk runs up and down the tree, taking messages between the eagle in the highest branches and the dragon Nidhog in the darkness below its roots. Nobody knows exactly what these creatures say to each other, but Ratatosk is very keen on gossip and takes pleasure in provoking both the eagle and the dragon. Finally, two white swans live at the Well of Fate and drink from its milky waters: they are the ancestors of all swans in the world.

There is little the gods can do about the creatures who wear away at the World-Tree, but every day three women of destiny – the norns – take water from the Well of Fate and mix it with white clay, and they use this mixture to coat Yggdrasil's roots to protect it from decay. Without their care the tree would be in a much worse state, though it is already rotting on one side. These powerful women are named Destiny, Becoming, and Upcoming, and their days are busy: because as well as tending to the World-Tree, they are responsible for weaving out the life-span of every person on this earth. They have a beautiful hall close to the Well of Fate, and their work will only come to an end when the great tree shivers and the world sinks back into the abyss.

3

Gods and Goddesses

Health to the Æsir! Health to the Asynjur! Health to this plentiful earth! ('The Lay of Sigrdrifa', 2)

Odin and his brothers Vili and Ve were the first of the gods, born to the giants Bor and Bestla, and Odin is father to many of the Æsir. He is married to the goddess Frigg and their sons are the beautiful Baldr, admired across the worlds, and the blind god Hod who is tricked into killing his brother. Odin also fathers children outside his marriage to Frigg: Thor is known to be the son of Odin and the earth-goddess Jord, who some say is really a giant and the source of Thor's great strength. Odin also forced a child on a princess named Rind, after it was prophesied that her son would avenge the death of Baldr. Rind was not impressed with Odin's advances, so the god resorted to enchantments and tricked his way into her bed. The child that Rind gave birth to was named Vali: he played his role and took revenge for Baldr's death at only one day old, but Odin himself was exiled for crossing a line that the other gods won't cross. Other members of the Æsir are rumoured to be fathered by Odin, and several royal dynasties count Odin as their ancestor. The youngest generation of gods include Vidar – whose role is to avenge Odin's death – as well as Modi and Magni, sons of Thor. They only play a minor role in the stories of the gods, but they will return after Ragnarok and make sure that the legacy of the older gods is not forgotten.

The other major family of gods are the Vanir. Njord, the old god of the sea and its gifts, is the father of the famous children Freyja and her brother Freyr. Incest was common amongst the Vanir, and the mother of Freyja and Freyr is rumoured to be Njord's sister. Both father and son take wives from Jotunheim and many of the gods have mothers from the giant tribe. The giants often try, and fail, to marry or abduct goddesses and to weave the power of the Asynjur into their own family. It is unusual for gods to be fathered by giants, though both Loki and Tyr are exceptions to this rule. Other gods have an even stranger lineage: Heimdall is said to be the son of nine sisters known elsewhere as the waves, and the divine being Kvasir was made from the spit of the Æsir and the Vanir mixed together in a bowl. The gods are flawed like humans and they are hard to tell apart from men and women by their looks, but in other ways they're quite distinct from us.

Odin

An old man walks into a settlement wearing a wide-brimmed hat and a dirty cloak, and leaning heavily on a spear. He is led to the hall and approaches the high seat, greeting the giant who sits there: 'Wise Vafthrudnir, I have heard that you consider yourself to know more than most people, and I wanted to see for myself whether the rumours are true. But I'm thirsty – how about a drink before I test your wits?' The giant peers into the gloom of the hall, trying to get a better look at the old man standing in the shadows. 'You've some boldness for a beggar!' he exclaims, 'and I've a mind to teach you a lesson before I have you killed. We'll have a game of riddles, and then you'll see how wise I really am.' The giant calls for ale. 'Ask me anything, and I'll answer it. If you can pose a riddle that gets the better of the mighty Vafthrudnir, you might just leave here with your neck. You'd better hope you're smarter than you look!' The old man raises his head and strokes his beard. The firelight glints off his one bright eye and catches the hint of a smile. Outside a raven calls and is answered by another.

Odin is the oldest and foremost of the gods. With his brothers Vili and Ve he created the world from the body of the giant Ymir and breathed life into the first humans. He lives in the most splendid of the many halls of Asgard surrounded by his hand-picked warriors, and though he is honoured by nobles and war-makers, poets and priests, Odin does not parade around the nine worlds in rich clothes and fine company. He walks the roads of Midgard as a solitary traveller dressed in travelling clothes, and he goes by countless different names – the Wayfarer, Blind Guest, Greybeard, Sage; even those who recognise Odin call him the All-Father. In this disguise he is very hard to tell apart from any other visitor seeking shelter from the rain. But what Odin is really looking for is knowledge. It is what drives him to the hidden corners of the world, to the hovels of those gifted in foresight and to the halls of the wisest kings. There may be beings in the nine worlds wiser than Odin and with longer memories, but no one is quite as relentless in their desire to understand the world. Odin is obsessed with what will happen and how he can best prepare himself. He always wants to know.

Through his endless search for knowledge, Odin has learned spells and enchantments that are hidden from humankind. He knows how to dull blades, quench fires and calm restless seas; he knows how to make a woman fall madly in love with him; and he knows how to raise a person from the dead so they can speak with him again. When the Vanir tribe sent the severed head of Mimir back to Asgard, Odin knew how to preserve the head with herbs and spells so that his wise friend could continue to offer him advice. Odin will go to consult the head one final time before Ragnarok, but the knowledge of what is to come will not help Odin or any of the gods to avoid their fate.

As well as knowing a great deal about the distant past and the future of the world, Odin is also able to look out from his high seat Hlidskjalf and see the lives of all people as they are unfolding. Two ravens called Hugin (Thought) and Mugin (Mind) sit beside him, and every day they fly out over the world and return with news. There is very little that passes the All-Father by. Odin rides the eight-legged Sleipnir, the best of all horses, and he is often accompanied by two wolves which he feeds with his own hand at his table in Valhalla. Other possessions prized by Odin and sacred to mankind are the ring Draupnir – the Dripper – which produces eight new rings of equal weight in gold every ninth night, and the rune-engraved spear Gungnir, which Odin threw to start the first war in the world. A spear thrown over an advancing army dedicates the ones who fall to Odin.

Odin knows that knowledge often comes at a heavy price. He walks around with one good eye: he dropped the other one in Mimir's Well in exchange for wisdom. And that wasn't the only sacrifice that Odin made. To learn the art of writing he hung himself for nine nights on a branch of Yggdrasil, exposed to the wind and rain and pierced with a spear. There's no one higher than Odin, so he offered the sacrifice to himself. He didn't take a single sip of water or a bite of food during his ordeal, and though he cried out with the pain of it there was no one there to hear. After the nine nights were up, Odin's suffering was rewarded and he dragged knowledge of the runes into the world. Writing is a skill that has never been forgotten and Odin has been known as Father of the Gallows ever since.

Odin's urge to understand has led him to break all kinds of taboos. He was once accused of practising a forbidden kind of witchcraft, beating on a skin drum in woman's clothes, and Loki also said that he was hungry for what lies between men's thighs. Odin does what needs to be done to learn more about the world: he thinks nothing of deception and often changes his mind or fails to honour a promise of victory; he doesn't treat his lovers well. Sometimes his actions make the other gods uncomfortable, and when, in his grief at the death of Baldr, Odin used powerful spells to rape the woman Rind and father an avenger, they banished him from Asgard for a time. Odin is the first to admit that he can't be trusted, but sometimes he's the one who gets caught out. He once arranged a date with the daughter of Billing, only to find a dog chained in her bed and armed warriors waiting to ambush him. He didn't see that coming, for all his knowledge of the future. Lust can make the wisest of the gods behave like fools.

The Mead of Poetry

The most famous of Odin's deceptions is also the story of the origin of poetry.

It was early in the cycle of the world, shortly after the short but destructive war between the Æsir and Vanir had ended in a stalemate. To seal their truce the gods from both tribes spat into a vat, and to keep this sign of their oath at the forefront of their minds the gods turned their spit into a man named Kvasir. This spittle-man was so wise that there was not a question he couldn't answer, and he travelled round the world spreading his divine knowledge far and wide. But for a man of such wisdom he had far too much trust in other people, and when he was invited to stay by two dwarf brothers named Fjalar and Galar, he didn't realise that they wished to take his knowledge for themselves. The dwarves asked to speak with Kvasir in private, and when they were alone they killed the wise being and drained his blood into three large vats. They added honey to the blood and from this mixture they brewed a special kind of mead which turns whoever drinks it into a poet or scholar. Odin realised Kvasir was missing, of course – but the dwarves had already got their story straight when the gods came calling: the wise being had suffocated on his own knowledge because there was no one in the world able to ask him enough questions.

Fjalar and Galar did not end their deception with the killing of Kvasir: they also took a guest of theirs – a giant called Gilling – rowing near their home, and when the boat hit some rocks near an island it tipped the giant overboard and drowned him. 'What has happened to my husband?' asked the wife of the giant when the dwarves returned to shore. 'He drowned,' replied Fjalar; 'Try not to make a fuss when there's nothing we can do to bring him back.' The giantess cried loudly at this news, and Fjalar put his fingers in his ears, but Galar dropped a mill-stone from the roof onto her head. When the son of the giants – a huge fellow named Suttung – heard about this, he came in a fury to the brothers' home. He took the dwarves out to the spot where his father had drowned and tied them to a rock where they would be covered at high tide. 'Please!' begged the dwarves: 'If you spare us, we'll give you compensation that will make you the envy of the gods! The mead of poetry will be yours – every little drop!' In this way, the dwarves saved their necks and the mead of poetry passed to the giant known as Suttung.

Odin learned about the existence of the mead at the same time that he found out that the giants had claimed it for themselves. But he also heard that Suttung had hidden the precious mead deep inside his mountain home, under the watch of his daughter Gunnlod – and this set the father of the gods to thinking. Odin told his plans to no one, but left one day to visit the home of Baugi, Suttung's brother, where nine slaves were busy cutting hay. He came in disguise and offered to sharpen the slaves' scythes for them; and after he did, they cut more cleanly than they ever had before. 'Who wants to buy this whetstone?' Odin asked the slaves, who were leaning on their scythes in the middle of the meadow taking a well-earned rest. 'I'll sell it for a very reasonable price.' The slaves all wanted to buy the whetstone, and Odin weighed it in his hand as they jostled for attention. Then he threw it up high into the air and walked away. The slaves ran with their scythes to catch it, but in the confusion they ended up slitting each other's throats.

Baugi now had no slaves to bring in the hay, and he was not in the best of moods. Odin stayed with him that night and made him a deal: he would do the work of the nine slaves, and in return all he asked was a sip of Suttung's mead. Baugi couldn't guarantee anything, as the mead was his brother's property, but he did agree to take this stranger to Suttung and to plead his case. Odin stayed on the farm for the summer, collecting the hay and doing the work of nine men as he'd promised.

When winter arrived, the farmhand claimed his wages: an

introduction to Suttung in his mountain home. It was a long journey to the great stone hall, and when they arrived Suttung refused outright to grant this stranger a sip of mead, however much he'd helped his brother. Baugi wasn't in the mood to press Suttung any further: 'Fair's fair, I've brought you here and it turned out as I thought.' But Odin had one more trick to try: he pulled a drill-bit from his cloak. 'The least you can do is help me drill into the mountain where the mead is kept: we'll get a sip without your brother knowing and no harm will be done. I'm not leaving empty-handed.'

Baugi reluctantly agreed and set to work. When he told Odin he had drilled through the mountainside, Odin blew into the hole and the dust flew back into his face. He put his hand on Baugi's shoulder, and said, 'I think you need to drill some more.' The giant carried on drilling and muttering beneath his breath, and this time, when Odin blew into the drill-hole, the dust blew out the other side and he knew that they had bored right through the mountain to Gunnlod's room. Odin quickly changed himself into a snake and slid into the hole; and Baugi wasn't quick enough to strike him with the drill.

Gunnlod had been locked away with the mead for some time and she was keen for company. Odin quickly seduced her with promises of marriage and status. He came to the giantess's bed three nights in a row, and each time Odin slept with Gunnlod and whispered sweet nothings in her ear she granted him a precious sip of mead. With the first sip the god drained the first vat of mead, and on the second night he drained another. On the third night, Odin drained the final vat and shook the last drips into his mouth. He turned to Gunnlod, who was lying there looking up at him with trusting eyes. This was too easy! He swallowed hard to keep the mead from rising up his throat, turned himself into an eagle and flew out of Gunnlod's mountain home as fast as he was able, which wasn't very fast at all: it's not easy to fly after downing three whole vats of mead. Suttung saw the bloated bird flying overhead and he suspected he was being robbed. 'Gunnlod!' he roared as he turned himself into a huge eagle. 'I'll deal with you when I get back!' Suttung gave a mighty beat of his wings and leapt into the sky.

The gods had climbed the walls of Asgard and were watching the pursuit. They were urging Odin on – it seemed like he would make it but he looked like he was ready to burst. Three huge vats were dragged underneath his flight path, and as the god flew over he vomited the mead straight into these huge containers. The giant Suttung had to break off his chase when they reached Asgard, but he came so close to catching Odin as they raced towards the home of the gods that the All-Father panicked and blew some of the mead out of his arse in the direction of Midgard. This mead is known as the 'bad poets' share'. It is there for anyone to claim, and there is plenty of it to go around. The sweeter mead that the gods collected in the cauldrons was shared out in Asgard and passed to the best poets in the world of men. When skalds make verse they fill themselves with the spittle and blood and sweetness of Kvasir and the gods, and bring forth honeyed words. This is perhaps the greatest gift of Odin to mankind, and it is why he is honoured by poets most of all. But there's little honour owed to him in Gunnlod's hall.

Frigg

Frigg is Odin's wife in Asgard, and the daughter of the forgotten god Fjorgynn. Frigg can see the fates of all the gods, and she is the most revered of all the Asynjur: Friday honours Frigg's name in English, and it is a name that's still on everybody's tongue. Frigg keeps her own bright halls in the marshland home of Fensalir, and she is associated with fens and pools and bogs. She is attended by four goddesses in Fensalir who carry out her business. Lofn has the power to arrange marriages between men and women in awkward situations; Hlin helps to protect people favoured by Frigg and to give them refuge; Fulla is a virgin goddess who keeps her long hair tied up with a golden band, and she is Frigg's handmaiden, carrying her casket and shoes. Gna is the final servant to be counted, and she is Frigg's envoy, riding the horse Hoof-Thrower through the skies and carrying messages to the farthest-flung regions of the world.

Like her husband, Frigg sometimes gets involved with the inhabitants of Midgard, but she is not afraid to take a different side when she and Odin intervene in the lives of humans. Once, the two young sons of a king named Hraudung got swept out to sea whilst fishing in the shallows. Frigg and Odin guided them to safety and adopted them, disguised as poor farmers. One of the boys – Geirrod – was championed by Odin, and the other – Agnar – was fostered by Frigg. Odin persuaded Geirrod to push his brother back out to sea in their fishing boat and claim the kingdom for himself, and Odin later taunted Frigg for the different fortunes of their adopted sons. Frigg was not impressed: 'I hear Geirrod has grown up to be a stingy fellow, rude to his guests and mean with his hospitality.' Odin wagered that this was a lie, and to prove it he set out to visit Geirrod's hall himself, dressed in his usual disguise. But Frigg's servant Fulla got there first and warned the king that a dangerous sorcerer was doing the rounds: they'd know him by the fact that dogs would be afraid to bark when he approached. When Odin entered the hall, the guard-dogs cowered in the corner, so Geirrod ordered the hooded man to be seized and tortured over a fire until he revealed who he was. In this way, Geirrod signed his own death-warrant: Odin was roasted for eight nights before he finally relented and revealed his name, at which point he forgot his championing of Geirrod and caused the king to fall on his own sword. No doubt Frigg watched all this from Odin's high seat Hlidskjalf with her laughter ringing across the heavens. The story of Geirrod serves as a reminder that the All-Father doesn't always get his way.

Frigg may seem powerless to stop Odin's many affairs, but there are different rules amongst the gods and Frigg has her own history. In the early years of the Æsir it is said that Frigg was a wife to both of Odin's brothers – Vili and the older Ve – whilst her husband was away. At least, that's what Loki claims. Fidelity is certainly not a strong suit of the gods, but Frigg's loyalty to her son Baldr is absolute. She goes to extreme lengths to protect the shining god from harm, and to even greater lengths to try to get him back from Hel when he's killed by Loki's schemes. Frigg usually succeeds in getting what she wants, even when her desires are contrary to Odin's, but in this case all her efforts will be in vain. Even the most powerful and protecting of the god-desses cannot stand up to fate: it always has the final word.

Thor

Thor, the red-bearded son of Odin, is the protector of gods and the homes of humankind; and his hammer-blows ring like thunder through the heavens. Thor is the one god always ready to do battle with the giants, even though his mother Jord was rumoured to be a giantess herself. Thor thinks nothing of cross-ing the wide rivers and mountains that border Jotunheim on foot, and he regularly leaves his home Bilskirnir (Lightning-Flash) in Asgard and journeys deep into giant-land to pick a fight with the strongest of its inhabitants. He needs to keep the giant population in check. He is helped in his battles by his hammer Mjolnir, a weapon which only he can wield and which is capable of flattening mountains and crushing the thickest of giant skulls. When Thor throws Mjolnir at his enemies the hammer always finds its way back to his hands. Its only defect is its curiously short handle, though it doesn't feel undersized when Thor strikes. To help him wield such a powerful weapon, Thor owns a pair of iron gloves and a belt that increases his already prodigious strength. He rides in a chariot pulled by two goats that have a very special attribute: they can be eaten every night, and as long as their bones are not damaged, Thor can use his hammer to bring the animals back to life.

One of the goats is limping slightly, and this is because Thor once offered to share its meat with a family of poor farmers who had let him stay for the night. One of the farmer's hungry children, not knowing when he'd get a taste of meat again, broke a leg bone to get at the marrow, and the goat has been lame ever since. Thor was raging when he realised what had happened and he claimed the farmer's children as compensation. Thjalfi and Roskva – brother and sister – became his loyal servants and they often accompany the strongest of the gods on his adventures.

Thor always prefers action to conversation and he's not the brightest tool in the smithy. His father Odin sometimes makes fun of his son's short fuse: he once pretended to be a ferryman and insulted Thor across the water. 'Who's that beggar wearing no shoes and a soiled shirt? Are you the god of slaves?' taunted Odin. Thor was fit to explode with anger, not knowing who it was who spoke to him this way – this ferryman who slandered his mother and called his wife unfaithful. Odin was careful to keep just out of reach.

It is not uncommon to hear of Thor breaking the heads of a whole family of giants – wives and daughters, in-laws and aunties – in a fit of rage. But whilst Thor is not known for his diplomacy or guile, it is often his brute force that keeps the peace. As Loki says of Thor: 'Faced with you alone, I'll walk away, since you do strike.' It is easy to make fun of Thor's tendency to strike first and think later, but without the god's great strength, the worlds of gods and humans would be a lot harder to defend.

Thor Loses His Hammer

Thor lost his hammer once and it almost caused the ruin of the gods. It was stolen by a powerful giant named Thrym, who hid it eight miles under the earth and demanded the goddess Freyja as a bride in exchange for its return. When Loki returned to Asgard with this news, Thor was hopping mad, but without his hammer he was powerless to do anything against this strongman of the giants. Thrym was undoubtedly a tough opponent even for Thor: he styled himself as the lord of ogres, and he kept a herd of gold-horned bulls in his fields, and a pack of bitches with golden collars at his side to show the world how hard he was. Freyja simply snorted with derision when it was suggested that she give herself up to this hoodlum in exchange for Thor's hammer, so the gods had to come up with a more cunning plan.

'Why not', said Heimdall, 'dress Thor in Freyja's bridal veil and hang keys around his waist? He'll get close enough to Thrym to kiss or thump him, whichever he prefers.' Thor turned a deep shade of red, and his fingers itched for his hammer, but there was little to be done as no one had a better plan.

Loki volunteered to be Thor's handmaiden. The role was right up Loki's street, and he wore his new clothes with a twinkle in his eye. But the gods had a much harder time dressing Thor: even with a heavy veil concealing his face, the hulking son of Odin hardly made a convincing bride, and Loki knew he'd have his work cut out trying to pass off this bristling figure as Freyja. When Thor angrily devoured a whole ox and eight salmon at the wedding feast and washed them down with three casks of mead, the quick-thinking Loki told Thrym that his bride had been starving herself in anticipation of the wedding. 'It's rare', said Thrym, 'to see such hunger in a woman, but I know that all her appetites are soon to be fulfilled.' Later in the meal, when Thrym bent toward Thor to steal a kiss and jumped back at the sight of two fierce eyes glaring at him from under the veil, Loki stepped in again. 'Mistress Freyja has been so excited for the wedding that she hasn't slept for eight nights. A man so good with the ladies should know what tiredness and lust does to the eyes.' Thrym was so caught up with the idea that he'd soon have Freyja as a wife that he recovered his composure, but he didn't try to kiss the bride again. Eventually, as the gods had hoped, Thor's hammer was brought in to the feast to consecrate the wedding, and as soon as Thor felt its cold weight in his lap he exploded from his seat and brained the groom where he stood, before turning and battering all the giants present at the ceremony. He even bashed Thrym's elderly sister for daring to ask for a bridal gift, giving her a hammer-blow instead of the precious rings she was expecting. So Thor won his hammer back, and whilst some might laugh to think of the great red-bearded god decked out in a wedding dress, it is hard to imagine the giants laughing much about that night.

Sif

Thor's wife is the goddess Sif, and it is proper to introduce her in connection with her husband as her name means 'relation', and reminds the gods of the bond of marriage. After Freyja, Sif is the goddess whom the giants desire the most: an unruly visitor from Jotunheim named Hrungnir boasted that he'd keep the two of them alive for his pleasure when he destroyed the other gods. Sif was once famous for her beautiful golden hair, and now she's famous for the golden threads worn in its place. Loki cut her hair whilst she was sleeping and Thor forced him to find a wig that grew like real hair to make up for this prank. It is one of the most ingenious objects ever crafted for the gods.

Though Sif claims that she has none of the flaws that the rest of the Æsir are afflicted with, there are rumours that she may have been a little too intimate with Loki: after all, he was able to get close enough to catch her sleeping and to cut her hair. Even Odin taunts his son with the knowledge that Sif takes a lover whilst Thor is away wielding his hammer in giant-land. Sif certainly had a husband before Thor: whilst Thrud is the daughter of Sif and the red-bearded god, Ull is Sif's son by another man. Little is known of Thrud, though Thor was not happy when she took off with a dwarf named Alviss whilst he was away from home: it took all her father's guile to break the match and turn the dwarf to stone. Thor also has children outside his marriage to Sif, including a son born to the giantess Jarnsaxa: he is called Magni, the strong one, and he is a fitting descendant of Thor. Magni proved his strength at three days old, lifting the limb of a fallen giant off his father's body – a feat that the other gods couldn't manage with all their collective strength.

Freyr

The gods would not be nearly as potent as they are without the reproductive powers of the Vanir, and especially the god of prosperity and plenty: Freyr. Freyr holds sway over the sunshine and the rain, and he helps the fertility of the earth and its inhabitants. Along with Odin and Thor, he is the most worshipped of the gods, and those who work the land are particularly keen to get on his good side. Freyr is prayed to for good harvests and for virility and health.

Freyr was given the gift of the bright realm of Alfheim when he grew his first tooth, and his most recognised possessions are Gullinbursti – the golden boar – and Skidbladnir – a majestic ship that can be carried in the pocket. He was once the owner of a shining sword that fought the giants on its own behalf, but he gave it away to his servant and ended up having to fight a giant called Beli with an antler instead. There will be much more serious consequences of this at Ragnarok, as Freyr will have to meet the fire-giant Surt without a weapon.

Freyr's Lust for Gerd

Freyr lost his sword for love, though the story's not nearly as romantic as it sounds. The god of the fields had taken to climbing up to Odin's high seat Hlidskjalf to spy on women in the worlds below; and one morning, as he scoured the home-fields of the giant known as Gymir, he spotted the most beautiful woman he'd ever seen. She was glowing with such good looks that sunbeams seemed to radiate from her forearms and light the space around her as she went about her chores. Freyr fell hopelessly in love with this giant's daughter, and spent his days lying in the meadow lost in thoughts of how it would feel to have those arms entwined around his neck. He didn't eat or sleep, and the rings around his eyes made him look like he was sick.

His father Njord and stepmother Skadi became concerned: they sent for Freyr's servant, a man of sunny disposition called Skirnir: 'Go and find out why my son's so pale', said Njord, 'and do whatever you can to bring about the cure'.

Skirnir had been Freyr's loyal servant since childhood, and he soon coaxed the truth out of his master. 'She may come from the giant race, but her arms look like the sun to me. I think I'll die if I don't have her: it's painful for a god to be denied in this way.' Skirnir knew the gods wouldn't be thrilled at a union between Freyr and a lowly giant-girl – and that he'd probably get the blame – but he offered to go to giant-land anyway and to talk to this girl on Freyr's behalf. 'I'll need your horse though, Freyr, and your sword as well, if I'm going to make it through the mountains and the walls of fire unscathed.'

The guard dogs began barking as soon as Skirnir drew close to Gymir's mountain home. Freyr's servant was preparing to be challenged by the old man himself, but it was the shining lady who came out to greet him: Gymir was away, and Gerd was mistress of the house. The keys dangled at her belt as she eyed the stranger up. The girl did not forget the courtesies. 'Greetings, stranger. I'll offer you a cup of ale, if you'll tell me quickly why you've come to my father's home, and with a sword that's hateful to the giants.' Skirnir wasted no time at all in getting down to business. He told Gerd that Freyr desired her companionship, and he offered three remarkable gifts as proof of his master's intentions. First, he revealed eleven golden apples, which have the power to grant eternal youth. But Gerd turned them down. 'I don't know how long my youth will last, but I'm not going to share a moment of it with Freyr,' was her reply. Next Skirnir offered another gift sacred to the gods: Odin's ring Dripper, which has the power to replicate itself. But Gerd turned this down too. 'I've enough gold here in my father's court, and the freedom to spend it as I want.' Finally, Skirnir grew impatient and unsheathed Freyr's inlaid sword: he offered her the gift of life itself, or death if she refused. But Gerd would not be bullied: 'I'd rather die than give in to Freyr's desires. Kill me if you must, and be prepared for my father's terrible revenge.'

Now Skirnir dropped all pretence at courtship. He pulled a switch of wood from his belt, and began to curse the giantess. 'See this, Gerd? It's a taming wand, and I *will* tame you with it. I promise you endless suffering, girl, subjection and humiliation if you turn my master down,' he said, carving runes into the wood. 'Your future without Freyr will look like this: I'll make you as barren as a dry thistle but leave you with an insatiable desire that is sure to drive you mad; you'll be raped by a deformed ogre with three heads, given nothing but goats' piss to drink, and be caged beneath the earth for all men to watch your suffering. How does that sound? You'll live like this in utter misery for as long as time itself.' Skirnir paused in his rune-carving. 'Do you want me to finish the curse, Gerd of the shining arms, or will you take my noble master as your husband? I can easily scratch these runes away, and with them the miserable future I'm about to seal for you.'

Faced with this threat, what could Gerd do but offer Skirnir the cup of mead and agree to his demands? In nine nights she promised to meet Freyr at the grove of Barri, and to become his wife. Freyr was happy at the news, though nine nights seemed an unbearably long time to wait. Did the god know what ugly threats Skirnir made on his behalf to force Gerd to consent?

Perhaps what's important is that Gerd of the shining arms takes her name from the fenced-in fields, and that her conquest by the god of sunshine and rain will make the land grow green. But can the gods' treatment of the giants be excused so easily? Freyr will be without his sword at Ragnarok, and perhaps the moral failings of the gods are what brings about their ultimate demise.

Freyja

Freyja is the most important of the Asynjur and one of the few whose exploits are as well-known as the gods'. Freyja is the daughter of an incestuous relationship between Njord and his sister (things were different then in Vanaheim), and she is the sister – and, perhaps, former lover – of the god Freyr. Like her brother, she has power over fertility and love, and she is said to have taught the Æsir the most taboo of magic arts. Freyja rides on a chariot pulled by two cats, and she owns a cloak made of falcon's feathers that allows her to fly at the head of the valkyries who serve her in her hall. Freyja is the most beautiful and desirable of all the goddesses, and she is the one to call on to intervene in love affairs, or when help is needed in the bedroom. Loki accuses her of getting into bed with all of the gods and elves at Ægir's feast – but then, she is the goddess of fertility, and Loki isn't one to talk. Though Freyja is mocked by a giantess for her many partners, her reproductive power is greatly desired by the inhabitants of Jotunheim, and giants often try to force her into marriage: but this is a line that Freyja will not cross, whatever liberties she takes at home.

Freyja may have had relations with many of the gods, but she misses her husband Od, the father of her two treasured daughters Hnoss and Gersemi. Od went on a journey and did not return, and Freyja searches across the nine worlds for some clues about where he ended up: in her wandering she goes by many different names, and few people realise that they are being visited by the most powerful of goddesses when she walks into their home. Freyja is so frustrated by her fruitless search that she cries tears of red gold for her missing husband. This bright gold and her string of lovers don't help much with the loneliness.

Freyja intervenes in war as well as in affairs of the heart, and it is another sign of her status that she chooses half of the warriors who die in battle to live in her majestic hall, known as 'The Place of Many Seats'. It is no less of an honour to be escorted to Freyja's realm of Folkvangr than it is to enter Valhalla. As a goddess of death as well as love, Freyja controls many aspects of people's lives, and she is often called upon to intercede in family affairs. She helps her loyal follower Ottar to learn about his noble lineage from a giantess, and even turns him into a boar so she can ride him to giant-land, and ride him back at home. She does this because she's pleased that he sets up stone altars to her and sacrifices oxen in her honour. Frejya also loves an erotic poem: and composing one is another way to find favour with this most passionate of goddesses and perhaps receive a visit from her.

The Brisingamen and the Eternal Battle

Freyja is the owner of the most famous of treasures: the Brisingamen. This gleaming necklace is said to have been crafted by four dwarves who were only willing to sell it if Freyja would spend a night with each of them in turn. Four nights later, Freyja left Svartalfheim with the precious jewel around her neck.

Now, Freyja was not one to hide her light from anyone, and

she paraded her new necklace around for all to see. Loki wondered how she'd come across such a rare and precious piece of jewellery, and he soon found out about the unusual contract she'd made with the dwarves. He went to Odin with the news: 'Steal it from her,' said Odin, 'that will be punishment enough.'

Loki did what few of us would think to do: he turned himself into a fly so that he could squeeze through a crack into her room. He bit Freyja on the neck so that she turned over in her sleep: then he promptly unclasped the Brisingamen and stole out with the heavy necklace hanging from his neck.

When Freyja awoke to find that the Brisingamen was missing she stormed up to Odin's hall. 'I know that you're behind this, Odin. Give the necklace back to me, if you value the peace that reigns in Asgard!' But Odin looked back at her with his one bright eye and knew exactly how to make her anger work to his advantage. 'I'll tell you where the necklace is hidden, Freyja, if you'll do something for me in return.' He stroked his beard. 'Find two heroes to fight a battle with each other that lasts until the end of time. Then we'll talk again.'

Odin knew that it was no small thing to cause a conflict that would last that long, but Freyja could draw on the powerful sorcery of the Vanir. She caused a king called Heidin to kidnap a princess named Hild and to take her away against her father Hogni's will. At the break of day, Hogni brought his war-band to the island of Hoy in Orkney where Heidin was waiting with his hand-picked men. Hild tried to get the men to come to terms and offered a gift to her father, but it was too late: Hogni had unsheathed his sword Dainsleif, which cannot be returned to its scabbard until it gets its taste of blood. The two armies fought a long and bloody battle, and by the evening the shadow of the high sea-cliffs fell on the bodies strewn across the heath.

Although Hild – whose name means 'battle' – was powerless to stop the bloodshed, Freyja taught her spells so that she was able to resurrect the dead and staunch their wounds; and by the morning all the men were healed. However, for them *every* morning is the morning of the battle, and they soon begin to fight again. In this way the battle of Hjadningavig is set to continue forever, or at least until the warriors are called away by Odin.

If Odin was satisfied that Freyja had fulfilled her side of the bargain, Loki was not so co-operative, and he refused to give the necklace up. Freyja had to send Heimdall as her champion to challenge Loki for the Brisingamen: rumour has it that they fought by the seashore in the shape of seals, and that they will pick up where they left off at Ragnarok. Freyja got her necklace back in the end: it must have been a splendid treasure to be worth the trouble that it caused.

Baldr and Hod

None of the gods – not even Loki – could find a bad word to say about Baldr the Good. In fact, Baldr, the second son of Odin and Frigg – is often called the shining god as he is so beautiful that he seems to glow. His skin is pale white, and his eyebrows so fair that the mayweed, the whitest of flowers, is named 'Baldr's lashes' in his honour. He also has the temperament to match his shining appearance: he is the most merciful of the gods, and he lives in Breidablik, the broad gleaming land where nothing impure can thrive. His only flaw, if it can be called a flaw, is that none of his judgements last for long, perhaps because he's simply too forgiving. He's married to the motherly goddess Nanna, and they have a son called Forseti. Though Baldr's life is blessed in being unremarkable, it is really only a prelude to his early death.

Baldr first had a premonition about his fate when he began to be troubled by dark dreams. Never one to dismiss a portent, his father Odin set off to Hel to find out whether something was amiss. The signs did not look good. When Odin entered Hel's domain, he saw tables strewn with arm-rings and an empty throne decked with gold, as if waiting for a visit from a noble guest. Mead was being prepared in great vats. A ferocious dog barked as he approached, and its chest was matted with fresh blood. Odin's worst fears were confirmed when he summoned up a prophetess from her grave outside the gates of Hel. 'Don't you know – the throne is waiting for Baldr,' she said, 'and the best of mead is being brewed for his arrival. If you want to know more, I'll tell you that your own son Hod will be his killer, and that revenge will come from another of your sons, yet to be born. Now let me sink back into my grave, and don't disturb me for such a little thing again!'

Fate had now been set in motion, and though the gods were powerless to change its course, they did what they could to protect Baldr the Good. Frigg sent emissaries around the nine worlds requiring everything – from the smallest stones to the greatest rushing rivers – to swear an oath not to harm her son in any way. The oath was so powerful that the gods made great fun out of standing Baldr at the centre of the hall and pelting him with anything they could lay their hands on: the stones and weapons all bounced harmlessly off Baldr's radiant body, as they'd sworn not to do him any harm. Loki couldn't stand the fact that this flawless god was being mollycoddled and protected in this way – what was so special about him, anyway? In the guise of a woman, he travelled to Frigg's hall in the fens and tricked her into admitting

that there was one small plant growing nearby that she hadn't
thought to ask for an oath: the mistletoe. It seemed so young and
harmless. The woman's eyes lit up like a serpent at this news.

Loki wasted no time in finding himself some mistletoe and
whittling it away until he had a slender spear. At the feast that
evening, the gods started their game of throwing the tableware
at Baldr, whilst his blind brother Hod sat listening to smashing
of cups and the laughter of the gods. Loki came and sat beside
him. 'I can tell you'd like to join in the fun, Hod.' He raised the
blind god from the bench and placed the spear in his hand.
'Here: throw this at your brother: I'll guide your arm.' The slender spear flew straight on its course, and Baldr didn't even try to
get out of its way. He stared in disbelief at the dart protruding
from his chest, and the blood blossoming across his pale skin.
He died in the heart of Asgard, in the one place where he should
have been safe from harm, and though Loki stood at his shoulder, it was Baldr's brother who struck the fatal blow. The gods
stood silent under the weight of their grief, and the light itself
seemed to fade across the plains of Idavoll.

The killing of Baldr was the greatest disaster to befall the
gods, and not only because the Æsir lost the most perfect member of their family: the tragedy is that Baldr didn't die fighting
his enemies, and the only revenge the gods can take is against
themselves. When Odin fathers another child to kill the blind
Hod and avenge the death of Baldr – a feat the infant accom-
plishes at just one day old – it is the All-Father who loses another
son: one who is as blameless as the first. What hope is there for
the gods when the laws of vengeance unravel at the seams, and
no action brings release? Odin knows better than anyone: with
the death of Baldr, Ragnarok comes one step closer and can no
longer be forestalled.

Baldr's Funeral

Baldr's funeral took place at the shores of Asgard, and was attended by all the most important gods. Even frost-giants and mountain-giants came in numbers to pay their respects to the blameless Baldr. The funeral procession was led by Freyr riding a chariot pulled by his golden boar. Odin and Frigg followed the god of the fields, escorted by the valkyries and by Odin's ravens; Heimdall joined the procession on a horse with a golden forelock; Freyja drove her harnessed cats. Thor alone travelled there on foot to consecrate the pyre of his younger brother. The gods wanted to lay Baldr to rest in the richly decorated ship Hringhorni – but it was so large that it could not be launched by any of the gods, so an ogress was fetched from Jotunheim. She arrived at the funeral riding a wolf with venomous snakes wound about its neck as reins, and the four battle-scarred warriors charged with restraining the wolf had such difficulty holding on to it that they had to kill the beast to keep it from ruining the proceedings. The ogress marched without ceremony to the grounded ship, grasped the prow, and launched it into the ocean with one heave, causing sparks to shoot from the rollers and the entire world to tremble. Thor was so upset at this that he wanted to smite the ogress there and then, but he was restrained by Odin – who was mindful of the fact that the gods had invited the troll to do this very job. Thor was still seething as he stepped forward to consecrate the funeral pyre, and when a dwarf called Lit got in his way, the god kicked the unfortunate creature into the ship to burn alongside Baldr.

There was more drama to come. Baldr's wife Nanna died from a broken heart on seeing her husband's body laid aboard the ship, and she was placed next to him amongst the flames. Odin added the ring Draupnir – the most precious of possessions – to the pyre, a fitting gift for the most radiant of gods. He whispered something into the ear of his dead son, but none of those present was close enough to hear, and no one will ever know what Odin said. The smoke from the pyre was swallowed by the clouds.

Baldr's body was cremated and sent to the land of the dead with all the splendour owed to a son of Odin, but his mother Frigg still had hope that Hel could be persuaded to release him from her realm. She sent an emissary, the messenger god Hermod, down to Hel, riding on Odin's horse Sleipnir. After travelling for nine nights and crossing the Gjoll bridge, Hermod arrived in Hel to find Baldr and Nanna already presiding over the honoured place prepared for them, and he was received by Hel herself. The goddess of death had some sympathy for the plight of the Æsir, and agreed that Baldr could return to the land of the living if – and only if – he was as universally loved as Hermod claimed. To prove it, all creatures across the world would have to mourn. Hermod returned from the halls of Hel with the ring Draupnir as a token for Odin and a linen garment for Frigg, and breathlessly relayed his message. Emissaries were sent to every corner of the nine worlds. It wasn't hard to persuade all life to shed a tear for the loss of such a perfect god, and even the coldest metal learned to weep for Baldr: this is why iron is often wet with condensation when it is brought into the warmth. But there was one creature who would not weep – an old giantess calling herself 'Thanks' sat skulking in her cave and insisted she would not mourn for any son. 'Let Hel keep what she has', was her cold reply. It is hard to imagine someone being this heartless – unless the old woman was Loki in disguise.

Loki

Loki is a slippery character, and all who deal with him need to have their wits about them. He's an outsider in the family of gods: against the usual way of things, his father is a cruel giant called Farbauti, whilst his mother is the goddess Laufey. It is a sign of the gods' suspicion of his father's line that Loki takes his mother's title and is known as Loki Laufeyson. The gods are right to hold Loki at arm's length. His eyes light up at the prospect of trouble, and like a maladjusted child he sometimes breaks things just to watch the fallout from his actions. But the trickster also feels bound to honour oaths he's made, and he's a quick-thinking foil to Thor in many of his adventures in giant-land, offering ingenious solutions to problems that leave the Æsir at a loss. He is married to the loyal Sigyn, and their sons go by the names Nari and Narfi: both of them are punished for their father's indiscretion and come to gruesome ends. Loki also took a lover amongst the giants and fathered three monstrous offspring who will end up being the great adversaries of the gods at Ragnarok. Perhaps more surprising is that Loki has given birth himself: most famously to the eight-legged Sleipnir, but also to a brood of ogresses which he conceived after eating a woman's half-cooked heart.

Loki is always changing his appearance, and he favours the forms of birds, fish and biting insects. He has been known to turn himself into a woman on more than one occasion, and he is as comfortable playing the role of a handmaiden as he is seducing goddesses with his handsome looks. He is both a thief and a provider of great wealth; a valued companion and a devious, backstabbing, murderous rogue. He is the sworn brother of Odin; yet he will also side with the forces that destroy the gods at Ragnarok. Loki disrupts the order of Asgard with his many personalities, and by doing so exposes the limits of the Æsir's flawed and fragile rule.

Loki Wins Treasures for the Gods

Many of Loki's early pranks are harmless, or end up benefitting the Æsir in some way. It is true that he cut off Sif's golden hair whilst she slept, but when Thor threatened to break every bone in his body, Loki more than made amends. Not only did the son of Laufey find dwarves to create a golden headpiece that would grow like normal hair, but he also persuaded these master crafts- men to make Odin's charmed spear Gungnir and Freyr's ship Skidbladnir. Gungnir had the property that every spear-thrust would find its mark, and Skidbladnir had an advantage over other ships: it could be folded up like cloth and carried in the pocket, and when its sail was unfurled it would always find a wind blowing from the right direction.

Loki didn't stop there, either. He wagered his head with a dwarf named Brokk that his brother – a master blacksmith by the name of Eitri – could not make three treasures as valuable as Sif's hair, Gungnir and the ship Skidbladnir. Brokk accepted on behalf of his brother, and was given the job of pumping the bel- lows of the forge whilst the blacksmith worked. First Eitri placed a pigskin in the forge, and Brokk pumped away at the bellows. Thinking to distract Brokk and win the wager, Loki turned himself into a fly and bit the dwarf's hand; but Brokk continued to pump the bellows, and out of the forge came a remarkable object: a boar with golden bristles that could race across the sky faster than a chariot and illuminate the way with its shining hide. Next, the blacksmith put gold into the forge, and Brokk pumped at the bellows again. This time Loki bit Brokk twice as hard on the neck, but the dwarf simply grimaced and continued working the bellows, and Eitri pulled the ring named Draupnir from the forge. Draupnir is more like a living thing than gold has any right to be: it drips eight gold rings of equal weight on each ninth night. Finally, the blacksmith placed iron into the forge, and warned Brokk that if he stopped working the bellows even for a moment, this most prized creation would be ruined. Loki once more turned himself into a fly and bit Brokk as hard as he could on the forehead, so that blood dripped into his eyes. This was more than the dwarf could bear and he took his hands off the bellows for an instant to swat the fly away. Eitri was making the famed hammer Mjolnir, and it is because the dwarf stopped blowing for an instant that the handle is so short.

When it came to deliver these three objects to the gods – the ring to Odin, the golden boar to Freyr, and the hammer to Thor – it was agreed that even with its defect, Mjolnir was the best of all possessions, as it would aid the gods most in their conflict with the giants. Brokk had won the wager, and now Loki had something of a problem – as he'd offered the dwarf his head in payment. 'How about taking my weight in gold instead?' Loki suggested, knowing that the dwarves love precious things. But Brokk refused: he wanted exactly what the trickster god had promised.

Loki asked for a moment to himself, and took the opportunity to jump out of the window and flee across the sky and the seas in his magic shoes. Just as Loki thought that he had slipped the noose, he heard a booming voice behind his ear: Thor's. 'Hello, Loki. How's the air up here? Let's get you home now to honour your agreement.' He nudged Loki in the back with his new hammer. 'But . . . but I returned Sif's hair,' Loki stammered, 'and you got that hammer in the bargain! How's this for gratitude? You gods are all the same!'

'A debt must be paid,' was all that Thor would say. He bundled Loki into his chariot and kept a firm grip on him until they reached the gates of Asgard. However, Loki had been thinking as he sped across the sky, and a mischievous glint came into his eye. He jumped out of the chariot and walked back into the hall with his head held high.

The dwarf was sitting whetting his knife on his belt, and he grinned when he saw Loki coming in. But there was something in the trickster's gait that quickly wiped the smile from Brokk's face. 'You are welcome to take my head as promised, Brokk, but there's one thing to bear in mind: I didn't offer you my neck. Take care you don't break the bargain, or the gods will have you killed.'

Brokk circled Loki with his knife in hand, but whichever way he looked at it, he couldn't work out how to cut off Loki's head without damaging his neck. The dwarf realised that he'd been duped and he was furious: before he left for Svartalfheim, Brokk took a strip of leather and with the help of his brother, Awl, punched holes in Loki's lips and sowed his clever mouth shut. This thong on Loki's mouth is called Vartari, and for all the good that Loki did in bringing the treasures back to Asgard, the gods may have wished that Brokk had pulled the thong tighter and sealed Loki's mouth for good.

Loki Insults the Gods

Nowhere is Loki's growing hostility towards the gods clearer than in his disruption of what should have been the happiest occasion: a feast attended by Æsir and elves in the shining sanctuary of Ægir. In this great hall the ale flowed of its own accord, and instead of firelight the sheer quantity of golden tableware was enough to illuminate the hall. Everyone present remarked on what a good job Ægir's servants were doing, and everyone was very happy with the way the feast was turning out: everyone, that is, except Loki, who killed one of the servants out of sheer spite. The gods were furious that Loki would disrespect their host in this way and ruin such a pleasant feast, and they drove him away to the woods with the threat of violence. But Loki wasn't done with his mischief, and walking in the cool air of the forest, he had plenty of time to recall all the worst things he'd heard about each of the gods. He walked back to the hall and found that the party had resumed: the ale was flowing, and the gods were taking turns to retell their great victories and slapping each other on the back. But they soon fell silent when they saw Loki watching from the doorway.

'I'm thirsty after my long walk – bring me a drink!' Loki demanded. He was greeted with silence. 'What, not a word from all you puffed-up gods? You've two choices, as I see it: force me to leave and violate this sacred place, or find me a seat at the table.'

Bragi was the first to respond, as spokesman of the gods: 'The Æsir have their standards to uphold, and we won't be pouring ale again for you in Ægir's hall. Go now and keep the peace, and recall that the gods were generous to you tonight in letting you leave on your two legs.' Loki feigned a hurt look, but his eyes were flashing with malice as he turned to the high seat. 'Odin – don't you remember that we are blood-brothers, and that we swore that each of us would never drink ale without the other? I thought you were a man to honour such a sacred bond.'

Odin stared into this cup with his one good eye. 'Fine – let him have a drink, before he unleashes his tongue on all of us.'

Nobody would pass the cup to Loki, so he helped himself, and stood on the table for a toast: 'Hail gods, hail goddesses, and all the most sacred powers . . .' He bowed to the room with mock sincerity. 'Hail all the sacred powers,' he continued, '. . . except for that one god, Bragi, who doesn't know how to give a welcome, and now sits trying to hide himself.'

Bragi gave the trickster a pleading look. 'Listen, Loki, I'll grant you a gift of a horse and arm-rings if you'll only sit down and not cause any more unpleasantness amongst the gods.'

'Horses and arm-rings!' sneered Loki. 'I'd be surprised if you had either to give away: of all the gods and elves gathered here, you're always the last to fight for gold, and the slowest to shoot your bow.'

'If we were outside this sanctuary, Loki, I'd kill you for that slander.'

'You're a mighty warrior when you're sitting down, Bragi, but you're nothing but a prancing poet when you stand: you'll leg it when you have to face a real man. Come and start something if you're upset!'

At this point Idun thought to intervene: 'Bragi – don't rise to his bait, and don't bring dishonour to your family by trading insults with Loki in this sanctuary.' But Loki had words for her too: 'Shut your mouth, Idun! Let me tell you now: of all the gods, you are craziest for sex. I know this, since you draped your perfumed arms around the killer of your brother.'

The gods all stared into their cups. They knew what he said was true, and that they were in no position to judge. And so it went on, with Loki insulting each of the gods in turn in the sanctuary of Ægir's hall: not afraid to break long-held silences or to make lasting enemies of those he once called friends. Gefjon and Frigg he accused of being unfaithful, Freyja of being a prostitute for all the gods, and of farting in surprise after she was caught in bed with her brother; Odin he called a lady-witch and a pervert; he mocked Njord for having giant-daughters piss in his mouth, and the goddess of the fields he called a shit-smeared serving girl: he's the real father to many children of the gods, or so he said. It is only when Thor came back from Jotunheim and threatened to smash Loki with his hammer in that sacred place that Laufey's son finally backed down. But Thor came late to the party, and the damage had already been done. Loki had said many things that could not be unsaid, and he had laid bare the failings of the gods for all to see. But worst of all, in his cruel words to Frigg he had revealed his role in the death of the innocent Baldr and this was a crime that the gods would not easily forgive.

The Binding of Loki

After Ægir's feast the gods found it hard to look each other in the eye, but they were all determined on one thing: Loki had to be punished. They hunted the trickster across the nine worlds and when they found his hideout by a waterfall in Jotunheim, Loki's luck finally ran out. The god had taken to bathing in the form of a salmon, out of fear that Odin would spot him from his high seat Hlidskjalf. So great was his paranoia that he spent his days inventing cunning tools that might be used to catch him. One day he wove a fishing net, and he was sitting in his hut staring at this new invention when he heard the gods approach. Loki threw the net in the fire and jumped into the water, but the criss-cross pattern in the ashes told the gods exactly what they needed to know. They built a net and dredged the mountain pool, and soon Loki was cornered. He tried to make a mighty leap upstream, but he wasn't quick enough for Thor, who caught the salmon by the tail in his vice-like grip. This is why the tail of this fish tapers and why the salmon always tries to leap upstream.

Once the gods had Loki in their power they exacted a terrible revenge. First they set three stone slabs upright in the floor of the cave and drilled holes in them. Then they turned Loki's son Narfi into a wolf and set him loose to savage his brother Nari. They tied Loki down by threading the guts of his disembowelled son through the holes in the stone: the guts turned to rigid iron bonds fastening themselves around Loki's shoulders, waist and legs. The goddess Skadi – remembering Loki's role in the killing of her father – found a snake to hang above his face and drip venom into his eyes and mouth. Loki's loyal wife Sigyn cannot set her husband free from the magic bonds that hold him, but she sits at his head holding a bowl to catch the venom. From time to time she has to take the bowl away to empty it, and when she does Loki writhes in pain so that the whole earth quakes. This is Loki's punishment, but he will escape at Ragnarok, and he will captain a ship that brings the sons of Muspell from the giant-lands to lay waste to the dwellings of the gods. And so, at the end of time, the great mischief-maker will get his revenge.

Tyr

Tyr is the god of glory in battle; the most courageous of the Æsir. His father may have been a giant, but the gods can be certain of Tyr's loyalty – unlike Loki's. He is most famous for sacrificing his right hand to help restrain the wolf Fenrir – a monster that the gods had reared, but who grew too large to handle. Tyr was the only one of the gods bold enough to approach the wolf to feed him, and he was the one god to step forward and place his hand into Fenrir's mouth when the gods attached a leash around the great wolf's legs. Of course, Tyr lost his hand when the wolf realised he'd been tricked. It says a lot about Tyr's loyalty that he was willing to sacrifice so much in order to protect the gods from harm: not only giving up his hand, but also his good word.

Tyr is often known as the one-handed god, or the leavings of the wolf, but this nickname is not meant as an insult. At Ragnarok, Tyr will pit himself against another wolf – the great Garm, chained in Gnipa Cave – and though he will lose his life, the battle will be fierce and one-handed Tyr will also cause the death of his opponent. It is only fitting that he should meet such a heroic end, and those warriors who show no fear in battle and stride out at the front of the war-band are said to have the courage of this god. There is a runic letter named after Tyr, and it was known to be good luck before a battle to consecrate a weapon to the god, or even to carve this rune onto the blade. Tuesday takes its name from Tyr, and it must have been a good day to pick a fight.

Heimdall

Heimdall is known as the watchman of the gods and the guardian of Asgard. He was born to nine sisters, daughters of the sea-giant Ægir, and raised on the edge of the world, where he was made strong by the rich earth and the ice-cold sea and a diet of boar's blood. Heimdall lives in the place called Himinbjorg, perched beneath the skies and overlooking Bifrost, the rainbow bridge that leads from Midgard to the home of the gods. Heimdall drinks fine mead in this solitary place and guards the road to Asgard. The boughs of the World-Tree run close to Himinbjorg, and the white mud that runs down Yggdrasil cakes Heimdall's back as he props himself up against the tree to keep his endless vigil. For this reason he's known as the whitest of the gods, but the most striking thing about this watchman is that his teeth are all made of shining gold.

Heimdall will never be caught napping on his watch: he is always alert and needs less sleep than a bird. He can see things that are a hundred miles distant, whether it is day or night, and his hearing is even better than his sight. It is said that he can hear the grass pushing up through the earth and the wool growing on a sheep's back. Anything louder than this Heimdall hears easily, and no one steps onto the rainbow bridge without his knowledge. Like Odin, Heimdall also made a sacrifice at Mimir's Well in order to gain these extraordinary gifts. Whereas Odin sacrificed an eye for inner wisdom, Heimdall left his ear in the well. Heimdall's most famous possession is the Gjallarhorn, which he will blow at the onset of Ragnarok to warn the gods that the giants are approaching. He owns a splendid horse named Golden-Forelock, and carries a sword called 'Man's Head'. Heimdall has a particular enmity with Loki, whom he accused of being drunk at Ægir's feast, and with whom he once fought over Freyja's necklace. This feud will last until Ragnarok, when the two gods are destined to fight one another in the final battle.

Heimdall and the Social Classes

Heimdall, like Odin, has many names. He is called Gold-Tooth, and Wind-Guard, and Loki's Foe, and on one adventure to the world of men he was known by the name Rig. Rig went to the seashore and followed green roads until he came to a hovel. The door was hanging open, so the god walked in. He found a fire in the hearth and a grey-haired couple huddled round it, dressed in cast-off clothes. They were called Great-Grandmother and Great-Grandfather, and they brought the god rough bread and boiled meat to eat. Rig spent three nights in that poor household, sleeping between the old couple in their flea-ridden bed and giving them advice. Nine months later, Great-Grandmother gave birth to an ugly child: she called him Slave. He carried wood, and grew up with a crooked back and rough hands. He took as a wife a girl with sunburned arms and muddy feet called Serving. Together they had many rough-looking children, and from them come the estate of slaves, who put manure on the fields, cut turf and look after the animals.

Rig travelled the roads again, and came to a hall. The door was not locked, so in he went and found a fire in the hearth and a couple working away next to it. The man had a well-groomed beard and a well-fitted shirt: he was working wood. The woman wore a woollen dress fastened by brooches and she sat spinning. They were called Grandmother and Grandfather, and they brought the god the best food they had to offer. Rig spent three nights in that household, sleeping between the couple on a clean bed and giving them advice. Nine months later, Grandmother gave birth to a boy with bright eyes: she called him Farmer. He ploughed fields and timbered barns, and grew up strong and rosy-cheeked. He took as a wife a girl with her own dowry and keys at her belt called Daughter-by-Marriage. Together they had many upstanding children, and from them come the estate of farmers, who tame animals and settle the land.

Rig went on his way once more, and came to a fine hall facing to the south. The door had a ring, and the god pushed it open. The floor was covered with fresh straw and a couple sat looking into each other's eyes and enjoying the leisure that they had. The well-dressed man was stringing a bow and shaping arrows for the hunt. The lady of the house wore rich clothes and a pendant lay on her bright chest: she sat admiring her beautiful arms and straightening her sleeves. They were called Mother and Father, and they brought the god roast meats and fine white bread to eat, and wine served in decorated cups on an embroidered tablecloth. Rig spent three nights in that fine household, sharing a high-sided bed with the couple and giving them advice. Nine months later, Mother gave birth to a boy with piercing eyes: she called him Lord and wrapped him in silk. He practised with a bow and took hounds to the hunt, and he grew up able to swim and to wield a sword. Rig came back to this son when he was of age, and taught him runes, and told him of his origins. He encouraged his son to claim land for himself, and Lord rode to neighbouring lands with a spear held high and brought war to the surrounding tribes. Lord ruled over eighteen settlements, and doled out rings and horses to his followers. A wife was brought to him by emissaries who had travelled from another land. She was wise and radiant with elegant hands and her name was Erna. They loved each other and together they raised a dynasty, and from those descendants come the race of nobles who rule and know the art of war. The youngest of those children knew runes and secret knowledge: he knew more even than Lord, and he gained the right to be called after the god that was known to men as Rig, or King. Territories across the water awaited his conquest. But all the estates of man, from the humblest of slaves to the most warlike king, can trace their roots back to Rig, or Heimdall. For this reason, the watchman of the gods is also known as the progenitor of humankind.

Njord and Skadi

Njord is one of the few named Vanir gods, and the father of Freyr and Freyja. He came to Asgard as a hostage after the first war, but he was raised in Vanaheim where the laws on love between members of the same family were much more relaxed. He is accused by Loki of fathering Freyr and Freyja on his sister, and of allowing the daughters of a giant to piss in his mouth: it is hard to know which of these insults is more shameful. Njord is famed for his wealth, which seems to flow endlessly from his lands. He calls the ship-enclosure of Noatun his home, and he is thought of as the god of open waters and its winds, the sea's fish and its riches. He can calm both storms and fire at will: sailors and fishermen often speak his name.

Njord's love of the sea is almost as famous as his wife Skadi's love of the high mountains that she calls home. Skadi is the daughter of a famous mountain-giant called Thjazi, and she was very close to her father growing up. When the gods killed him for abducting Idun, it was Skadi herself who marched to Asgard in full armour to demand compensation. The gods offered her marriage into the Æsir tribe to make up for her loss: but she had to choose her husband by the look of his feet alone. Skadi hoped to secure the most beautiful god, Baldr, as a husband, and so picked the shiniest pair of toes. But the feet belonged to the old Vanir god Njord, whose feet were washed clean by walking in the surf beside his seaside home.

Skadi's marriage to Njord is not a happy one, and their differences would be hard for any couple to overcome. Skadi wanted to live in the mountains where she had grown up, but Njord wanted to live close to the sea that he cherished. They tried dividing their time between the two places, living for nine nights in the Home of Thunder up in the high mountain passes and three nights in Noatun where the water lapped against the shore. But Njord found the mountains oppressive and the crying of the wolves grated on his ears. Skadi couldn't stand the constant churning of the sea and she found it hard to get any sleep because of the screeching of gulls. They decided to go their separate ways.

Skadi is happy at her father's ancestral home in the mountains where she spends much of her time skiing and tracking wild animals: she is known as the god of skis and of hunting with a bow. Odin is said to visit her here in the mountains, and a powerful clan in Norway trace their descent from this love affair. It is hard to make Skadi laugh and it was another condition of her reconciliation with the gods that Loki had to do just that. The trickster ended up tying his testicles to the beard of a goat and playing a squealing game of tug-of-war. This raised a smile from Skadi, and she laughed out loud when the goat tugged Loki's balls so hard that he fell into her lap. Despite this, Skadi never forgave Loki for his role in her father's death, and she is the one who decides to hang a serpent above Loki's face when he is bound by the gods. Skadi is not a goddess to be pushed around.

Ull

Ull is another god associated with hunting and with travelling across the snow and ice. Ull likes to ski and skate and he uses his shield as a sled. Ull is the son of Sif and stepson of Thor; he is handsome and graceful in his movements and his skills of archery are famous. He lives in the place called Yewdales where the best wood for bows can be found, and he is a reliable god to call upon in a duel.

Bragi and Idun

Bragi is the god of poetry and eloquence, and he is known as the first skald in the world. The word for poetry, or *bragr*, is named after him, and he gives the gift of wisdom and mastery over verse to those who honour him. He has such a way with words that his tongue is said to be charmed and his beard is longer than any other god's. Because of his eloquence, he has the honour of greeting those who enter the halls where the gods are assembled, and he is the first to challenge Loki when he arrives at Ægir's feast. Loki accuses Bragi of being a coward during this exchange of insults, at which point his wife Idun intervenes. She is in turn accused of being mad for men, and for draping her arms around her brother's killer.

Idun's name means 'forever young' and she is most famous as the guardian of the golden apples of eternal youth, which she carries in a casket made of the same wood as the World-Tree. The gods should take better care of Idun and her apples than they do, as they rely on this fruit to prevent them growing old. They twice came close to losing the source of their power: once when Idun and her apples were taken by the giant Thjazi, and once when Skirnir offered eleven apples to Gerd as a marriage gift. Without Idun, the gods would grow old and grey and wizened, as they do in the brief time that she is missing.

Gefjon

Gefjon – the giving one – is most famous for her skill with a plough. She is gifted in the second sight that so many powerful women have, and knows the fates of men as clearly as Odin does. She is said to receive in the afterlife all women who die as virgins, and to be a virgin herself, though that's a claim the gods take with a pinch of salt. Loki accuses her of throwing her legs over a youth who gave her some jewellery, and another story tells of her sleeping with a Swedish king in return for land.

Gefjon disguised herself as a woman of the world, and she travelled to the kingdom of Gylfi. Gylfi had so much rich land that he was careless with it: in return for Gefjon's company the king offered her as much Swedish soil as she could plough in a day and a night with four oxen. This was a foolish bargain to make with a goddess, and Gefjon taught him a lesson about kingship: she fetched her four strapping sons out of giant-land and turned them into bulls to help her plough – and they were larger than any bulls seen before in Midgard. With them, she ploughed up the land itself and carried it west to the nearby sea, where it became the island of Sjælland. The wound in Gylfi's kingdom filled with water and became Lake Mälern in Sweden, and its bays match the outline of the new land that she created. Gylfi tried to visit Asgard to learn more about the gods and their trickery, but he was fooled again by Odin and he never got his land in Sweden back.

Mimir and Hœnir

Mimir is known for his head, the well that is named for him, and little else. Mimir means 'the one who remembers', and when he still had his head on his shoulders he used to travel every day to drink at the waters of the well that takes his name. Mimir's Well lies in Jotunheim beneath one of the roots of Ygg-drasil, and it is a place where great knowledge can be found – for a price. Somewhere in its depths is Odin's eye and Heimdall's ear and much more besides. Mimir was one of the Æsir sent as a hostage to the Vanir tribe after the war between the gods. He was accompanied by the long-legged Hœnir, who was pretty as a picture, but didn't have much to say for himself. The Vanir soon realised that Hœnir wouldn't make any decisions of his own without the advice of Mimir, and they thought that they'd been cheated in the exchange: they'd given some of their most important gods to the Æsir tribe, and in return they'd been given a man too wise for his own good and a pretty mute! They decapitated Mimir, and sent Hœnir back to the Æsir with the severed head. Odin was able to preserve Mimir's head with herbs and spells, so that it is still able to give him counsel, and he learns a great deal about runes and sacred knowledge and the fate of the gods from his reanimated friend. The fate of long-legged Hœnir is not talked of much – he probably wouldn't tell his story even if he was asked. But this quiet god shares the honour of being one of the few to survive Ragnarok, and he brings with him knowledge from the earliest time, when he and Odin walked the world together.

The Children of the Gods

The youngest generation of gods are not as famous as their parents, but their time is sure to come. Vidar and Vali are the sons of Odin, born to mothers outside Asgard; Magni and Modi are the strong sons of Thor; whilst Forseti survives his parents Baldr and Nanna who both burned on the same funeral pyre. All of these gods are associated with revenge and with renewal. Vali is born to avenge the death of Baldr – a feat he carries out at one day old by killing his half-brother Hod. It is told that Odin raped the woman Rind to father Vali, and that Vidar was born to a giantess, but one friendly to the gods. Vidar is a strapping lad,

almost as strong as his brother Thor, and he accompanies his
family to Ægir's feast. His main role is to avenge his father's
death at Ragnarok. Vidar was given an iron-clad shoe when he
was little, and as he has grown it has been reinforced by leather
cut from the toes and heels of all the shoes worn in the world. He
will use this shoe to step on the lower jaw of Fenrir and to rip the
wolf's ravenous mouth apart. It is said that to help Vidar defeat
the wolf, the strips trimmed from a shoe should be thrown away
and not reused. By killing the great wolf, Vidar avenges his
father: although Vidar is known as the silent god, he once surprised the gods by declaring from horseback that he was ready to
take on the wolf.

Forseti is the son of Baldr and Nanna, and he presides over a
gleaming hall with a ceiling of silver and pillars of gold. He is
known for the ability to intervene in conflicts. He will be reunited with his parents after Ragnarok, when the world is reborn
and Baldr walks back along the road from Hel accompanied by
Nanna. Magni and Modi are sons of Thor, and reflect his great
strength and his temper. Modi is the angry one, and will take
ownership of his father's hammer with his brother Magni after
his death. Magni is the strong one, and he proved his right to
this title when he lifted a giant's leg off his father's body at three
years old, something no other god was able to do. Thor was so
pleased with this show of strength that he promised his horse
Golden-Mane to the boy, against the wishes of his grandfather
Odin. Magni and Modi have no need to avenge their father, as
Thor and the Midgard Serpent are set to destroy each other in
the final battle.

What these young gods all have in common is that they are
fated to survive the cataclysm of Ragnarok and to return to live
in the ruins of Asgard where they will witness the rebirth of an

eternally green land. The question is whether these avengers, strong as they are, will be more than shadows of their forebears. Will they be able to protect the world when the monsters return, or will it take a new god – the high one – to rule over this rejuvenated world?

4

The Giants

The Kinship of the Jotnar

We've already met with several giants – from the loutish Thrym to Gerd with her shining arms – and their stories are difficult to prise apart from those of the gods, as the fates of the two tribes are so closely intertwined: by descent, by marriage, and by their unending feud which will culminate in Ragnarok. The Jotnar have been the enemies of the gods since the killing of the first giant Ymir, but in many ways the Æsir depend on the giants for their own survival. Odin and his brothers are the sons of Bor and the giantess Bestla; the frost-giant Bolthorn is Odin's maternal grandfather; and the Father of the Gods is taught powerful spells by his giant uncle. The pattern of gods taking giant-wives begins before the nine worlds themselves are made, and the Jotnar are also forced to surrender many heirlooms to the Æsir: from the great cauldron in which the gods brew their beer, to the mead of poetry itself, stolen from the giant Suttung and tricked out of the protection of his daughter Gunnlod. The giants can trace their lineage back to the very beginnings of the world, and Odin also seeks to tap into their knowledge of the distant past and to learn from an elemental wisdom that is older than the gods. Even the earth itself is made from the flesh and bones of Ymir, the ancestor of all the giants whose blood flooded the valleys of the primeval world. The gods might be the creators, but without the giants there would be no seas or sky or mountains, and no Midgard built on fertile giant-flesh.

The Jotnar are all descended from the two giants who survived the deluge that killed the rest of their tribe: Ymir's grandson Bergelmir and his giant-wife. After Odin and his brothers had created Midgard, the surviving giants were banished to the edges of the world, and there are mountain-giants living in the crags and cliffs of Jotunheim, frost-giants in the frozen places, and fire-giants in the burning realm of Muspelheim. All of these wild lands – dark forests, scorched plains and barren mountains – are *utgard*: outside the enclosure that protects the world of humankind. Travel to these places is dangerous, and to enter Jotunheim the gods must cross surging rivers or barriers of fire. The giants sometimes travel to Asgard, and the arrival of three mysterious giant-women in the early years brought an end to the golden age of the gods.

The giants are responsible for many of the forces that sustain and pummel Midgard, from the eagle Hræsvelgr who sits at the edge of the world and beats his wings to make the winds, to the giant-girls who grind out salt at the bottom of the sea. The gods in turn impose some order on this chaos. They protect Midgard from the excesses of the Jotnar and turn raw knowledge and materials into the systems of a settled world. There is no moral equivocation in their dealings with the giants. The gods may cheat and deceive and steal from the Jotnar, but humankind will always ally itself with Odin and the Æsir, who offer protection against a hostile world. The gods certainly give the giants plenty of reason to be hostile, from the murder of their ancestor Ymir, to the abduction of giant-women and the breaking of oaths, and it is the giants who will take the final victory as the forces of chaos sweep the flawed structures of the gods aside at Ragnarok. It will be an orgy of destruction from which the world must be reborn: this is the fate that the gods are always trying to postpone, and this is why the conflict is more than just a war between two tribes.

Hrungnir and the Horse Race

Odin owns an eight-legged horse called Sleipnir, who is known to be the best of all horses: he runs so fast that miles disappear beneath his hooves and he can pass between the lands of the living and the dead. A horse like Sleipnir needs to stretch his legs, and one day Odin decided to take him for a proper ride – all the way to Jotunheim. This time, Odin didn't travel in disguise, but wore a golden helmet and rode openly across the sky. The other gods saw him leave and wondered what old One-Eye was up to.

It wasn't long before Odin reached the mountain home of a fierce giant called Hrungnir, who did a double-take when he saw the god racing through the sky above his home. The giant craned his neck and called up into the heavens, 'You don't pass the hall of Hrungnir without making yourself known! Tell me who you are, and where you found that horse?'

Odin rode at a leisurely pace towards Hrungnir. He began to provoke the giant before Sleipnir's hooves had even touched the ground.

'There's no need for introductions,' Odin said. 'But I'll wager my head that this horse is better than any of these brutes you fatten up in Jotunheim. Sleipnir could run rings around the best of them.'

Hrungnir took the bait right away. He owned a fine horse called Golden-Mane, and he thought he'd teach this puffed-up god a lesson. Odin had already set off at a canter, and Hrungnir jumped on Golden-Mane and raced after him, calling out all manner of insults to the Father of the Gods. Sleipnir sped across the land with his eight hooves moving so quickly that he looked as though he was not moving at all; and as fast as Hrungnir whipped his horse, and urged him on with curses, Odin was always a few paces ahead of him. Odin and the giant raced all the way to Asgard, and Hrungnir was in such a fury that he didn't notice that he'd left Jotunheim far behind and had entered the stronghold of his enemies.

Odin finally brought Sleipnir to a halt. There wasn't a bead of sweat on the horse. Hrungnir clattered to a halt behind him with Golden-Mane buckling at the knees.

'Welcome to our hall, mighty Hrungnir!' said Bragi, taking the reins of Golden-Mane and soothing the shaking horse. 'Come and share a cup of ale with the gods.'

Hrungnir barely acknowledged the welcome and barged his way into the hall, wiping the sweat from his brow with the cloth that was offered him, and calling loudly for a drink. Freyja brought out Thor's own cups to serve the giant his ale, and Hrungnir drained them all and demanded more. He soon became very drunk and started boasting to Bragi that he was such a powerful giant he'd uproot Valhalla and drag it off to Jotunheim, that he'd sink Asgard, and that he'd murder all the gods except shining Freyja and Sif of the Golden Hair, whom he'd take as his concubines. The gods regretted that they'd offered hospitality to this lout from Jotunheim, but Freyja continued to serve their guest despite his shameful words. Hrungnir grabbed her hand as it was halfway to filling his cup. 'First I'll drink the Æsir dry, and then I'll carry out my other threats,' he leered.

It's a sacred duty to treat guests well, but the gods eventually grew tired of this abusive giant and sent a messenger to Thor: there was trouble, and he needed to come home at once. By the time Thor arrived Hrungnir had become impossible to control, and was still calling out for more drink. Thor stepped into the hall. 'A giant!' he boomed. 'A giant at our table! A giant waited on by Freyja!' Hrungnir took a big swig from his drink. 'A giant drinking from *my cups*!' Thor was fit to burst with anger. 'Who let this madness happen? I'll beat them into dust!'

Hrungnir belched, and he turned unsteadily towards the god.

'Y'know, it was Odin, the big man himself, who gave me safe passage in your puny little hall, and I'll say this to you, Hammer-God . . .' – Hrungnir paused and blinked, and gave it another try – '. . . I'll say this to you, Hammer-God, you'll not get any honour from killing me here now without my weapons.' The giant wagged a meaty finger in Thor's general direction. 'If I'd only brought my whetstone and my *huge* stone shield, you'd be running from this place with your hammer dangling between your little legs.'

Thor could hardly believe what he was hearing, but furious as he was, he couldn't help but be impressed. No one had dared to speak to him like that before! When Hrungnir proposed a fight once he had sobered up, the god's eyes lit up. He'd return each insult with a blow that would shatter mountains and reach the ear of every giant in Jotunheim. 'Just be sure to keep your side of the bargain,' Thor shouted after him as the giant struggled to climb back on his horse. 'If you don't show at the appointed time, the shame of it will spread through all the worlds!'

Hrungnir galloped back to the land of the giants as fast as

poor Golden-Mane was able – and as he rode, the news that there was to be a duel between this giant champion and Thor spread far and wide. Hrungnir was the strongest of the mountain-giants: even against the mighty Hammer-God he had to have a fighting chance!

It had been settled that the fight would take place at the border of Jotunheim, on a plane marked out with hazel-rods. In preparation for the battle, the giants dug into the creek beds and created a huge being out of heavy clay – he was nine miles high and his chest was three miles wide, and he wore the clouds as hair. The giants imagined that such a creature would strike fear into the Thunder-God as he approached from Asgard, but they made a basic error – they gave their man the heart of a mare. It barely pumped enough blood to wake the great clay-creature up, let alone prepare him for the fight: he wet himself at the sight of the god advancing in all his thunderous rage. Not so with the giant Hrungnir: his heart was a valknut made of jagged stone, and his head was as hard as polished rock. His shield was made of stone as well, and he carried a whetstone as a weapon, slung over his shoulder like a club. He wasn't afraid of the burning sky, or the thunder and lightning that rolled around the mountains as Thor raced across the plane with his giant-killing hammer. Hrungnir waited, steady as a rock. The fight was on!

As the two adversaries stepped into the duelling ground, the thunderclouds gathered overhead and the mountains shook. Hrungnir had brought the great clay-giant to the fight, so Thor bought his servant Thjalfi – that was only fair. Before the fight began, Thjalfi ran over to Hrungnir to give him some advice.

'Listen, Hrungnir. I want to see a fair fight, so I'm giving you a tip. My master plans to embarrass you by tunnelling through the earth to strike you where it hurts. Do what you have to do to protect your rear end, and don't say I didn't warn you!'

Hearing this, Hrungnir took the stone shield off his arm and balanced himself on top of it, holding the whetstone in a two-handed grip ready to bash the god wherever he appeared from. He didn't have long to wait. Thor had mustered all his power in preparation for the fight, and all at once he exploded from the blocks and dashed straight at Hrungnir with his hammer held aloft. The sky crackled as he ran. Hrungnir was expecting Thor to plough into the ground, but the god was getting closer and showed no sign of changing course. The giant began to regret placing the shield underneath his feet, and now Thor was pulling back his arm to hurl the hammer at his head. Hrungnir barely had time to react when he saw Mjolnir flying through the air, but he trusted in the power of his own weapon. He threw the whetstone directly in the hammer's path, and there was a mighty crack as the weapons collided in mid-air. For a moment it seemed as though the power of the giants and the gods had cancelled each other out, but Mjolnir was made of far stronger stuff than the stone of the earth: it shattered the whetstone and kept flying on its path. One piece of the whetstone fell down to the earth, and this is the origin of all the whetstones in the world; but the other piece of the shrapnel struck Thor in the forehead and knocked him flat. Mjolnir struck a much harder blow to Hrungnir's temple: it smashed the giant's stone head into jagged shards which fell to the earth in a shower of flint. Hrungnir's headless body crumpled to the ground, and one of the giant's massive legs fell on top of the stunned Thor and pinned him to the spot.

Meanwhile, Thor's servant Thjalfi had taken care of the clay-creature, and his was by far the easier fight. He ran over to

Thor, who was awake and groaning. 'Get this thing off me!' he roared. But Hrungnir's leg was as heavy as a column, and Thjalfi couldn't budge it: neither could the Æsir when they came to help. Even Odin was at a loss, until Thor's infant son Magni climbed out of his mother's arms and lifted the leg as though it was a little thing. 'If only I'd been here earlier, Father, I could have boxed the giant for you and saved us all a lot of trouble.' Thor ruffled his son's hair and rewarded him with Hrungnir's horse. 'Now, how about getting this whetstone removed from my head?'

Magni might have been a strong lad, but more than strength was needed to dislodge the shrapnel stuck in Thor's temple. A prophetess who knew powerful healing spells was called upon to remove it. She was called Groa, and she was the wife of a man named Aurvandil who had been missing for many months. Groa spent a long time chanting over Thor, and he eventually felt the whetstone begin to work itself out of his head: the feeling was like waking from a dream of a pain that had already passed. Thor breathed a great sign of relief, and he started to tell the prophetess about his recent journey back from the north, where he'd met a man in need of help. 'This man, he weighed almost nothing, and so I carried him across the freezing Elivagar rivers in a basket strapped to my back, and dropped him off at the border of Midgard.' Groa wondered why Thor was telling her this tale; it was a little distracting. 'He was a nice man, and the only harm that came to him was a little frostbite in his toe, which was poking from the basket. I snapped it off and threw it up into the sky, where it is now known as the Morning Star.' Now Groa was intrigued. 'You might want to call the star by a more familiar name: Aurvandil's Toe.' At this Groa dropped her staff and squealed. 'You've found my husband? He's alive and mostly in one piece? I think I need to sit.' Groa was so overwhelmed with this news that she completely forgot the ending to her spell, and for this reason, the fragment of whetstone stayed stuck in Thor's head. When someone is careless enough to roll a whetstone across the floor, it makes the other half in Thor's head rattle. This is not the way to keep Thor on your side.

Skrymir and the Giant Glove

Odin once taunted his son across the water: 'I remember how you cowered in the finger of a giant's glove. You were scared to sneeze or fart!'

There's a story behind this insult.

Shortly after Thor had taken the children Thjalfi and Roskva to be his servants, and whilst his goat was still learning to walk with a lame leg, the son of Odin decided to travel by foot into giant-land. With him were his new servants and Loki, who was on much better terms with the gods in those days. The companions walked until they reached the encircling sea, then continued on the water until they reached a land that lay on the very borders of the world. There was a path that headed east, and before long the companions came to a great forest. Night was falling, and it was time to set up camp. Thjalfi, who was bounding ahead carrying Thor's bag, spotted an abandoned hall in the half-light, with a doorway almost as wide as its roof. The companions decided that it wasn't a bad place to shelter, and they soon settled down to sleep.

It wasn't long after midnight when they were woken up by an earthquake. The ground was trembling so much that the hall looked ready to collapse. 'Come this way!' shouted Thor, 'there's a side-chamber over here that looks more sturdy than the rest. We'll be safer there.' Thjalfi, Roskva and Loki hid in the shadows whilst Thor guarded the entrance with his hammer lying on his lap. The ground continued to rumble and the hall shook all through the night. Thor didn't sleep a wink.

At first light, the Hammer-God left the hall and went outside. In the light from the dawn Thor could see what they hadn't seen at night: the shadow they had taken for a low ridge was an enormous giant lying on his back. His chest was rising and falling, and he was snoring so loudly that the whole earth shook. Thor thought that it would be easier to tackle a giant of this size whilst he was still asleep, so he stood next to the man's head and swung his hammer high into the air. But just as Thor was preparing to let the hammer fall, the giant sat up. 'Is it morning already?' he asked. Thor was so startled at the size of him that he forgot to strike, and just stood there with his hammer raised. It took a while for the god to compose himself. He cleared his throat, and lowered his hammer as discreetly as he could. 'What do you call yourself?' he shouted up at the huge figure before him. 'I'm Skrymir,' replied the giant, 'and I don't need to ask your name – it's Thor of the Æsir. I recognise your hammer. But tell me, Thor, have you seen my glove? I'm sure I had it with me when I went to sleep.' Thor looked over to the hall where his companions were still hiding, and from this distance he recognised it for what it was. The side-room they had been sleeping in fitted snugly round the giant's thumb. Thor blushed a deep shade of red. Now he'd really have to find a way to silence this Skrymir for good, before the story spread round Jotunheim: the mighty Thor, hiding in a giant's glove!

'Are you going the same way as me, Thor of the Æsir?' the giant asked. 'If so, let us travel together – as it's a hard country this, for little folk.' Thor agreed to let Skrymir accompany them, but only for this reason: he'd have a better chance to kill him if he kept the giant close. Having settled this, Skrymir opened his enormous food-bag and began to eat his breakfast. Thor and his companions did the same with the bag that Thjalfi was carrying, and when the giant suggested that they pool their supplies, Thor was happy to do so – as their food had almost run out, and the giant seemed to have a great deal to share around. Skrymir tied up both bags into a single package and threw it over his shoulder with ease, striding out on the path and getting well ahead of the group. He had even set up camp under an enormous oak tree by the time that the gods caught him on the trail, and he was getting ready to bed down for the night. 'I've already eaten,' he told Thor, 'but you go ahead and help yourself from the food-bag.' The only trouble was that Thor was unable to untie the bag, however much he struggled with the knots and summoned all his Æsir strength. By this time, the giant was fast asleep and snoring loudly. Thor became more and more angry that he couldn't untie the giant's knots, and eventually his temper boiled over, and he marched over to the sleeping giant and struck him hard on the head with Mjolnir. Skrymir woke up looking slightly surprised. 'Did a leaf just fall on my head?' he asked, looking up at the canopy of the tree. 'Have you eaten well, my friend?' Thor glared at him and sat down under a nearby tree to dream of ale and roasted goat.

In the middle of the night, Thor woke from a fitful sleep. Skrymir's snoring was so loud that he shook the forest floor with each intake of his breath. Thor crept over to the giant, and raising his hammer high, thwacked him in the middle of his forehead. It was the hardest blow that Thor had ever given, and the hammer sunk deep into the giant's fleshy head. Skrymir sat bolt upright. 'What's happened now? Did an acorn just fall on my head?' he asked, looking up at the branches of the tree. 'And why are you awake?' Thor told him that he was just stretching his legs, and that it was still the middle of the night. The giant grunted and quickly fell back to sleep.

Thor was shaken. If he got a chance to strike the giant for a third time, it would be such a hammer-blow that no god would need to give another. The son of Odin pretended to rest, but he sat weighing the hammer in his hand. Near dawn, he heard Skrymir snoring again, and taking a long run-up, he leaped at the prostrate giant and flung Mjolnir with all his might. The hammer sunk up to its hilt, but the giant sat up looking confused. 'Did a bird dislodge a branch from the tree? It seems some twigs have fallen onto my head as I was sleeping.' Skrymir stood up and stretched – none the worse for being hit three times during the night by Mjolnir. 'If you're well-rested, we'd best be on our way, my little man.' The god massaged his hammer arm, with a look like thunder in his eyes.

It was not far now to the stronghold of giants that Thor had been searching for in this wild region of the world. The travellers would soon part company: the gods to the stronghold of Utgarda-Loki; and Skrymir to the north. The giant left Thor with some advice. 'I've heard you pipsqueaks whispering about my height, but you should know that in the land that lies in front of you, I'm considered average size. I'd turn back if I were you, and if you do enter into the hall of Utgarda-Loki, perhaps it's best not to brag about your Æsir strength.' The giant winked at Thor, picked up the unopened food-bag, and strode off into the trees. Thor had never imagined his hammer could be so useless against a giant, and he was not in a rush to meet this Skrymir fellow again.

Utgarda-Loki and the Trial of Strength

Thor and his companions continued their journey into Jotunheim and soon came across the stronghold. As Skrymir had
told them, it was a fortress built for giants of an incredible size,
and to see the sky above it the gods had to strain their necks so
far that they were in danger of falling on their backs. The gate
to the stronghold was just as large, and even with his great
strength Thor was not able to push it open. The companions
eventually had to squeeze themselves through the bars, which
were designed to keep out much larger creatures than the gods.
Inside the stronghold was a hall, and the gods entered to find
two enormous benches seating giants who were not small by
any measure. The companions walked up to the high seat and
made their introductions to Utgarda-Loki, but the giant did not
acknowledge them right away, small and insignificant as they
appeared to be. When he finally spoke, he did so with an
amused look on his face. 'Well, well. Is this little chap really
Thor, the mighty charioteer? I hope you are stronger than you
look! Listen to me, if you can hear all the way down there: I
have a rule that all visitors must obey. You'll be given hospitality, but only if you can prove that you are the best at something.
Doesn't matter what it is: you just have to beat the giant I choose
to stand against you.' Loki was the first to put himself forward.
He was hungry, so he suggested an eating competition, adding,
'And I'm so famished I'll finish my plate faster than any of the
giants!'

Utgarda-Loki nodded his head: it would be a skill indeed to
win this contest against the challenger he had in mind. He called
the giant named Logi up to the bench, and a large trough was set
on the table between the two contestants and filled to the brim

with meat. Loki and the giant Logi would start at opposite ends and eat their way towards each other – whoever got furthest would win the contest. Loki and his adversary ate as fast as they could, and met exactly in the middle of the trough. Only, whilst Loki had eaten the meat off the bones, the giant Logi had eaten the bones too, as well as his half of the trough! Everyone agreed that Loki had lost this contest to the giant: but at least the trickster wasn't hungry any more.

Next up was Thor's servant, Thjalfi. 'I'm known for being pretty fast,' he said. 'I'll run a race against anyone you choose.' Utgarda-Loki was pleased with this suggestion – running was a fine skill – but he warned Thjalfi that he'd have to be very quick indeed to win against the giant that he'd chosen. The party went outside for the race, to an area of flat ground with a racing track marked out. Utgarda-Loki had picked a rather small giant called Hugi to compete, but in the first race the giant was so far ahead of the boy that he turned round and came running back as Thjalfi was still racing up the track. 'You'd better put in some more effort, boy, if you're going to stand a chance,' said Utgarda-Loki – though he had to admit that Thjalfi wasn't particularly slow. In the second race, Hugi once more reached the end of the course with time to turn back, and this time Thjalfi was a whole arrow's flight behind him. Utgarda-Loki was impressed with the boy's ability, but knew he had no chance of catching Hugi. In the third race, Hugi had reached the end of the course before Thjalfi had even reached the mid-point. Everyone agreed that Thjalfi had lost the contest.

Now it was Thor's turn to compete, and Utgarda-Loki was keen to see what competition the god would choose, as his exploits were well known. Thor decided that he would like to challenge a giant to a drinking contest. That was simple enough for Utgarda-Loki to arrange, and he called for a horn to be brought into the hall. A servant came and placed the horn in Thor's hands. 'The best drinkers here in Utgard can drain the horn in one draught, though it takes some small giants two draughts. But no one here is so bad at drinking that it takes them three. Start when you are ready, mighty Thor.' Thor sized up the horn: it was unusually long, and so full that the liquid was almost spilling over the rim. Thor had built up quite a thirst watching the others compete, and he took long gulps from the horn, confident he could drain it in one go. But when he had taken as much drink as he could hold, he put down the horn and found that the level of the liquid was only a little lower than it had been when he started. 'You took some big gulps there, Thor,' said Utgarda-Loki, 'but I don't think you've made much progress. Have another go.' Thor raised the horn a second time, and drank for as long as he could hold his breath. It was hard to tip the horn up as high as he wanted, and the beer dripped and foamed in his red beard. When Thor lowered the horn, gasping for breath, it seemed that he had made even less of an impression on the drink, though now at least the horn could be held upright without spilling. 'Are you going to dare to take another drink, mighty lord of goats?' taunted the giant. 'If you do, it is going to have to be the biggest drink of all – and you are going to have to give a much better account of yourself in the other contests, if you want to keep your reputation as a mighty god intact.' At the thought that he would lose face in front of the giants, Thor grew enraged, and this time he didn't stop drinking from the horn until he was red in the face and couldn't take a drop more. He lowered the horn with a mighty belch, and saw that he'd made some impression on the drink, but nowhere near enough to drain the horn. He passed it back to Utgarda-Loki feeling utterly defeated, and more than a little queasy.

'Well, Thor, it is clear to me that your power is not as great as we've been told. But is there another trial of strength you can redeem yourself with?' Thor took a while to catch his breath before he replied. He suspected foul play. 'Such drinks would not have been called little by the gods, but I will undertake another test of strength.'

Utgarda-Loki left the hall, and returned with a large grey cat. 'Small boys here in Jotunheim like to play a game in which they lift the cat up off the floor. I wouldn't have thought to give such an easy test of strength to the mightiest of the Æsir, but I can see you need a boost in confidence, as you failed so badly at the drinking game.' Thor sized up the cat. He'd teach them a lesson, and throw the giant's pet against the ceiling. Thor cracked his knuckles and placed his hands on either side of the cat. The animal wasn't particularly heavy, but as Thor lifted the cat it arched its back – and however high Thor stretched himself, the cat's paws remained firmly planted on the floor. Eventually, straining all the muscles in his body, Thor managed to get the cat to lift a single paw from the floor. The task had not gone as Thor predicted, and Utgarda-Loki had more scornful words. 'As I expected! The cat is a large one, and Thor here is very short.'

Now Thor was angry, and he challenged any of the assembled giants to a wrestling match, no matter how small he might appear next to them. Utgarda-Loki cast his eyes over the giants, and shook his head. 'I don't see any man in this hall who would find it dignified to wrestle with such a weakling. But call my old nurse Elli to come here – perhaps Thor might have a chance wrestling with her ... though she's toppled men who seemed much stronger than this pint-sized god.' When Elli came stooping into the hall, the giants cleared a space, and Thor began wrestling with the old woman. The harder he grappled, the more she dug in her heels, and it was clear she had great staying power. Before long, Thor lost his footing, and the old woman forced him onto one knee. At this, Utgarda-Loki called a halt. He said that after this performance against an old woman, it would be pointless for Thor to wrestle anyone stronger. By now, it was late, and the giant found places on the benches for the companions to sleep, treating them well for the rest of the night – despite the fact that none of them had proved they were the best at anything at all.

The following morning, Utgarda-Loki laid on a hearty break-fast for his visitors, before leading the companions back to the gates of his stronghold, and escorting them out of his land. When they had travelled some way along the path, Utgarda-Loki asked Thor how he thought the visit had gone. 'I can't hide the fact we've all been shamed by what we found in your hall, and I wish I hadn't set foot in the place,' said Thor. 'Worst of all, I know that the news will spread, and I'll be mocked across the worlds.'

Utgarda-Loki looked back and saw that they were far from the stronghold. 'Now you're safely away from my home, I can tell you some truths. If I'd had any inkling of your power, I would not have let you anywhere near my hall, as it almost led to disaster for all the Jotnar. First, I'll tell you that I am the same giant – Skrymir – who you met in the forest on your way here. When you tried to undo the rucksack I was carrying, you couldn't do so, as I'd fastened it with magic, not with rope. When you struck three blows on my head with your hammer, I'm sure that any one of these would have crushed my skull, if I hadn't had the foresight to move a mountain in front of my head to shield the blows. That ridge that you see over in the distance with the three valleys carved into its sides – that is the result of Thor's three blows. I also deceived you in your trials of skill inside my hall, as the giants you faced were not what they appeared to be. In the first contest Loki measured up to Logi – wildfire – and the fire burned up the wooden trough as fast as it consumed the meat. When Thjalfi ran against Hugi he was actually running against my thoughts, and it is small wonder he couldn't keep up! When you drank from the feasting horn, Thor, the other end was lying in the ocean, and the fact you changed the level at all is a miracle. When you travel back to the water's edge, you will see just how much these three drinks emptied the ocean. From now on, people will call this the tide. I was almost as impressed when you lifted the cat – this was in fact the Midgard Serpent which circles the whole world, and you managed to lift it so far up in the air that it almost touched the heavens. It is also astounding to me that you stood for so long against your wrestling opponent, the old woman Elli. You were actually wrestling with old age itself, and it is well known that no man can defeat this opponent – yet you looked as if you might be a match for her. I've no desire to meet you again, and if you come to my halls in the future you'll find the doors barred and the giants ready to defend themselves. I'll use the same magic to conceal my stronghold as I used to trick you in the trials of strength.'

Thor had been growing more and more angry as he heard how they had been deceived, and his fingers tightened around the handle of his hammer. But when he raised Mjolnir to strike Utgarda-Loki, all he could see were rocks and a barren stretch of land. The giant was nowhere to be seen. When Thor turned the other way to run back to the stronghold, he saw that it too had disappeared, leaving an empty lava-field. Thor nursed his anger all the way back to the forest and across the encircling sea, and he vowed revenge for his humiliation: against the Midgard Serpent most of all.

Ægir, Ran, and the Nine Waves

Njord might be a sea-god, and the protector of sailors, but the seas also have a wild side, and it's not only the Midgard Serpent that seafarers are afraid of. The giantess Ran has a net which she uses to drag people from their boats and down into the depths. When a fisherman is lost at sea, it is said that he has been taken into Ran's embrace. She rules over the drowned in the darkness of the ocean. Ran's daughters have inherited their mother's nature, and personify the waves: their names are Rising, Roller, Sky-Glass; Surf, Swell, Wave, and Bleeding-Hair; Billow and Bitter-Surge are the last of them. The nine daughters of Ran can be companions to sailors on a sea voyage, but they can just as easily turn against a crew, and when they are agitated they lash the shore and toss longships around like toys.

Ran's husband is Ægir, and he is so closely associated with the ocean that his name can be used in place of the sea itself. Ships are known as Ægir's horses, and if a poet mentions Ægir's daughters, it is clear that he or she is referring to the waves. Ægir is a sea-giant, but in the same way that the sea provides sustenance to people who live by its shores, Ægir helps the gods to cater for their feasts. Ægir once visited Asgard as a guest, asking to be told tales about the gods and the creation of the world. It is said that the giant was greatly impressed with the splendour of Asgard and with the hospitality he received: the beer and the stories flowed freely, and Bragi answered all of Ægir's questions in a most respectful tone. He stayed as a guest for as long as he wanted, and in return, the sea-giant invited the gods and elves to a feast on his island home, where he would return the hospitality he'd received tenfold. When Ægir visited Asgard, the hall had been lit by the light of burnished swords: in the giant's hall it would be bright gold strewn on the floor that would take the place of the fire, and gold is still referred to as Ægir's Light. Ægir also promised to provide the gods with as much food as they wanted and as much beer as they could drink. A date was set for the gods to visit his hall. There was only one issue: Ægir did not own a cauldron big enough to brew beer for all those who wanted to attend, and he asked the gods to find one. He must have known they'd have to search in Jotunheim and put their lives in danger. Ægir might have been a willing host, but for all that he was still a giant, with a giant's grudge.

Hymir and the Cauldron

Thor received a tip-off from one-handed Tyr: he'd heard of a cauldron that might just do the trick. Tyr's mother was named Hrod, and she lived with a wise and fierce giant named Hymir near the edge of the sky and the encircling sea. Hymir was renowned for two things amongst the giant race: for having an incredibly thick skull; and for owning a pot for brewing mead that was a mile or more deep. Tyr thought this would be just the thing to keep the beer flowing at Ægir's feast, but Thor knew that if they were to win this cauldron from the giant Hymir they would need all the strength and cunning they could find.

The gods rode far from Asgard in Thor's chariot, across the icy rivers that had flowed since the beginning of the world. After leaving their chariot with a farmer by the name of Egil on the

edge of giant-land, Thor and Tyr continued on foot, walking
deep into Utgard and eventually reaching the windswept home
of the giant Hymir. The first person they met in that place was
Tyr's giant grandmother, and the god was taken aback by her
appearance: she had more heads than was usual. Nine hundred
of them, to be exact. Tyr's mother Hrod was a much more
friendly sight: she was dressed all in gold and had glowing skin,
and she immediately offered her son a drink of ale after his long
journey. 'You're welcome, son, along with your fierce-looking
friend. We weren't expecting visitors, but still, I'm glad you've
come.' Hrod was clearly nervous, and she paced back and forth
between the table and the window where she watched the evening approaching. 'Hymir will be coming back from the fields
soon,' she mused, and bit her already ragged nails. When Hrod
heard her giant-husband's footsteps outside, she ushered the
two gods into a tub hanging from the rafters. 'You'll be safer
there if he comes home in a mood!'

The giant burst into the room like a blast of winter air. Hymir
was a fearsome sight: his stern face was covered in rime blown
off the sea, and his cheeks tinkled with the long icicles that had
formed in his beard. 'Who's that you were talking to?' he
demanded. Hrod avoided the question. 'Welcome home into the
warm, my husband.' Hrod hung up Hymir's cloak and took a
deep breath. 'I've got some news that you'll be pleased to hear:
Tyr has come to visit! And by the way, he's brought a friend: the
eldest son of Odin. Isn't it nice to be surprised by guests!'

Hymir did not react well to this news. In fact, he glared so
icily at the place where the gods were hiding that he shattered
the beam from which the pots and jars were hanging, and they
all crashed to the floor. The only one that wasn't broken into
pieces was the sturdy tub in which Tyr and Thor were hiding.

The gods crawled out, brushing themselves off and muttering a greeting. Thor was bristling to take his hammer to the giant's skull, but he remembered the reason why they'd come.

'Mighty Hymir! We've come to ask a favour, which you might consider when you've finished smashing up your home. We'd like to borrow your famous cauldron for our feast.' Hymir continued to glare at the visitors. He knew very well that Thor was the widower of giants: and yet here he was asking for a favour. The boldness of the man! But Hymir was bound by the rules of hospitality, and he grunted at his wife. 'They can stay tonight, and you'd better hope they won't make trouble. I'll set them trials in the morning to test their strength.' He called to his servants to kill three of the fattest bulls from the home fields – they were to cook them quickly and serve them for supper. 'Let's see what appetite this great god has!' Hymir mumbled to himself. He was somewhat surprised when Thor ate two of the bulls all by himself. The god leaned back in his seat. 'Now I'm pretty full, my giant friend – I'll go and lie down if it's all the same to you, and get some rest before the challenges begin.' Hymir glared at him. They'd have to go hunting for more food in the morning, but the god had proved he was no pushover when it came to giant portions.

The story of Thor's fishing trip with Hymir, and their encounter with the Midgard Serpent is perhaps the most well-known of any of the myths, but here is not the place to tell it. Suffice to say, that when the shaken giant and the Thunder-God returned to shore, they had food enough but their relationship had not improved one little bit. Hymir was now more determined than ever that Thor should return to the gods empty-handed and with the shame of having lost. He began by asking the god to drag the whales that they'd caught to shore: Thor dragged the whales with one hand, and with the other he pulled their boat right up to Hymir's hall. He didn't even bother to empty the bilge, and the heavy prow cut a furrow through the fields. The giant might have been impressed with this feat of strength, but he certainly didn't let on. 'You think you're strong, but there's only one true test of strength, and that's whether a little man like you can break my glass goblet. I'll let you have a go, and if you succeed then you're welcome to my cauldron. And if you fail, you'll leave my hall – and the next time I see you or that one-armed god they call my son it will be to break your heads.'

'What a strange thing to ask, and what an easy task!' thought Thor. He picked up the glass goblet and weighed it in his hand, and without even rising from his seat, hurled it at a stone column in Hymir's hall. The pillar shattered into pieces, but the glass goblet lay intact amongst the rubble. Hymir laughed and continued eating, and Thor's mood did not improve one bit.

Later in the meal, whilst Hymir was busy mopping up his plate, Tyr's mother approached with some advice for Thor. 'You're the strongest of the gods, but you'll never find a way to break that cup unless you use my husband's skull. It's far harder than a pillar, and as thick as anything.' Thor took Hrod's advice. He waited until Hymir leant back from the table with his belly full, and summoning up all his strength, slammed the goblet against Hymir's forehead. The giant upended the table as he fell backwards and Tyr roared with laughter. The giant's skull was still intact, but the goblet had been smashed to smithereens. There was no doubting Thor's strength now, or that he'd passed the final trial of strength. Hymir was very sore – not only had he lost his favourite goblet, but now he'd have to honour his agreement and give the gods his cauldron. It brewed ale on command and was not a little thing to give away. But Hymir had a final test for Thor. 'Take it!' he said, rubbing his forehead and tasting iron in his mouth. 'The cauldron is yours . . . if men as small as you can manage to carry it away.' Tyr tried twice to lift the giant cauldron, but had no luck. It wouldn't budge an inch, even though Tyr was no weakling. But Thor had a different approach. He swung off the rim of the cauldron and turned it upside down so that he was trapped inside. Bracing his head against the bottom of the cauldron and digging his heels into the ground, Thor managed to lift it clean off the floor and to walk out of the house with its rings jangling around his feet.

The gods had transported the cauldron in this way almost to the edge of giant-land before Hymir's men caught up with them. The gods saw the dust rising from the lava-field before they saw the mountain-giants themselves. Thor sighed and rolled the cauldron off his shoulders. He took Mjolnir in his hand. The hammer flew, and one-handed Tyr made every sword-blow count. The gods littered the plain with those giants the poets call the 'whales of the lava', and sent Hymir's clan packing off to Hel. That's how the mighty Hymir lost his life, and that's how the gods got hold of a cauldron big enough to brew the ale in Ægir's hall.

Hymir's wife, the gold-decked Hrod, who had helped Thor and Tyr to outsmart her husband, may have returned to Asgard with her son. But Hymir's daughters took up the feud on their father's behalf. The story goes that these young women once took turns to piss in Njord's open mouth as he dozed at the edge of the sea. There can be no reconciliation between the giants and the gods.

Geirrod and his Giant-Daughters

The daughters of giants can be as fierce as their fathers. The story of Geirrod and his daughters starts with Loki, as so many tales of the giants do. It was summer, the days were long and lazy, and Loki was bored. He decided to visit Jotunheim to see if things were livelier over there, and he borrowed Freyja's cloak of falcon feathers for the journey. Disguised in this way, he flew to the mountain stronghold of the giant Geirrod. Surely there must be something happening in this cavernous hall? What Loki didn't realise is that he was about to be the entertainment.

Loki wasn't bold enough to fly right into the hall itself, so he perched on the cliff-face next to a high window and peered down into the cavern below. His eyes took a while to adjust to the darkness, and when they did, Loki saw the giant Geirrod looking right back at him. It seems there wasn't much going on in Jotunheim either. 'Climb the rocks and fetch me that odd-looking falcon!' Geirrod ordered his men. Loki wasn't that alarmed. He felt very safe perched so high up on the rock-face, and he decided it would be amusing to stay put and watch the giants struggle up the cliffs towards him. He'd enjoy watching their faces as he escaped at the last minute. Only, when he tried to fly he realised that his feet were stuck – and by then it was too late. He was bundled into a bag and dumped on the cave-floor in front of Geirrod.

Loki had not taken off his cloak of feathers, and from the outside he looked just like a falcon. But Geirrod peered into his eyes and saw that they were the eyes of a man, not of a bird. 'Tell me who you are, or things will get much worse!' he said. But Loki wouldn't say a word, and so the giant threw him in a chest and starved him for three months. The giants are an old people, and they can be as patient as stones. If Loki thought it was tedious in Asgard, it was nothing compared to three months locked inside a chest. When he was pulled out, blinking and dishevelled and stinking like the grave, he was much more inclined to talk. The god revealed who he was. 'I'll spare your life,' said Geirrod, 'if you do something in return. Find a reason to bring Thor to my home, and make sure that he leaves his hammer behind.'

'That's not going to be easy,' said Loki, 'but I'll do my best if you'll only let me out of this filthy chest.'

'Swear on it!' said Geirrod.

Loki swore so many oaths, on so many sacred things, that eventually Geirrod was convinced and set him free.

Loki returned to Asgard and didn't tell anyone where he'd been. Speaking to Thor, he soon found an opportunity to fulfil his promise to the giant. 'Listen, Thor. I've heard of this place, not far from here, where all the talk is of your strength and how it's hardly to be believed. There are two beautiful daughters there who blush whenever your name is mentioned, and I'm sure you'd get the best of welcomes in that splendid hall.' Thor was eager to set out, and tied his hammer to his belt. 'One last thing – it would be a sign of good faith if you left Mjolnir behind – to let them know you come in peace.' A shadow passed across Thor's face, but he did as Loki asked.

The gods travelled along the green paths towards Jotunheim. Thor took his servant Thjalfi as a companion, and followed Loki's directions to the east. On the edge of Jotunheim they met the giantess named Grid. Like so many giantesses she was caught between two worlds: she owed loyalty to the Jotnar tribe, but she was mother to the silent god Vidar who will avenge Odin against the wolf. Of all giantesses, Grid was most inclined to help the gods: she took Thor and Thjalfi in for the night, and when the fire had burned low in the hearth she told Thor the truth about Geirrod. 'He was my husband once, and he's not a man to trifle with. If I know that cunning son of trolls at all, you're about to walk into a trap.'

It was too late for Thor to turn back now and fetch his hammer, but Grid lent him a belt of power and iron gloves, which would help Thor greatly in his dealings with the giants. She also gave him a thick staff, known as Gridarvol, which would cause the death of Geirrod's daughters. Armed in this way, Thor and Thjalfi set out to cross the freezing rivers known as Elivagar, and made their way to Geirrod's stronghold. The journey into Jotunheim is a story in itself: Thor waded through the icy waters with Thjalfi clinging to his back; and he had to use Grid's staff to brace himself against the surging current and prevent them both from being swept away. The thundering god was wearing the belt of power and he shouted into the tumult that he'd swell with such rage that he'd touch the heavens if the waters didn't stop. But the river kept rising as the two men advanced, and it didn't seem like your average mountain flood. When they reached the middle of the swirling torrent, Thor saw what was causing the waters to rise. Geirrod's daughter Gjalp was straddling a ravine in the mountains, and adding a great torrent of piss to the frozen waters. 'A river must be plugged at its source,' Thor remarked. He pulled a stone from the river-bed, took aim and hurled it at the splay-legged giantess, where it found its mark and stemmed the stream. From then on the crossing was easier, and Thor was able to drag himself out of the river using rowan trees that were growing at the water's edge: since this time rowan has been known as 'Thor's lifeline'.

By the time the companions arrived at Geirrod's stronghold in the mountains they had dried off, but they stank like goats, and instead of being invited to the hall they were directed to a smaller cave where the animals were kept. There was a single chair in the centre of the room, and Thor was keen for a sit-down after his exertions in the river. But no sooner had he stretched out his legs than the chair began rising to the roof of the cave, and Thor could see that he was about to be crushed against the rock. Luckily, Thor still had the staff that Grid had given him, and he braced it hard against the roof. The strongest of the gods pushed down with all his might until he heard a crack and a terrible scream. Geirrod's daughters, Gjalp and Greip, had been beneath the chair and he had broken both their backs. Were these the blushing daughters Loki meant for him to meet? Thor's beard bristled and his eyebrows cast a shadow on his face.

Geirrod acted as if nothing untoward had happened, and invited Thor and Thjalfi into the warmth of the hall. The giants were busy feasting, and there were fire-pits running the length of the cavernous space: the roof could hardly be seen for all the smoke, and great stalagmites stretched into the darkness. 'Welcome, Thor, to my great hall. We're all eager to see how strong you are, so shall we start the contest?' Geirrod reached down, plucked a white-hot lump of iron from the fire with a pair of giant tongs, and threw it right at Thor's head. After his tussle with the giant's daughters, Thor had come prepared: he was already wearing the iron gloves that Grid had given him – and a good thing too, as he was able to catch the glowing iron in mid-flight. Geirrod jumped behind a stalagmite, but Thor threw the hissing metal back with such force that it punched straight through the rock and through the giant's chest as well, sending him crashing into the cave-wall. Thor didn't leave that place until he'd dealt out punishment to all the giants feasting there:

many got to know Grid's staff. Perhaps amongst the thrill of all these broken heads, Thor forgot that it was Loki who'd proposed the trip to Geirrod's hall – and without his hammer Mjolnir.

Thjazi and the Theft of Idun's Apples

Many of the showdowns between the gods and the giants come about because one tribe has something the other tribe desires. What the Jotnar want most from the gods are their women, as well as the apples that keep the Æsir young. Idun is the guardian of these apples, and she is as much a force for renewal as the fruit that she shares out. The Æsir know her value all too well, as she was abducted once by the giant Thjazi. It only took a few days for Idun's magic to wear off, and the gods began to bend with age like ancient apple trees.

Thjazi was the descendant of a long line of mountain-giants, and his father's name was Olvaldi. Olvaldi was very wealthy in gold mined from the mountains, and when he died he divided his wealth by letting each of his giant sons take mouthfuls of gold in turn: gold is still called 'the speech of Thjazi' for this reason. Thjazi was known for being the father of Skadi of the skis, and for taking the form of a great eagle in his mountain realm of Thrymheim, where the thunder rolls around the crags. It was as an eagle that he engineered the theft of Idun and her apples.

One day, Odin, Hœnir and Loki were travelling far from home across a barren land. There wasn't much to eat in this wild place, and when the three gods descended into a valley and came across a herd of cattle milling round an old oak tree, they thought themselves lucky. They caught and killed an ox and laid its carcass in a cooking-pit, but when they broke open the oven, the meat wasn't at all cooked, and they had to replace the embers and seal the pit again. A second time they opened the oven – and still the flesh couldn't be prised off the bones. The gods wondered what magic or trickery was preventing the fire from cooking, and a voice answered them from the tree above. 'I am the reason your meat will not cook.' The gods looked up and saw a huge eagle sitting in the branches of the tree. 'I will arrange it so the oven heats your meal, as long as you give me my fill of the raw meat first,' the eagle said.

The gods agreed, and the eagle descended from the tree with a great clatter of wings, and tore at the carcass with its sharp beak. The eagle had the appetite of a giant, and gulped down two thighs and both the shoulders of the ox in no time. Loki wasn't going to stand for this, and he swung a stick at the eagle before he could polish off the remainder of their dinner. Thjazi jumped away from the blow, but the stick got tangled up in his feathers, and before Loki knew it, the eagle was flying high up into the air with the trickster god clinging onto the other end of the branch for dear life. The eagle swooped down to the valley floor, and flew so low and fast that the ground swept past in a blur and Loki's feet whistled through the grass and bounced off stones and tree-roots. He thought that soon his arms would be wrenched out of their sockets, but he could not let go for fear of hitting the ground at such speed. He cried out to Thjazi for mercy, and the eagle had a proposition.

'I'll let you go, Loki of the stick, but only if you do something for me in return.'

'I'll do whatever you like,' said Loki, 'only let me go while I've still got arms and legs to do it!'

'You must find a way to bring me Idun and her apples,' said Thjazi, 'and it is not a little thing.'

Loki saw an outcrop of jagged rock approaching and quickly

gave his vow to help the eagle. Thjazi beat his wings and circled back to the oak tree, where he set Loki down close to his companions. The trickster would not speak about what had happened, and just sat nursing his shoulders as Odin and Hœnir laughed and ate their meal.

Loki's gift was knowing what made the gods tick, and he soon found a pretext to lure Idun out of Asgard. He told the goddess that he'd found a tree in a forest outside Asgard and that the apples growing on this tree seemed to him to be even more beautiful than the apples of eternal youth. 'That's impossible, Loki: there's no fruit more desirable,' she said, but Loki caught the doubt in her voice. 'If you don't believe me, why not come and see for yourself? Bring your famous apples so that we can compare.' Loki led Idun away from Asgard, and as soon as they were out of sight of its walls, the giant Thjazi arrived in eagle form and grabbed Idun in his talons, sweeping her away to his eyrie up in Jotunheim. The mountain-giants thought this a great victory.

The Æsir knew that Idun had been abducted when they woke up to grey hairs and wrinkles in the place of smooth and glowing skin. 'The last time I saw Idun,' said her husband, 'was when she talked with Loki Laufeyson.' Loki was found and dragged to the assembly. He couldn't help but be amused. 'Are you going to beat me with your walking sticks?' he asked, 'or nibble me to death with your gums?' But the gods threatened him with powerful spells that would drive him to the brink of insanity, and he saw that they had never been more serious. 'I know that Idun is with the giant Thjazi, and tricking him will not be easy. But I'll fly to Jotunheim if you'll lend me your falcon cloak, Freyja. You won't be needing it for love-making, unless I manage to get Idun back.'

In falcon form, Loki flew to the stronghold of Thjazi in the mountains; and, as luck would have it, he arrived when Thjazi was out fishing on a mountain lake. Loki found Idun alone and in very bad humour: it was not improved when she saw who had come to rescue her. 'No time to talk right now!' said Loki. He quickly turned her into a nut and grabbed her in his beak, took her apples in his talons, and flew as fast as he could for the realm of the gods. Thjazi had taken in his catch and was rowing home when he saw a falcon flying in a hurry from his hall. He wasted no time in assuming eagle form, and raced after Loki in a giant rage, leaving the boat bobbing in the middle of the lake. The air resounded with each flap of the giant eagle's wings, and his anger could be heard far away in Asgard.

The Æsir reacted as quickly as their ageing bodies would let them. They piled kindling inside Asgard and stumbled up the stairs with flaming torches. Loki looked as if he would fly straight over the ramparts and into Asgard, but at the last minute he changed direction and flew along the walls. The giant eagle was not quite so agile, and he continued straight over the ramparts, where the gods had kindled their bonfires. The eagle's feathers caught fire as he tried to gain height, and the giant Thjazi tumbled out of the sky, landing inside the walls where he was beaten to death by the waiting gods. This killing was very famous, not least because it led Skadi to seek compensation for the murder of her giant-father, and because Thjazi's eyes were thrown into the heavens to make two of the brightest stars. Most importantly, the gods got Idun back from the giants – and with her, their youth and their vigour. Thor flexed his muscles and swung his hammer arm; Freyja rubbed the wrinkles from her hands and felt her blood begin to warm. Bragi smoothed his beard – he felt a poem coming on. Idun was just happy to no longer be a nut.

Frodi and the Giant-Girls

Humans have few dealings with the giants, and on the rare occasions when they make their way to Midgard, men show that they have little skill in harnessing the Jotnar's power. King Frodi was a king of the Skjoldung dynasty, descended from Odin, and he ruled over what is now Denmark and became the most powerful king in the north. His rule was so secure that a gold ring could be left lying on the heath and no one would think to steal it or to do harm to any other person. For this reason the name Frodi has come to be associated with the peace that reigned across the north.

One summer, Frodi went to Sweden on the invitation of King Fjolnir, and whilst he was there his eyes were caught by two slave-women of very sturdy build. These slave-women were called Fenja and Menja, and although Frodi didn't realise it at the time, they were descended from the giants of Jotunheim. He bought the slave-women from Fjolnir and set the two of them to work in Denmark. They were told to turn two millstones that were so large that nobody else in the kingdom was able to work with them. The mill – called Grotti – had the property that it would grind out whatever the owner wanted; and what Frodi wanted was more of the same for his kingdom: peace and prosperity. But Frodi worked the two giant-women too hard, only letting them rest for as long as a cuckoo remains quiet in the woods. The giant-women thought that this situation could not go on for long. One evening they chanted a song over the mill, and it began grinding out an army to do battle with their master. The sea-king Mysing led that enchanted army, and by the end of that same night he had killed Frodi and taken Denmark's riches for himself. So ended the peaceful reign of Frodi. But it can't be said that Mysing fared much better with the giant-girls. He took them and the mill Grotti with him on his ship and asked them to grind out salt, which was rare in those days and as precious to him as gold. The sisters ground through the evening, and by the middle of the night they had ground a great pile of salt onto the deck. They asked Mysing if they should stop and grind out something else, but he angrily told them to keep grinding and mind their place. The giantesses redoubled their efforts, and before long the ship was weighted down with salt and it sank to the bottom of the ocean. The giant-girls sank with the ship, and with no one to tell them to stop, they are still grinding away at the bottom of the ocean. Since then the sea has always been salty, thanks to the two giant-girls and the greed of men.

Surt

There are other giants named in the mythology – such as the fighting Hrym, and the mysterious Beli killed by Freyr with an antler for a sword. There are many giantesses, too – from Angrboda, the old witch of the Iron-wood, and Gunnlod, tricked by Odin out of her precious mead, to the mysterious giant-girls who bring discord to the early world. Some would even call the monstrous brood of Loki giants, but there's something different about these creatures: the giants' power can be harnessed and their bodies plundered by the gods, but the monsters are a force apart. They can unravel the world, swallow the sun and moon, and command the legions of the dead: their power is only to annihilate and their victory is death.

There is one more giant who must be mentioned, and he is the one to speak of last. Surt is the most powerful of the fire-giants, and he rules over the realm known as Muspelheim. This burning-hot land lies far to the south, and not even the gods can travel there. Surt – the Charred One – guards this realm. He owns a flaming sword called 'curse of kindling', which burns like an otherworldly sun. Surt's enmity towards the gods is as old as the worlds, and he will lead his people – the sons of Muspel – to wage war at Ragnarok. Surt will unsheathe his flaming sword, burning everything before him and leaving nothing but blackened earth and smoke behind. He will fight with Freyr in the final battle, and though Freyr will manage to extinguish Surt's flame before he dies, the rainbow bridge will lie in ruins and the destruction of the world will already be complete.

5

Monsters and Supernatural Beings

The struggle between the gods and giants underlies all that happens, from the world's creation to its end. But gods and giants are not the only agents in the mythical world. There are creatures living in the World-Tree that are both destructive and benign; there are rock-dwelling dwarves and elves inhabiting the brightness of the sky; valkyries who stalk the battlefield to take away the bravest of the dead; and prophetic women who can see far beyond the foresight of the gods. And there are Loki's brood, the terrible children Fenrir, Jormungand, and Hel: three monsters who will never be tamed or bent to Odin's will, and who threaten the very fabric of the world. But it's typical of Loki that he gives birth to good as well as bad, and the story of the magical horse Sleipnir is where we'll begin.

Sleipnir

The horses owned by the Æsir are listed by Odin, and their names – Glad-and-Golden, Silver-Tuft and Swift-of-Hoof – make it clear how much they are prized by the gods. Thor's horse can run just as fast through water and air as it can over land, and Freyr's horse can pass through fire and come out the other side unscathed. But there is no doubting the identity of the prince of horses. His name is Sleipnir, Odin's ride, and his eight legs make him easy to identify. He can outrun all other horses and pass between the worlds of the living and the dead. Just as Yggdrasil is the finest of trees, Skidbladnir is the best of ships, and Odin is the foremost of the gods, so Sleipnir is the best of horses.

The Master Builder

Sleipnir was born to the most unlikely of mothers and his story is tied up with that of the master builder and the hard bargain this giant made with the gods. It was early in time, and the walls of Asgard destroyed in the war between the Æsir and the Vanir had still not been repaired. It worried Odin that the Jotnar would quickly overrun Asgard if they attacked, and he walked the broken earthworks wondering what kind of wall would be needed to keep out trolls and mountain-giants. One day a mysterious travelling stonemason crossed the rainbow bridge with an answer. He proposed to build a wall of stone so high and strong that it would make the home of the gods impregnable, and to do it in the space of just three seasons.

The All-Father gathered the gods together to consider the builder's proposal. The price the man demanded was high – he not only wanted to be given the sun and the moon, but also the goddess Freyja and her golden tears – and this was not a price that the gods were willing to pay. However, Loki sat looking thoughtful as he listened to the news. 'We know that the builder can't possibly complete the task that he's set himself,' he said. 'So what's the problem here? Why not watch him labour, and take bets on just how far he gets? He won't win Freyja, and we'll get a head start on our wall.' It seemed win-win the way the son of Laufey told it. So the gods came back to the builder with an offer: he could have the sun and the moon and Freyja too, but only if he finished the wall by the first day of summer. 'Can I use my horse, at least?' asked the giant. The gods agreed, and Odin and the builder swore oaths to each other in front of many witnesses. Both sides were pleased with the deal they had struck.

It shouldn't have been possible for one man to build such a towering wall in such a short space of time, even if he was a giant, as several of the gods suspected. But there was the small matter of the builder's horse, named Svadilfari. If the builder was strong and steady in his work, the horse was twice as strong, and never needed rest. The builder started work on the first day of winter: he laid the stones by day and used Svadilfari to drag great boulders to the wall by night; and the work progressed at a fast pace through the winter and the spring. The wall was high and wide and unassailable, just as the builder had promised. With three days to go until the start of summer, the wall had almost reached the gates of Asgard – and now the gods began to panic. They couldn't possibly give Freyja to the builder, let alone the sun and moon: the heavens would be ruined. But they had also sworn solemn vows. There was no doubt they were in a fix, and as they sat blaming each other for this turn of affairs, the gods remembered that it was Loki who had spoken most strongly in favour of their deal with the builder. Odin drew the trickster close. 'You'd best come up with a plan, Loki, or you'll suffer a much worse fate than that awaiting Freyja and the moon.' He described in great detail how a slow death in Asgard could unfold, and the trickster swore he'd make things right.

Svadilfari was in great health, and showed no signs of tiring, but Loki knew that all stallions have a weakness. The gods watched the son of Laufey walk into the forest and watched a beautiful mare walk out the same way he'd gone in, swishing her tail and whinnying. When Svadilfari saw the mare, he couldn't resist his instincts: he broke free from his harness and chased Loki beneath the unfinished wall, much to the amusement of the gods. Loki led Svadilfari on a dance across the plains, and it was soon clear that the work on the wall would be delayed. When the builder realised that he wouldn't be able to finish the work without Svadilfari, he flew into the kind of rage that only mountain-giants are capable of – and then the gods were sure about what kind of being he was. They forgot their solemn pledges not to do the builder harm, and called on Thor to come back from the East and rid them of this raging tradesman.

It only took one blow from Mjolnir to shatter the giant's skull into a thousand pieces and to send him tumbling down to Hel. In this way, Thor paid the builder his wages and the gods escaped a bargain that would have seen the whole world ruined for the price of an impregnable wall. Only, the wall was never finished, and never will be finished: there's a weakness in the stronghold of the gods, and this will play its part at Ragnarok. As for Loki, he became pregnant by the giant stallion Svadilfari, and some months later he gave birth to a beautiful grey colt, which happened to have eight legs. And that is the story of how Sleipnir, the very best of horses, came to be.

Loki's Monstrous Children

Sleipnir is an animal treasured by Odin, and the gods counted themselves lucky that Loki was there to help them outwit the master builder. But Loki's other children were not such welcome additions to the world. Loki was not content with marriage to the loyal Sigyn, and paid regular visits to Angrboda, an old giantess who lived in the Iron-wood where the wolves come from. After Loki's visits she gave birth to three children feared across the nine worlds: their names are Hel, Fenrir and Jormungand. When the Æsir found out that these monstrous children were being raised in Jotunheim and being taught to hate the gods, it was decided that something should be done. Odin took the fierce daughter Hel, and sent her down to the underworld to rule over the dead. Jormungand – a serpent even at this time, though not the world-entwining monster it would become – was thrown into the deepest part of the encircling sea. The wolf Fenrir was the child Odin feared the most, because he saw that their fates were tied together. He decided that Fenrir should grow up amongst the gods – for what better way to keep evil at bay than to keep it close at hand?

Hel

Loki's daughter is dreadful to behold. Half her body is as black as a carcass from a bog, and the other half is as pale as a bloated corpse, and her moods are at one with the drizzle and the dark of Niflheim. She is the ruler of the realm of the dead, where she holds court in the rain-lashed hall of Eljudnir and is obliged to host all those who die of illness or old age. The unhappy dominion of Hel is vast, and the hosts of the dead that she counts as guests include Baldr, and his wife Nanna, who followed the shining god down beneath the roots of Yggdrasil and sits beside him in a seat of honour. Hel owns a terrifying wolf called Garm, who is leashed in the mouth of a cave outside the gates of Hel and is always on guard in case the dead should try to leave.

Garm will howl at the approach of Ragnarok and break free from his leash as all the inhabitants of Hel march out with their monstrous brethren. Hel is friend to no one and protective of her dominion of death, but even she had some sympathy for the untimely arrival of Baldr in her halls. Hel gave the gods a chance to free the son of Odin from her realm, but the fact that not all creatures wept for Baldr and her conditions were not met serves as a reminder of just how hard it is to bend the laws of death.

Fenrir

Hel is sometimes referred to as sister of the monstrous wolf, the second of Loki's children with the giant Angrboda. Fenrir is the most feared of all wolves. One of his sons, the wolf Skoll, chases the sun through the sky and will consume it whole at Ragnarok. Another son called Hati chases the moon and will also catch up with it eventually. Fenrir himself, the fame-wolf, will be the killer of the All-Father in the final battle: an act that is all the more monstrous as it was Odin who raised this creature in the home of the gods.

Odin was used to feeding the most ferocious of wolves at his table, but soon after the gods adopted Fenrir it became clear that he was no ordinary wolf. The gods were alarmed at the rate at which he grew, and before long Tyr was the only man brave enough to approach this monster from the Iron-wood. The gods decided that something had to be done before Fenrir became impossible to control, and they devised a plan to shackle him with a chain of bolted iron. They called this shackle Læding, and asked Fenrir if he would like to test his strength against it. Fenrir looked at the iron shackle, and decided that it would not hold him back. The wolf only had to plant his feet and flex the muscles in his legs and the shackle snapped in two. The gods would need a stronger fetter. The next shackle they forged was twice as strong: they named it Dromi. The gods asked if Fenrir would like to test himself against this impressive chain and gain endless fame for his strength, but the wolf was unsure. It was a magnificent piece of forged iron, each link as weighty as a boulder and as large as a man's head. Still, the wolf reasoned that he'd been growing in strength since he broke Læding, and the thought of being renowned for such a feat persuaded him to try. He allowed the gods to wind the chain around his legs, and when everything was secured he strained against the heavy shackle, beating it against the ground and twisting his legs with all his might. The fetter burst open with such force that the pieces flew far into the distance. It is because of these feats that we call completing a difficult task 'loosening yourself from Læding' or 'breaking free from Dromi'.

The gods needed help if they were going to make a shackle that could not be broken by the strongest creature in the world, and they turned to the greatest metalworkers in the world: the dwarves. Freyr's servant Skirnir travelled down beneath the roots of Yggdrasil to the land of Svartalfheim, and found the ancestors of Durin hammering at their forges in the half-light. The dwarves agreed to fashion the shackle known as Gleipnir: it is made from six materials that are very hard to find. The first of these is the sound of a cat's footprints; the second is the beard of a woman; the third is the root of a mountain; the fourth is the sinew of a bear; the fifth is the breath of a fish; and the final element is the spit of a bird. If the cat makes no sound and the fish has no breath and women have no beards, it is because these things were taken by the dwarves to make their magic fetter. Gleipnir was stronger than any object made before or since, yet it was as smooth and flexible as silk. The gods were very pleased.

Odin had chosen a special place for the final trial of Fenrir's strength: an island called Lyngvi in the centre of a pitch-black lake. The gods passed Gleipnir round and tested it, remarking how strong it seemed, but also encouraging Fenrir by saying that it would not be impossible to break. 'And what if I can't free myself?' asked Fenrir. 'We hardly need to fear a wolf that can't break a ribbon: we'll let you go, of course,' said Bragi in his silky voice. Fenrir was not convinced: if this ribbon had been made strong with powerful magic as he suspected, he'd quickly find himself abandoned on this island in the lake. But rather than having his courage and strength called into question, Fenrir demanded that one of the gods put his hand between his jaws as he was being bound. 'It will be a sign of your good faith, as I fear I'm being tricked.'

The gods looked at each other and it seemed that no one was willing to make this sacrifice, until Tyr stepped forward and stuck his hand between the wolf's sharp teeth. The gods wound the ribbon Gleipnir round Fenrir's legs, and the more the wolf strained to break himself free the tighter it grew. The gods all laughed at the wolf's struggles: all except Tyr, that is, whose hand had been bitten clean off at the wrist. Since then, the wrist has been called the 'wolf bone' in honour of the god who sacrificed his hand.

When the gods felt sure that Fenrir could not escape from Gleipnir, they took the loose end of the shackle and tied it to a large stone called Gjoll, burying this stone deep in the earth. One of the gods managed to slip a sword into Fenrir's gaping mouth as he lunged at Odin. The sword lodged upright, and wedged Fenrir's jaws open so that he could do no harm. From his gaping mouth an endless stream of drool drips to the ground; and it is the source of the river Van which carries Fenrir's expectation of revenge across the world. He will remain bound by the shackle until the end of time, when all bonds will break and he will be released to take vengeance on the gods.

Jormungand

The third of Loki's monstrous children is Jormungand, the Midgard Serpent. When Odin threw Jormungand into the deepest part of the encircling sea he thought to banish the serpent to a place where it could do least harm. But in the vast depths Jormungand was able to grow unchecked and to stretch along the ocean floor, and it eventually grew so large that it was able to encircle the whole world in its coils. When the serpent moves the deep oceans surge, and it is known that when Jormungand uncoils itself and rises from the depths the seas will inundate the land and the world itself will unravel at the seams. It is wise to leave the serpent undisturbed. Only, Thor knows that he is destined to meet Jormungand at Ragnarok and he is impatient to test his strength against the serpent's massive bulk.

Thor's Fishing Trip

Thor had been tricked once in a trial of strength in the halls of Utgarda-Loki when he found himself unable to lift the Midgard Serpent and drag it from the ocean floor. Thor took it very hard that he had been shamed in this way, thinking he was lifting a cat off its feet, when really he was pulling at the coils of Jormungand. Fate said that the two were set to meet at Ragnarok, but Thor said otherwise. He'd meet the serpent on his own terms.

It was during Thor's visit to the home of the frost-giant Hymir that he found the opportunity. Thor had eaten Hymir out of house and home and the giant complained loudly that he'd have to go fishing to satisfy such a greedy guest. Thor stopped in the midst of cleaning his plate: 'I'll row out with you into the encircling sea,' he said; 'two pairs of hands are always better on a boat.' Hymir wasn't sure that Thor would make much difference at the oars, small as he was: 'You'll probably freeze if you go out as far as the giants are accustomed.' Thor's eyes flashed when Hymir told him this: he wanted to bash the giant with his hammer there and then, but at this time he had bigger fish to fry. 'It's not certain which of the two of us will turn the boat around,' he replied through gritted teeth. For bait the giant told Thor to go into the fields and find what he could, so the next morning Thor marched up into the shieling and chose the most impressive animal in Hymir's herd – a jet-black ox – grabbing its horns and ripping its head clean off. With his bait trailing behind him, Thor returned to the shore. It was clear that he was not fishing for minnows.

Hymir had already launched the boat and Thor had to wade into the shallows to catch him up. Both men glared at each other, but Hymir had to admit that Thor was pretty handy with the oars. The boat sped through the water until they had rowed far from the shore. Hymir looked down into the glassy depths and was sure that Thor would soon want to stop, but the god kept rowing and Hymir's face darkened. 'This is a good spot to cast our lines,' the giant said at last. 'These are the fishing grounds where I catch the biggest whales.' But Thor pretended not to hear and redoubled his efforts at the oars. Hymir worried that if they went much further into the open seas they would risk disturbing the Midgard Serpent with their lines.

Eventually Thor stopped rowing: the boat was now far out of sight of the land. Hymir cast his lines and soon caught two whales, but Thor had baited his line more cunningly. He attached the ox-head to a heavy hook and let the line sink to the very bottom of the ocean. Sure enough, the Midgard Serpent rose from its slumber on the ocean floor, opened its eyes in the gloom, and closed its jaws around the ox-head, at which point Thor pulled hard at the line. When the serpent felt the pain of the hook and realised that it had been tricked, it jerked its head and the god's elbows slammed into the gunwale. Now Thor became really angry. He summoned his divine strength, and bracing his feet against the floor of the boat he hauled the line with all his might. The strain was so great that Thor's feet broke through the strakes at the bottom of the boat, but he held fast and reeled in the line, and eventually he dragged the great serpent to the surface of the churning sea. Jormungand reared up out of the water, and for a moment the two great adversaries stared at each other: close enough to touch, and separated by a single line that quivered under the tension of Thor's grip. The ocean trembled, the seabed shook, and the earth let out a groan. Thor raised his hammer behind him to deliver the killing blow – and at that moment the giant Hymir reached forward with his fishing knife and cut the line with a resounding 'snap'. The serpent immediately sank back beneath the surface and the waters calmed.

The journey back to shore was not a happy one, and Hymir didn't say a word as he worked the oars. Thor had come within a hair's breadth of killing the Midgard Serpent and changing the events that had been foretold. But who's to say that Jormungand's death throes would not have unravelled all creation, and hastened the very event that the gods fear most? Perhaps in this case, it took a giant to balance out the reckless ambition of a god.

Women of Fate

Higher than the monsters, higher even than the gods and god-desses, higher than the branching limbs of Yggdrasil itself, stands fate. Fate controls everything, and fate is always in the hands of women.

The valkyries are the shield-bearing women who decide the fate of warriors in battle. They decide who should live and who should die to swell the ranks of the Einherjar. These women ride across the heavens in helmets and burnished mail, and their spears catch the light as they are drawn like birds of carrion to battle. They are called Victory-Storm, and Battle-Cry, Spear-Shaker and Mail-Coat-of-Conflict, and the names they take reflect their love of war. Most of the time these warrior-women obey Odin, though they have been known to take opposing sides in battle, and even to grant the All-Father the victory he wants whilst taking the life of a hero from the winning side. It is said that the war-king Hakon was brought to Odin's halls in blood-stained mail after routing his enemies: he died a victor, and the valkyries offered him cool ale and called on Odin to welcome an undefeated warrior to a seat of honour in Valhalla. Odin's look was fierce as he came to greet the king.

Freyja is known as the foremost of the valkyries, and she owns a cloak of feathers that allows her to traverse the nine worlds as swiftly as a bird. The valkyries that serve her and Odin have also been known to wear garments that turn them into white-necked swans, and it is in this disguise that they are most often seen by men. Valkyries sometimes fall in love with human heroes, though they are usually unwilling to tie themselves to marriage and give up the freedom to decide who lives and dies. When the valkyrie Brynhild disobeyed Odin's orders, the father of the gods punished her with marriage: she'd sleep for years and only wake when a hero came to claim her.

Though Odin holds some sway over the valkyries who serve in Valhalla, there are other women of fate whom Odin must consult about his own fate. The volur – whose wands mark them out as women of rare power – are especially gifted in prophecies. Odin sought an audience with one prophetess raised by giants at the beginning of the world to hear the ancient history recounted and to learn about the future. She knew about the gaping void before the start of history; she knew that the moon would be swallowed and the sun grow black; and she knew that Baldr would return once the world had been reborn.

The prophetess also spoke about those women called the norns who determine all that happens: both good and bad. Their names are Destiny, Becoming, and Upcoming, and they sit by the Well of Fate tending to the World-Tree, casting lots, and weaving out the lives of every being on this earth. When the thread woven by the norns runs out, there is not a human or a god powerful enough to change this destiny. Fate cannot be worked around.

Before great battles, the valkyries can sometimes be seen weaving on looms of their own: whilst the ravens were gathering over Irish lands a man named Dorrud watched twelve riders converge on the ruins of a building. When he looked in at the window, he saw valkyries chanting as they worked a loom strung with entrails and weighted with men's heads. The pin-beaters were arrows dripping blood. The valkyries wove with their swords drawn and wound the names of champions into a web of war: as they did so the skies darkened and the clouds turned red as gore. When the women were done with their song they ripped the weft to shreds and each rode away with her own piece: six to the north and six to the south.

As the two armies faced each other through the early morning mist, the warriors knew that what the valkyries had determined for each of them would come to pass.

There are other women of fate who help a woman bring a child into the world and who should be prayed to for ease of birth, as well as female spirits who incite humans to great deeds and to evil, appearing in dreams from the world of the dead. These women of fate are together known as the disir, and they don't belong to any race but walk amongst the gods, the giants and the elves. A blood-sacrifice should be made to the disir, and if they are not happy with what's offered it won't be long before they take a sacrifice themselves.

Elves

Of all the supernatural beings in the world, the elves are closest to the gods and the most mysterious. They live in the bright realm of Alfheim and they shine like the heavens. If a person has glowing skin and bright eyes, or a beauty that seems not to belong to this world, they are said to be related to the elves. The god Freyr is said to rule over Alfheim, and the elves can often be found in Asgard sharing the same table as the gods. They are listed among the guests at Ægir's feast, and they are witness to the shaming of the gods by Loki. As beings of the light and sky, elves have little reason to interact with people, and when they do it is not always to help. Their wisdom as well as their beauty is renowned, but there is a danger in interacting with the elves and in travelling to the forests and hidden valleys to seek them out. Elves can enchant and seduce, make people lose their minds, and cause invisible harm to humans and their livestock. Their binding magic is reckoned to be no less powerful than the enchantments of the gods, and sacrifices are made to both the Æsir and the elves.

Volund the Smith

One of the few elves whose name is widely known is Volund, the greatest of all craftsmen. Volund was one of three brothers who went out on the bright snow to hunt game. The brothers built a hunter's cabin by a frozen lake, and before long three mysterious women came to the lake. They were valkyries, and they had taken the form of white-necked swans. The swan-maidens each chose one of the shining brothers as a lover: the valkyrie known as 'Strange Creature' draped herself round Volund's neck. The brothers lived there with the swan-maidens for seven years, but by the eighth year the valkyries had grown restless and could hear the call of battle and the call of fate. In the ninth year they left, flying away as silently as they'd arrived. Volund's two brothers were distraught and left to seek their lovers – the middle brother Egil was a famous archer and thought he'd be able to track the swan-women down – but Volund stayed by the lake and threw himself into his work. The ringing of the anvil could be heard day and night as he twisted red gold into serpent shapes, making bright rings for his lover in the hope that she'd return.

Nidud was a king in Sweden at the time, and news came to him of a mysterious craftsman up by the lake who could be heard working at his forge day and night. The king sent men to Volund's home, and their burnished shields caught the light of the waning moon as they entered the clearing by the lake. They admired the bright rings hanging the length of Volund's hall, and took one of them. When Volund returned from the lake he counted the rings and found one missing – and he stared so long into the fire hoping that his lover had returned that he fell asleep, and woke to find that he had been surrounded by Nidud's men.

The warriors tied Volund up and dragged him to their king's hall. When the elf was brought before the king, he saw that Nidud had given the missing ring to his daughter Bodvild, and that he'd strapped Volund's sword to his own belt. Whenever the elf caught sight of his possessions he showed his teeth, and the look in his eyes was like a serpent's. The queen was scared of this fierce man: she asked her husband to cut the elf's hamstrings so that he couldn't escape or do them harm. Volund's sinews were cut behind his knees, and he was imprisoned in a smithy on an island just off the shore, where the king forced him to work precious metals and to create objects that made Nidud the wonder of the surrounding tribes.

Volund worked without sleep, nursing a hatred for his captors. Nidud wore Volund's sword openly, and the princess Bodvild wore his lover's ring: this hurt him the most. One day the young sons of Nidud came to watch the craftsman at work. They asked to see what he was making, and Volund showed them a glimpse of precious things. He asked them to come again in the morning in secret: he'd give them each a treasure made especially for them. The boys came to the smithy early and without an escort; and whilst they were looking into the box of gold rings, Volund severed their heads from their slender necks. He buried their bodies beneath his anvil, but kept their heads for a project he'd been planning: he inlaid the skulls with silver and crafted two exquisite cups for Nidud. He turned the boys' eyes into strange gems that he sent to Nidud's queen, and for Bodvild he made a beautiful bracelet out of their milk teeth.

Soon Volund had a chance to double his revenge: Bodvild, the king's daughter, came to him with a request to repair the elf-ring that had broken. Volund sat her down in his smithy and plied her with drink until she was unable to stand. Volund's brother Egil had been collecting feathers for the blacksmith to make wings in his workshop, and the elf raised himself up off his crippled legs with a beat of his arms and raped the daughter who'd taken his ring, leaving her weeping and alone on the island as he flew into the sky.

Volund visited the hall of Nidud before leaving for the bright clouds of Alfheim. Nidud wanted to know what had happened to his boys: he was bent over with grief. Volund first made the king swear oaths that he'd not harm his daughter and then revealed that she was pregnant with his child. Then he told the king to go to the smithy: there he'd find the anvil stained with blood and the mangled bodies of his sons buried in the mud. He revealed that the king had been drinking from silver cups the size of small boys' heads; when the queen had been admiring her jewels, she'd been admiring their unseeing eyes; when Bodvild had shaken the delicate bracelet on her arm, her brothers' teeth had been tinkling like silver tears. Nothing he could have said would have been harder for Nidud to hear than this, but the plight of Bodvild – the one who'd worn the ring intended for the swan-white maid – was harder still. Volund flew away, his terrible revenge complete.

Dwarves

Before the gods gave the dwarves consciousness they were little more than maggots writhing blindly in the dark of Ymir's flesh. The first of the dwarves that the gods created was named Motsognir, and Durin the second – the dwarf who recorded the names of the elders Nyi and Nithi, Dvalin, Nar and Nain, and of all those who came after. With the spark of life came wisdom and a love of crafting precious things, but the dwarves remember their origins in the earth and prefer to live below the ground in caves and rocks and caverns under Yggdrasil. Whilst the dark land of Svartalfheim is home to the dwarves, they can also be found under the mountains of Midgard, where they mine precious metals and make their homes in dripping halls amongst the rocks. Dwarves are renowned as blacksmiths and jewellers, and they create objects that breathe life into base metals. Sif's golden wig – which grows like real hair – was made by the sons of Ivaldi the dwarf, as was Odin's spear Gungnir and Freyr's ship Skidbladnir. When Loki challenged the dwarf-smith Eitri to match this accomplishment, he produced the hammer Mjolnir – which seeks out Thor's hand – along with Freyr's golden boar and the ring Draupnir which replicates itself. The dwarf-made fetter that bound Fenrir surpassed anything the gods were able to devise themselves, as does Freyja's famous necklace. The dwarves may even have played a role in the creation of humankind, crafting likenesses in wood to which the gods gave life. The dwarves are usually willing to help the gods, but sometimes they exact a high price for their work: the dwarf Brokk sowed Loki's mouth shut after being denied the trickster's head as payment, leaving him with a crooked mouth, and the brothers Fjalar and Galar killed the wise being Kvasir to make the mead of poetry.

A pale-faced dwarf named Alviss even had the nerve to claim Thor's daughter as a bride, and very nearly won her hand. Thor would only agree to honour a match agreed without his blessing if Alviss could answer all the questions that he posed. Thor took his time, asking for the names by which the sun and moon, night and day, wind and sea and fire were known amongst the different beings of the world. Thor had not forgotten that the dwarves were created early in the world and that their wisdom is renowned: but he also knew that the rock-dwellers have a weakness. Alviss lived up to his name of 'All-Wise' and answered every question Thor could think to ask, but the dwarf became so carried away with proving his wisdom that he forgot to find shelter beneath the ground when the sun came up, and was promptly turned to stone. The dwarves' habit of living in the darkness makes them ill-suited to the light. Along with the most famous of dwarves, such as the beings North, East, South and West, who hold up the sky at the four corners of the world, there are many more who are remembered only by their names. The poets recall Gandalf and Vindalf, Thorin and Oak-shield, but their stories have all been forgotten.

The Sons of Hreidmar and Andvari's Gold

One story that's remembered is that of Hreidmar and his sons. Hreidmar was a powerful man living in the early days of the world, and he had three sons named Otr, Regin and Fafnir, who were able to change their shape. One day, Otr had taken the form of an otter to catch salmon at a nearby waterfall. At this time, the gods Odin, Hœnir and Loki were travelling through Midgard, exploring its hidden places and learning more about the world. They followed a river into the mountains and came across the pool in which Otr had been hunting. He was dozing on the bank with a salmon at his feet and didn't hear the gods approach because of the roar from the waterfall. Loki picked up a stone and threw it at Otr, killing him with one blow. The gods picked up the otter and the half-eaten salmon, and went searching for a place to spend the night.

Over the hill was the home of Hreidmar, and when the gods saw fires burning in the twilight they walked up to the hall and asked the farmer for hospitality. Loki proudly presented Hreidmar with his catch, not knowing that he was holding out the body of the farmer's son. Hreidmar called in his other sons, Regin and Fafnir. 'Do you see what these visitors have brought us as a gift? Do you recognise his pelt?' Hreidmar and his sons then rushed the gods and overpowered them, taking Odin's spear and Loki's magic shoes. When the Æsir learned that the otter Loki had killed was Hreidmar's son, they offered to pay whatever ransom the farmer thought appropriate. The farmer demanded a heavy price in return for their lives. 'I'll have the otter skinned and the hide sown up to make a bag. You'll fill this bag with treasure and cover the outside so that I can no longer see my son for all the gold. That's the only way that we'll be reconciled.'

Loki was responsible for Otr's death, and he was sent to find the ransom whilst Odin and Hœnir stayed behind as hostages. Loki headed for Svartalfheim, the land of the dwarves, where there was gold to be found in great quantities. He had heard of a certain dwarf named Andvari who owned a hoard large enough to repay their debts to the farmer. Loki found Andvari swimming near his home in the form of a pike, and the fleet-footed god easily caught the dwarf and marched him back to his cave. Andvari had no choice but to show Loki where his treasure was kept, and to hand it all over to the god. But out of the corner of his eye Loki noticed the dwarf pocketing something. He gestured for the dwarf to hand over whatever it was he was hiding, and after many protests Andvari opened his hand to reveal a golden ring. He begged Loki not to take it, as the magic ring could replicate itself and would allow him to regain his wealth:

but Loki took the ring, along with the rest of the gold. The ring was known as Andvaranaut, Andvari's gift, and it was not a gift made in good faith.

As Loki was leaving, the dwarf called after him and cursed the gold. 'It will cause the death of anyone who owns it,' he shouted, 'and you'll regret ever stepping foot in Andvari's hall!' Loki shrugged his shoulders: he was not planning to keep the gold himself.

Loki returned to Odin and Hœnir and showed them the hoard; and Odin admired the ring Andvaranaut so much that he decided to hang on to it. The gods then filled the otter bag with gold, and piled the rest of Andvari's hoard over the top so that the hide was covered. Hreidmar came to inspect the ransom: he noticed a single whisker poking out of the pile of gold, and would not consider granting the gods their freedom until it was covered. Odin took Andvaranaut, turned it in his fingers, and placed it over the whisker. He looked at Hreidmar with a glimmer like red gold in his eyes. 'Now our debt is paid,' he said. Hreidmar's sons gave Odin back his spear and Loki back his magic shoes, and once the gods were out of danger, Loki took great pleasure in telling Hreidmar that the gold was cursed and that it would destroy whoever owned it.

Hreidmar took the gold and the ring Andvaranaut, and locked them away for safekeeping: if the gold was cursed, that was even more reason to keep it under his watchful eye! But it wasn't long before Hreidmar's sons came to their father and asked for a share of the ransom – after all, they were Otr's brothers. Hreidmar, though, would not part with a single coin. 'Otr was my son, and now the gold is also mine, and will belong to no one else until the day I die!' Seeing there was no way to get round their father, the brothers took hold of him and cut his throat. Regin thought the gold should now be divided equally between the two brothers, but Fafnir mocked Regin for killing his own father and told him that he wouldn't get a penny. Fafnir had already tried on Hreidmar's magic helmet, which caused dread in any creature that looked at it, and Regin was not immune. He fled to the land of the Danes and left Fafnir alone with his cursed inheritance. Fafnir for his part walked deep into the heath and turned himself into a dragon, so that he could protect his precious treasure from ever passing into another's hands.

Better that the dwarf's gold had remained with Fafnir and the curse had been buried with it in the heather! But a hero would come to claim the hoard, and Andvari's gold would pass into the world of men. The hero's name was Sigurd of the Volsungs and his story is the most famous of the legends of the North.

6

Sigurd and the Volsungs

After the gods paid Otr's ransom with Andvari's gold, their debt was discharged. They turned their attention to other things. But Odin did not forget the hard bargain Hreidmar had made, and Regin did not forget that he'd been deprived of his inheritance. It was not the dragon's fate to lie peacefully on his hoard of gold, but it would not be a god or dwarf that would come to challenge him: that task would be left to a hero from the world of men. In the story of the Volsungs, the gods take a step back into the shadows, a family rises under the watchful eye of Odin, and a human hero takes centre stage. Myth blurs into legend. This is the story of Sigurd of the Volsungs: it is a story that begins with the rise of a great dynasty and ends with a terrible feud between in-laws; and there's far more human drama here than Sigurd's fame as a dragon-slayer suggests.

The Volsung Line

Like so many legendary heroes, Sigurd traces his descent back to the gods. Sigi was the great-great-grandfather of Sigurd, and he was said to be the son of Odin. One day, Sigi went out hunting with another man's slave; and when the two men laid out their kills in the evening, the slave had proved himself to be the better hunter. Sigi killed the slave and buried him in a snowdrift; and because he kept quiet about what he had done, it became murder. The body turned up, as bodies tend to do, and Sigi was declared an outlaw. He would not have survived long if Odin hadn't appeared and guided his son far away from his ancestral home to a place where warships lay waiting. Odin gave Sigi a troop of warriors to lead, and the hero won victory in many battles.

Sigi made war on the surrounding tribes until he'd carved out a great kingdom named Hunaland. He ruled over it for many years, and had a son called Rerir: a strong and capable man, as fond of war as his father had been in his prime. When Sigi's in-laws saw that the king was growing old and frail, they killed him, intending to rule over the kingdom in his place, but the young Rerir gathered an army and took revenge, killing every one of his father's attackers, even though they were his uncles. Rerir took all the power and wealth that his father had wielded, but he couldn't conceive a child with his queen, and it seemed that there would be no heirs to continue the line of Sigi and of Rerir.

Rerir prayed to the goddess Frigg, who was sympathetic to his plight. With Odin's blessing, she sent a valkyrie named Hljod down to Rerir in the form of a crow. Hljod dropped an apple in Rerir's lap, and the king looked up at the crow and knew the meaning of the gift. He ate some of the apple and slept with his queen, and it was soon clear to everyone that she was carrying a child. The couple waited in expectation for the birth, but a year passed and there was no sign that the child was ready to be born.

In fact, the pregnancy lasted for so long that Rerir himself died before he saw the birth, and the queen became increasingly desperate. After six years carrying the child, she begged for it to be cut from her womb. The huge infant was named Volsung, and he kissed his mother on the cheek before she died.

Despite losing both his parents, Volsung had a head start in life: he was able to walk from birth, and he quickly grew to be a formidable warrior. He rose through the ranks to rule over Hunaland with the same spirit as his father, fighting many battles and securing his lands. Once his rule was secure, Volsung ordered a magnificent hall to be built as a symbol of his power, and it was famed across the world for the huge tree that stood at its centre. The tree's branches were covered in blossom and grew up through the rafters, and it was called Barnstokk in the common tongue. When King Volsung was at the height of his power, the apple-bearing valkyrie named Hljod came back to Hunaland and married Volsung. They had a happy marriage, and Hljod secured the Volsung line with ten children: nine sons and a daughter. Each of the young Volsungs stood out from the crowd, but the most accomplished of all were the first-born: twins named Sigmund and Signy.

The Sword in the Tree

When the twins had grown up, Volsung arranged to marry his daughter Signy to a powerful king named Siggeir, who ruled over the land of the Geats. Signy was not happy with the match. A great wedding feast was prepared in the hall of the Volsungs, and a great many followers accompanied Siggeir across the sea to the celebrations. Towards the end of the evening, when the hearth fires were burning low around the great trunk of

Barnstokk, an old man with a grey beard entered the hall. He wore a dirty cloak with a hood pulled low over one eye, and as he walked towards the centre of the hall the guests saw that he had no shoes on his feet. Nobody knew whether to welcome him or not. The mysterious old man drew a sword from under his cloak and plunged it straight into the tree. He turned to address the guests and told them that whoever was able to pull the sword free from the trunk would receive it as a gift. The man then left with as little ceremony as he had arrived, disappearing into the darkness outside.

Many men jostled to take their turn at attempting to free the sword. The heroes tried first; and later, men of less renown had a go: they were all disappointed. Then Volsung's eldest son Sigmund stepped forward: the sword seemed to loosen itself at his touch and he pulled it free. Everyone agreed that it was the finest sword they had ever seen, and Siggeir offered to buy it from the young Volsung for three times its weight in gold. Sigmund refused – it was clear that it was meant to be wielded by a Volsung and not by Siggeir: the King of the Geats could offer whatever he liked, including all his wealth and lands, but Sigmund would never relinquish the sword. Siggeir was angry at the Volsung boy's insolence, and whilst outwardly he laughed it off, he was already planning to avenge the insult. The next day, Siggeir surprised the Volsungs by announcing his departure. 'I'll leave this morning with my new bride, and not trouble you for further hospitality. But the Geats will return the invitation before too long: this wedding feast will be continued at my expense.'

Signy warned her father that if he let her go to Geatland, it would cause strife in their family for years to come, but Volsung brushed aside her misgivings and agreed to come and visit

Siggeir in three months' time. There is little accounting for the stubbornness of kings.

The Death of Volsung

Volsung and his sons travelled to Siggeir's kingdom as they had promised, taking three well-crewed ships and arriving on the shores of Geatland early in the evening. When they disembarked, Signy greeted them with the news that Siggeir had gathered a huge army and planned to offer his guests sword-points instead of feasting cups. She urged her father and brothers to sail home and come back with an army. 'Nonsense,' replied Volsung, 'I've made a vow never to flee from fire or cold steel, and I'd rather all my sons died in battle than be taunted back home as cowards. Every man must fall at the appointed time: the Volsungs will not ask for any quarter.'

He sent Signy back to be with her husband, and the Volsungs camped near their ships. They did not have long to wait for battle: as dawn broke, they found a great army bearing down on them, and ran forward in their mail to meet the onslaught. The small band of Volsungs fought so bravely that it is said they broke the ranks of Siggeir's army eight times that day, but eventually the numbers became so overwhelming that Volsung was cut down in the press of bodies, and his sons were taken captive. Signy came to her husband and pleaded that for her sake, he might hold off from killing her brothers all at once. 'Wouldn't it be better to celebrate your capture of these noble prisoners, and give me time to reconcile myself to their deaths?' Siggeir thought his wife was mad not to allow the Volsungs a quick death, but he was happy to humiliate his enemies by laying a great trunk over their legs as makeshift stocks, and leaving them out in the open for anyone to see. The brothers sat trapped by the tree-trunk until night came, and just as they were settling down to sleep a great she-wolf ran out of the forest and devoured the brother sitting closest to the tree-line. It was as easy as picking a morsel off a spit. Each night, the same wolf came and attacked one of the brothers, until after nine nights only the eldest Volsung was left sitting beneath the trunk: Signy's twin brother Sigmund. Signy would have to intervene.

The queen sent a man to her brother with a bowl of honey hidden in his cloak. The man covered Sigmund's face with the honey and poured some in the hero's mouth. When the she-wolf came to devour the last of the Volsung brothers, she licked Sigmund's face and his open mouth to reach the honey, and when Sigmund felt the tongue of the she-wolf between his teeth he knew what to do. He bit down hard and held on tight as the animal thrashed around in agony. Even when the wolf braced against the tree-trunk so forcefully that the wood split down the middle, Sigmund still held on, and eventually he ripped the wolf's tongue out by the roots. Some say that the wolf was Siggeir's mother in disguise.

Sigmund Gets an Heir

Siggeir now believed that all the Volsung brothers were dead, but Sigmund had escaped to the forest where he was plotting his revenge. His twin sister learned where his hideout was, and when her son was ten years old she sent the boy out to Sigmund to see if he could be any use to his uncle. Sigmund received the lad warmly enough, and set him to making bread whilst he collected firewood. When the hero came back to the hideout, he asked the boy how the bread was getting on. 'Not so well,' the boy answered. 'There was something alive in the flour and I couldn't get the baking done.' Sigmund knew that such a timid boy would be no use to him, and his sister agreed: 'Take the boy away and kill him,' was her cold reply. And Sigmund did as she asked. The same thing happened with the second child of Signy and Siggeir, and he was also given to the wolves.

Signy knew that she would have to take matters into her own hands if the Volsungs were to be avenged. She took the shape of a sorceress and went to her brother in the forest. Sigmund took her in and found that he desired the company of a woman. They shared a bed for three nights, and when Signy returned to Siggeir's halls she was pregnant with her brother's child.

When this son of the Volsung twins was born, he was named Sinfjotli, and his fate was very different to that of the boys that came before him. When he was ten years old, his mother tested his mettle by sewing the cuffs of his shirt to his wrists and passing the needle through his skin. Sinfjotli endured her rough treatment without comment, and still looked at his mother with an impassive face when she ripped the cuffs from his arms along with a great ribbon of skin. 'Grandfather Volsung would not have flinched,' he said, 'and neither will I.'

Signy sent the boy into the forest to his uncle, and like his brothers before him, Sinfjotli was asked to take the sack of flour and make himself useful. When Sigmund came back from collecting wood, he smelled the aroma of baking bread and asked Sinfjotli whether he'd noticed anything strange about the flour. Sinfjotli shrugged. 'It seemed there was something alive in there, so I kneaded it in with the dough.' Sigmund was impressed: he'd put the most venomous of snakes into the sack, and now he knew he'd found a nephew worthy of the family name. Little did he know that the boy was his own son, and Volsung on both sides.

Sigmund and Sinfjotli Take the Form of Wolves

Before Sigmund took revenge he decided he needed to toughen up his nephew even further. The two men lived like wolves, preying on travellers and killing them for their possessions. One day, whilst looking for plunder, the two of them came across a hovel, not knowing that it belonged to a sorceress. Inside the hovel were two sleeping men and two wolf-skin cloaks. Sigmund and Sinfjotli put on the wolf-skins and were straight away turned into wolves: the spell they'd been placed under could not be broken for ten days. They went their separate ways to continue raiding and foraging for food, but agreed to call for help if they met more than seven men. Sigmund was soon cornered by seven hunters and called to the boy for help. Sinfjotli ambushed and killed all the men. Before the ten days were up, Sinfjotli was cornered by a band of eleven men, but rather than calling for help, he attacked them all and won the fight, though he received many injuries. When Sigmund discovered the wounded Sinfjotli, he was angry that the boy hadn't called for help: but Sinfjotli mocked the older warrior. As a young wolf pup, he had taken on eleven men, when the fully-grown Sigmund was scared to tackle seven! Sigmund saw red and attacked the boy, biting him on the throat and badly wounding him. Even though the ten days were up, the heroes did not emerge from the wolf-skins.

Sigmund dragged his son to back to their den and was at a loss over how to heal his wounds. Luckily, a raven appeared with a leaf, and when he laid it on Sinfjotli he was healed. Sigmund watched the raven fly towards the treetops and suspected that Odin had helped their family once again. The two men emerged from their wolf cloaks some days later, and burned them on the fire so that no one else would fall under their spell. Sinfjotli was now fully grown: he'd tasted the blood of men and was ready to take vengeance.

The Revenge of the Volsungs

The Volsungs left their forest hideout and went to Siggeir's hall, where they hid in a store-room to prepare themselves for battle. Two of Signy's young children were playing with golden arm-rings in the hall, and it happened that one of the rings rolled into the room where Sigmund and Sinfjotli were arming them-selves. The children saw the warriors and ran to their father to warn him, but Signy scolded them for telling tales and shooed them out of the hall, straight into the arms of Sigmund. She told her brother that the children had betrayed them and that they should die. Sigmund wanted nothing more to do with killing Signy's children, but Sinfjotli didn't hesitate, and he butchered his brothers right there, dragging their disjointed bodies into the hall in front of Siggeir. The Volsungs now fought fiercely against Siggeir's followers, but they could not get close to the king and were captured alive.

Siggeir wanted the Volsungs to die the worst kind of death after the harm that they had done to his family, and he settled on burying them alive in a mound with a large stone standing between them, so that they would have no company in their suf-fering. Signy managed to sneak a bale of straw into the mound as they were being buried, and when Sinfjotli felt in the straw he found a large parcel of pork concealing Sigmund's famous sword: the gift he'd pulled from the tree all those years ago. The two men grasped the sword from either side of the stone and slowly sawed their way through the rock. Once they were united, they were able to dig their way out of the mound, and went straight to Siggeir's hall – still caked with the soil from their own graves. The Volsungs set fire to the hall and blocked the only entrance. Signy came to the doorway to greet her brother and her child, but she would not leave with Sigmund. She recounted the lengths she had gone to in order to avenge her father Volsung: incest with her twin, the killing of her own children, and now the burning of their father. She declared herself unfit to live with the shame: she'd show her husband Siggeir a last loyalty and die by his side in the fire. With this, she turned and walked back into the smoke.

The Poisoning of Sinfjotli

It is told that Sigmund returned to Hunaland and reclaimed the kingdom once ruled over by his father Volsung. He married a woman called Borghild and had a son Helgi, who commanded the troops in his father's kingdom, and went on to carry out many great deeds alongside Sinfjotli. Sinfjotli was by his side through the wars waged against the neighbouring tribes, and greatly increased his reputation in battle. But he fell in love with a woman who had also been promised to Borghild's brother – and went to war against her people, killing Sigmund's brother-in-law and returning with the dead man's bride. Borghild pretended to be satisfied with the gold that Sigmund gave to compensate her for this loss, but at the funeral feast she insisted on serving the ale herself. She approached Sinfjotli and asked her stepson to drink from the horn as a pledge of good faith. Sinfjotli could see that the drink had been tampered with, and he let his father drain the ale for him: Sigmund had a stomach of iron. Borghild came a second time and taunted Sinfjotli – other men should not drink the pledge for him. Sinfjotli could see that the drink was murky, and his father once again drank it down. When Borghild came a third time, it was obvious to Sinfjotli that the drink was poisoned, but by this point Sigmund was blind drunk. 'Strain it through your moustache, son!' was his helpful advice. Sinfjotli drained the horn and fell down dead.

Sigmund was distraught. He wanted to carry his son's body to the forest where they'd lived and hunted together, and asked an old man sitting in a boat for passage across the fjord to the wild lands on the other side. But the boat could only take one, and the body disappeared into the mist, piloted by the stranger in his wide-brimmed hat. That was the last that Sigmund saw of his son, but he soon banished Borghild and ruled over his kingdom with the cold resignation of a man who has nothing left to lose.

The Defeat of Sigmund

Sigmund looked for another wife in his old age, and found a suitable match in Hjordis, daughter of a powerful king named Eylimi. Eylimi invited Sigmund to a feast with his followers, but when the Volsungs arrived they found that there was another suitor by the name of Lyngvi, son of Hunding. King Eylimi realised that he could expect trouble from the Volsungs or from Hunding's tribe, whichever match he made, so he gave Hjordis the right to make her own decision. She chose Sigmund, old and grizzled as he was, and they were married with great feasting. But the jilted suitor Lyngvi gathered a great army and marched on Sigmund, intending to lay low the pride of the Volsungs once and for all. The old Volsung warrior did not flee, but marched to war with King Eylimi. The battle was fierce, and although Sigmund commanded a much smaller force, he fought like a wild beast at the front of his men, blowing the horn of the Volsungs and smashing through the ranks of the invaders. Spears and arrows rained down, but the norns shielded Sigmund from their blows and he left countless men bloodied by his hand. It looked as though Sigmund might prevail against all the odds, until a man walked into the melee. He had a wide-brimmed hat and a single eye, and no weapons touched him as he bore his spear through the carnage. He came to the thick of the fighting and held up his spear as Sigmund swung his sword, shattering the famous blade to pieces. Sigmund realised then that his luck was over, and before long the tide of the battle turned against the Volsungs. Sigmund fell alongside King Eylimi and most of his followers.

Sigmund's wife Hjordis had hidden in the forest during the battle, but as night fell she walked amongst the dying and the dead until she found her husband. Sigmund was fatally wounded, but was still able to speak and to comfort her. He told her that Odin had allowed him victory in many battles, but now meant for him to join the ranks of the chosen in Valhalla. He told Hjordis that she was pregnant with a son of the Volsung line, and that she should keep the pieces of the broken sword safe so that the blade could be re-forged: with it, their son would carry out deeds that would be known to everyone.

Hjordis stayed with her husband through the night, and in the morning she was still sitting there amongst the corpses when a great fleet of ships arrived. She quickly swapped clothes with her serving maid, and when the warriors approached she pretended to be a slave. The men were from a raiding party sent by King Hjalprek in Denmark, and his son was in charge of the war-band. They treated the women well, and Hjordis and her servant led the Danes to where the wealth of the Volsungs was hidden: it was greater than anything the warriors had seen in all their years. The women were taken back to Denmark, but Hjordis' disguise did not last long. She was fairer than the woman who wore noble clothes, and had better manners. When she came to tend the fire early one morning, the king asked her how she judged the time back home when there were no stars. Hjordis answered that her father had given her a gold ring whose surface turned cold just before daybreak. With this, she revealed that she was no serving girl – but the knowledge of her noble lineage only increased her standing with the Danes.

The Fostering of Sigurd

When Hjordis gave birth, the boy was taken to Hjalprek, and the king remarked on the boy's keen eyes. The boy was named Sigurd, and as a child he excelled at everything. His foster father in King Hjalprek's court was another exile: the dwarf named Regin. Regin had fled to King Hjalprek after his clash with the gods and the loss of Otr's ransom to his brother Fafnir. The dwarf was a skilled blacksmith and had many useful things to teach the young hero, tutoring him in languages and the art of writing runes. But Regin always had one eye on the gold that had been stolen from him, and before long he began to urge Sigurd to help him recover his inheritance.

Regin's plan was to make Sigurd so unhappy with his lot as a fostered child that he'd ride against the dragon to increase his standing. The problem was that Sigurd saw no need to be resentful of his position. After all, Hjalprek always gave him whatever he needed – and to prove it Sigurd asked the king for a horse befitting his stature as a Volsung. 'Young hero, that's the least thing you could ask,' said Hjalprek. 'Go out into the fields and choose any horse you like.'

Sigurd set out early the next day, and met an old man with a long beard sitting by a river. The old man suggested that they drive all the horses off the heath and into the river; and when they did so there was only one horse that remained standing fast against the current. It was a wild grey stallion who had never been ridden. The old man told Sigurd to take that horse as his own, as the stallion was descended from Sleipnir and the hero would not find better. Men with more winters in the world would have recognised the old wanderer for who he was, and as soon as Sigurd took hold of the stallion the old man vanished. Sigurd called the grey horse Grani, and he turned out to be the best of horses, just as Odin had predicted.

Regin continued to cajole Sigurd into taking on the dragon Fafnir and claiming the gold hoard that he guarded: the dwarf promised the inheritance would pass to Sigurd at the proper time. Sigurd thought that by encouraging him to face such a daunting opponent at such a young age, Regin was asking a great deal of him; and he wondered why his foster father knew so much about this treasure hoard. Regin told Sigurd the whole story – about Loki's killing of his brother Otr and the ransom of gold that the gods had paid, taken from the dwarf Andvari. He told Sigurd that his father had died at the hands of Fafnir, and that his brother had turned into a great dragon in his greed, stashing the gold away within his lair on Gnita Heath. He told Sigurd that he had been left without an inheritance, and had been forced to flee his ancestral home and offer his services as a blacksmith to King Hjalprek. He told the boy a great deal, but didn't dwell on the curse of Andvari that accompanied the gold.

Regin Forges the Sword that was Broken

Sigurd was sympathetic to his foster father's plight, and asked the dwarf to put his skills to use by forging him a sword that would be up to the task of dragon killing. When Regin delivered the first blade, Sigurd shattered it on an anvil and told his foster father that it would be useless. Regin returned to his forge, muttering beneath his breath, and made another sword. Sigurd treated this one exactly as the first, and once more the anvil broke the blade. So Sigurd turned to his mother for help: he asked her for the pieces of his father's sword, Gram, that she'd collected from the battle all those years ago. Seeing that her son was turning into a very promising man, Hjordis passed over the broken sword; and Sigurd asked Regin to stop his tinkering and make a blade more worthy of a hero. Regin was angry at his foster son's insolence, but he did as he was asked, and when he drew the re-forged sword from the furnace for the final time its edges seemed to burn. Regin told Sigurd that if this sword didn't fit the bill then he was no blacksmith, and when Sigurd struck the anvil a third time the blade cut clean through the heavy iron and its oak stand – right to the floor. To test its edge, Sigurd threw a tuft of wool into a river and held the blade downstream. The wool cut cleanly in two. Sigurd was very happy with the sword, and promised to keep his word to Regin and reclaim the gold from the dragon Fafnir. But first he had another task: to take vengeance for his father Sigmund's death.

Sigurd Claims His Inheritance

Sigurd went to King Hjalprek to ask for his assistance in making war on Lyngvi and on Hunding's sons. He wanted his enemies to know that they hadn't wiped out the great line of the Volsungs. Hjalprek gave Sigurd a great force of fighting men arrayed in mail, and provided ships to take them across the sea. Sigurd captained the finest of these ships: its sails were painted in ochre and blood-red, so that it could be seen from far away. The fleet had good passage at first, but before they reached the land a great storm blew up and the water turned the colour of fresh gore. Instead of reefing the sails as the wind ripped at them, Sigurd ordered them to be hoisted higher, and the masts groaned as the longships ploughed the surging waves. As they sailed past a promontory, a lone figure hailed them from the cliffs and praised Sigurd as unequalled amongst men. He asked Sigurd to lower the sails and take him aboard, and when Sigurd asked his name he replied with a riddle shouted to the winds, and called himself by many different names. As soon as this man was taken on board, the storm ceased, and the ships had safe crossing to the land of Hunding's sons. When Sigurd found that the mysterious old man had vanished, he suspected that he knew his real name.

When Sigurd and his forces came to land, they burned and plundered settlements and left scorched earth in their wake. People fleeing the destruction came to King Lyngvi, telling him that a great army was ravaging the land and that at its head was the last of the Volsung line, Sigurd son of Sigmund. Lyngvi gathered his forces and marched straight into battle. Arrows and spears blackened the sky above the two armies, axes swept through the air and split shields and helmets. Many men fell on both sides, and always at the centre was Sigurd with his sword Gram. After the battle had raged for some time, Sigurd advanced past his own banners, deep into the ranks of the enemy: he felled both men and horses with the keen edge of Gram, and his arms were soaked in blood to the shoulders. Men fled before him: they had never seen such a warrior before. Sigurd cut his way right up to Hunding's sons at the centre of their forces: he split the eldest prince's helmet and his body with one blow, and cut down each of the remaining brothers one after another. Sigurd won a heroic victory and many spoils of war, and his vengeance was complete.

Sigurd Kills the Dragon

Not long after Sigurd's return home, Regin brought up the issue of the dragon's hoard once more. 'Isn't it about time that you fulfilled your promise to your foster father, and put that sword to the test?' Sigurd had not forgotten the vow he'd made, and the two men soon set out for the heath where the dragon was known to dwell. They followed the track to a watering hole by some cliffs, a place where Fafnir was known to come and drink. Sigurd remarked that the prints of the dragon looked gigantic, and he wondered whether Regin's description of his brother as a middling serpent had been an honest one. Regin suggested a plan to Sigurd: he should dig a pit and sit concealed in it, so that when the dragon slithered over him he could stab it from below and pierce its heart. Sigurd wondered how he would escape the corrosive blood of the dragon if he was cowering below it, but Regin told him he lacked the courage of his forefathers if he was scared of such a little thing. So Sigurd set about digging the pit as the dwarf had advised, and Regin ran off to a hiding place on the heath. Whilst Sigurd was digging the pit, an old man with a long beard approached him and asked him what he was doing. Sigurd told him of his plan to kill the dragon and the old man gave him some guidance. 'Dig some channels running from your hiding place – here and here – so the blood will have a chance to drain away. Otherwise your plan is sound enough.' Sigurd thought this wise advice, and did as the old man had suggested. When he looked up from his work, the man had vanished into the wide skies of the heath.

The first thing Sigurd noticed was that the birds had stopped singing in the trees. There was a sound like rocks rolling down a mountainside, and the heather crackled as the dragon slid along the track. Sigurd set his helmet straight, and flexed his sword arm. The pit suddenly grew dark, and the hero thrust up through the brush with all his might, feeling the keen point of Gram sink into the soft flesh of the dragon's haunches. The death throes of Fafnir were something to behold: his tail smashed the rocks around him and his blood sprayed out in poisonous streams, withering the gorse and hissing as it sank into the dust.

When the dragon's tremors began to weaken, Sigurd clambered out of the pit. 'Who are you, to take the life of Fafnir, and what family are you from?' the dragon asked, his voice surprisingly clear, and smooth as silk. 'I have no family, and I'm called the noble beast,' Sigurd began, but he ended up telling Fafnir the truth, both his name and his lineage – for what harm could a dying dragon do?

Even up here on the heath, Fafnir had heard the story of the Volsungs, and he praised the deeds of Sigurd. 'You've done well to rise to such great heights as a fostered boy without a father of your own,' he said. 'I might not have a father,' Sigurd answered, 'but that hasn't held me back, as you'll have noticed.'

Fafnir warned Sigurd that though there was enough gold in the hoard to make his wealth the envy of the world, the same gold would be his death, and the death of all who owned it. 'I'll also give you this warning, if you'll listen: my brother Regin is sure to kill you now you've served your purpose. I know our family well, and you'd be better off riding away on Grani and never setting eyes on the cursed hoard of Andvari and the ring Andvaranaut. Take it from one who knows.'

Sigurd saw how human the eyes of the dragon looked. He also recognised the truth in Fafnir's dying words. But he took the gold anyway. He was a hero, after all, and every hero desires to have wealth until the moment of his death.

Sigurd Roasts the Dragon's Heart

Regin waited until he was sure his brother was dead before emerging from his hiding place in the heath. 'You've done well, foster son,' he said, 'and won great renown today.' But Regin also found that he was troubled by the sight of his brother lying bloodied on the ground, and twice he muttered, 'Though you've killed my brother, I am hardly blameless.' This annoyed the hero, and as he wiped his sword on the grass, Sigurd reminded Regin that he had been the one to put his life in danger – and at his foster father's request. 'No man could have killed that dragon without the sword I made!' Regin snapped back. 'It's not clear,' said Sigurd coldly, 'whether any sword is a match for a stout heart.'

They left the argument at that. But Regin still stared at his brother with a look of anguish on his face. He drank the blood of the dragon, and when Sigurd cut out the heart, he asked his foster son to roast it on the fire.

Sigurd sliced up Fafnir's heart and stuck it on a spit hung over the flames. As it roasted, he watched Regin out of the corner of his eye. When the juices began to run clear and sputter in the fire's heat, Sigurd pushed his finger into the meat to see if it was cooked, and the juice was so hot that it burned. Sigurd put his finger to his mouth, and when the dragon's blood touched his tongue he realised that he could understand the conversation of the nuthatches in the tree beside him. And this is what the birds were saying to each other:

'Look at Sigurd sitting there – splattered with blood and cooking for his foster father! He'd be better off eating the heart himself, and gaining some sense.' 'Look at Regin sitting there, plotting to betray his foster son. Sigurd's got no idea: he's far too trusting!' 'Sigurd would be wise to take the treasure from Fafnir's lair and carry it to Hindarfell, where the valkyrie Brynhild is waiting for a hero to wake her. He should think of what's best for himself, not what's best for Regin.' 'If he spares one brother after killing the other, he deserves what's coming!' 'Cut off the dwarf's head, and keep the treasure for yourself, Sigurd! That's what I'd advise . . .'

Sigurd heard all this and decided that it was not his fate to die at his foster father's hand. So he drew Gram and severed Regin's head from his body. The dwarf did not enjoy Andvari's gold for long.

Fafnir's lair had an iron door, which stood wide open, and all the pillars in that cavern were made of iron too. There Sigurd found the helmet of terror that Fafnir had owned, as well as a coat of golden mail – and so much gold that Sigurd wondered how a single horse could carry it away. He piled the gold into two large chests and loaded it onto Grani's back. But when he tried to lead the horse away, it would not move an inch, and no amount of whipping would persuade him. It wasn't until Sigurd jumped into the saddle to use his spurs that Grani trotted off – he'd been waiting for his master to add his weight, and since then, gold has been called Grani's burden, which is no burden at all.

Sigurd Wakes the Valkyrie

Sigurd travelled deeper into Hindarfell, as the nuthatches had advised him to do. He wanted to wake the sleeping valkyrie and to learn what she had to teach him. After reaching the top of the heath, Sigurd turned Grani south to the land of the Franks, and before long they came across a stronghold that glowed with the blaze of a fire. Sigurd passed into the stronghold and found a sleeping figure lying there. The figure was dressed for battle, and it was only when he removed the helmet that Sigurd saw that the warrior was a woman. The chainmail she was wearing had grown so tight that it seemed to bite into her flesh, and when Sigurd ran his sword blade through the heavy mail it opened up like cloth.

The valkyrie woke and greeted the dawn, and then turned to welcome Sigurd son of Sigmund. 'No need to look surprised!' she said. 'Who else would be carrying the dragon's helmet and holding Fafnir's ruin in his hand?' Sigurd asked the valkyrie her name and what had led her to be imprisoned in this way, and Brynhild related her story.

'Two kings were going to war, and one of them had been promised victory by Odin. But I had a soft spot for the other king, and I allowed him to win the battle. As punishment, Odin stabbed me with a sleep-thorn and vowed that my career as a valkyrie was over: I would never determine another victory, and my fate was to be married.' Brynhild gave Sigurd a pointed look. 'But before I succumbed to Odin's potion, I made a vow of my own: I would only marry someone who did not know the meaning of fear.' She looked around her. 'I've been sleeping for some time.'

What Sigurd wanted most of all right then was the wise

valkyrie's advice. She brought them both ale mixed with charms, and taught Sigurd much about the origins of runes and how they could be used – for writing and for luck, for ease of birth and for carving on a weapon to secure a victory in battle. She told him to guard his wine cup against poison, and to watch out for women who wished him harm; and she taught him how to treat sickness and calm waves. She told Sigurd to choose carefully between speech and silence: for a hero's words are as important as his deeds. She told him more: to be kind to his kinsmen, and not to become embroiled in arguments at meetings, but instead to mete out punishment another day. She told him not to sleep beside the road because of the evil spirits that live there; and not to trust the child of a man he's killed: even the youngest wolves are still capable of biting. Sigurd would have to be careful not to provoke his in-laws – if, of course, he was ever to marry. 'It seems to me,' replied Sigurd, 'that the woman I'd most like to take as a wife is sitting right beside me.' What better match could there be than the greatest of all heroes and the wisest of the valkyries? Brynhild agreed to this proposal, and they made solemn vows that no one else should come between them.

Sigurd rode away from Brynhild in his golden mail, carrying a shield emblazoned with the likeness of a dragon so that his most famous deed would be known to everyone he met. People described the way his weapons and his burnished helmet shone, but more impressive still was the way he held himself: he sat high in the saddle, and few could bring themselves to meet his piercing gaze. His shoulders were as wide as those of two men side by side, and it was said that he was so tall that when he walked through a field of full-grown rye the hilt of his sword barely brushed the tips. He was the strongest of men, and he matched his skill in battle with a hero's way with words. He had knowledge of events that were yet to happen, and he knew the language of birds: it was hard to take him by surprise. But most of all, Sigurd stepped up to all dangers and was not afraid. This was the measure of a hero.

For several years, Sigurd travelled between tribes, staying with great chieftains, hunting and fighting, and earning great renown. He visited Brynhild once more in these years: she was staying at her foster father's home, and he found her working on a golden tapestry recounting his deeds as a hero with a small child looking on. Those who knew Brynhild warned Sigurd that she preferred the play of battle to the game of love, and the hero found that she was reluctant to talk again of marriage. She was a shield-maiden after all, and it was not in her nature to give up wearing a helmet alongside warrior kings. Besides, Brynhild had the gift of foresight: she'd seen that the two of them were not meant to be together. Sigurd replied that he would marry Brynhild or no one; and as a proof of his pledge, he handed her Andvaranaut, the greatest treasure from Fafnir's hoard, once worn by Odin himself. Sigurd and Brynhild spent several nights together and repeated their vows to one another; and to protect the pledge, Brynhild surrounded her hall with a ring of fire through which only Sigurd would be able to pass.

The Gjukungs

Sigurd now travelled across the Rhine to the kingdom of Gjuki. Gjuki had three sons named Gunnar, Hogni, and Guttorm, and a daughter called Gudrun who was destined to be the queen of many tribes and the death of many kings. Gjuki's sons were tested warriors, and braver than all other men. But when Sigurd entered the hall at Worms in his golden mail, he towered above the other heroes. Gjuki was happy to welcome such a man to his hall, and Sigurd struck up a fast friendship with the brothers. They could always be found fighting alongside one another and bringing honour and riches to Gjuki's tribe. Sigurd told the brothers that he was promised to a valkyrie, but their mother Grimhild thought that it would be much better if the dragon-slayer married into the Gjukung family and brought his gold with him to the tribe. She devised a plan to bewitch Sigurd and make him forget his vows: this would clear the way for Sigurd to marry her only daughter Gudrun.

Events came to pass in this way. Grimhild drugged Sigurd's beer and he forgot his love for Brynhild. The queen then egged her husband on to offer Sigurd their daughter's hand in marriage, and to give him the power and status worthy of a son. Sigurd could not refuse such an offer from King Gjuki, and he and Gudrun were soon married. Gudrun was more than a match for her husband. Like him, she was proud of purpose, and beautiful with the beauty of cold iron. They had a child called Sigmund and secured the Volsung line, but when Sigurd gave his wife some of Fafnir's heart to eat, she saw something of what was waiting in her future, and grew more withdrawn. For their parts, Gunnar and Hogni were delighted with the match: they pledged to be like brothers to Sigurd and to always have his back.

Now Gudrun was married off, Grimhild turned her attention to the status of her sons. She suggested to Gunnar that it was time to marry, and the woman that she had in mind was Bryn-hild: that same valkyrie who had sworn vows to Sigurd. Gunnar didn't argue with the match: Brynhild was the most beautiful of women, and everyone – including Sigurd, who was still bewitched by Grimhild's spells – encouraged him to seek her hand. She could hardly refuse a hero such as Gunnar.

Sigurd Rides Through the Flames

It was widely known that Brynhild would only marry the man of her own choice, and that only the bravest hero of all could pass through the ring of flame she'd placed around her hall. Sigurd and the brothers rode up to the heath and saw golden trusses rising above a wall that was part fire and part mist. Gunnar spurred his horse and tried to ride into this wall of flames, but the horse drew back at the last moment, and no amount of coaxing could persuade him on. Gunnar borrowed Sigurd's horse and tried again, but Grani turned round to stare at his master: he would not pass through the fire without Sigurd on his back.

The heroes were facing a dilemma. 'Let's try this,' said Gunnar. 'We'll swap clothes and take on each other's forms, then you can ask for Brynhild's hand on my behalf.' So Sigurd and Gunnar changed appearances: Sigurd jumped on Grani's back and rode hard at the wall of fire. There was a great roar: the ground shook violently and flames rose up to the heavens as Sigurd passed through. No one had dared to cross the wall of flames before, but Sigurd was the bravest of men: there was no denying that.

Brynhild sat in her high seat carved in the likeness of a swan and held a sword in her hand. 'Sigurd!' she called, as the hero led his horse into the hall. But then she looked again. 'Not Sigurd, but Gunnar son of Gjuki!' said Sigurd, removing his helmet. The valkyrie was angry. She tried to send this imposter back the way he'd come. 'Well, whoever you are,' she said, 'I'm fresh from killing men in Gardariki, and I've no desire to change my life of war. You'd best be on your way.' But the man who called himself Gunnar did not move. 'If you really are the bravest of warriors, you know you'll have to kill all my other suitors: and there are more than a few,' she said next. But the hero still stood fast. 'Great valkyrie,' said the disguised Sigurd, doing his best to sound like a son of Gjuki, 'did you not promise to marry the man who passed through the flames? And am I not that man? And does that not make me the bravest man alive?' At this, he saw her soften.

The valkyrie could hardly deny his logic, and she let him stay for three nights. It had been a long time waiting behind the wall of flames, but the hero insisted on laying his unsheathed sword between them as they slept, which Brynhild thought was strange behaviour. 'The fates have ordained that we shouldn't touch until our wedding day: the sword is there to help me keep this pledge,' was this curious man's reply. Of course, Sigurd was still under the influence of Grimhild's spells, and the fact that Brynhild had already borne his child had escaped him.

After the three nights were over, Sigurd took his sword from the middle of the bed and prepared to leave. He might have had trouble recognising his former lover, but he knew the ring Andvaranaut: he slipped it from the valkyrie's hand as she slept, replacing it with another ring from Gunnar. He rode back through the flames to join his companions. Gunnar was very pleased with the way that things had turned out, and the two men changed back their appearances before riding home with news of the match. Brynhild in her turn went to her foster father Heimir and told him how Gunnar had ridden through the flames to claim her hand, though she'd pledged herself to Sigurd. Heimir replied that there was no changing things now, and that she'd have to marry Gunnar, but that he would foster the daughter that she'd had with Sigurd and keep her safe from harm. Aslaug was her name.

Brynhild Learns of the Deceit

The day of the wedding feast arrived, and it was to be a grand occasion. Many people came to watch the celebrations in Gjuki's hall, and Sigurd was there to see Gunnar pledge himself to Brynhild. Once the vows had been exchanged and the couple sat drinking wine and enjoying each other's company, Sigurd's mind was finally cleared of Grimhild's enchantments, and he remembered everything that had passed between him and the valkyrie. His face darkened but he didn't say a word.

Brynhild lived amongst the Gjukungs as Gunnar's wife, and for a time peace held in the court of Gjuki. Brynhild bit her tongue whenever she saw Sigurd in the hall, but she found it hard to hide her scorn for her former lover, and she couldn't resist provoking Gudrun. One day the women were bathing in the Rhine, and Brynhild waded out deeper than all the rest. This annoyed Gudrun. 'Do you think you're special, Brynhild? Why don't you come over and bathe with us?' 'I've every right to hold myself apart from other women,' replied Brynhild. 'After all, my husband Gunnar is the bravest hero in the world. He rode through the flames and performed great feats whilst Sigurd was still a nobody relying on handouts from powerful kings. I was lucky not to marry far beneath myself.' Gudrun could not contain her anger. 'It would be wiser for you to hold your tongue, Brynhild, than to talk that way about my husband. Everyone knows he's the greatest hero in the world.'

Then she told Brynhild the truth – that Sigurd had ridden through the flames disguised as Gunnar, and that he had stolen back the ring Andvaranaut and given it to her. Gudrun showed the valkyrie the ring on her own finger, and it was unmistakably the work of dwarves: it flashed and twisted like some living thing. Brynhild looked at the heavy ring on her own hand and turned as pale as a corpse. She walked away from Gudrun and the rest of the women, and didn't speak another word that day.

Brynhild's terrible mood darkened the hall of King Gjuki, and Gudrun thought that such behaviour was not fitting for someone in her position: was the woman not content with having all the wealth and prestige of the Gjukungs at her disposal, as well as a husband she had picked herself? Sigurd warned his wife against further provocations, but Gudrun was not easily dissuaded, and decided to confront the valkyrie. Nothing good came from the conversation. 'I've been tricked,' said Brynhild, 'into marrying the lesser man. I've been betrayed by Sigurd, and deceived by the Gjukungs who thought only about what was best for them. I resent you, Gudrun, for taking the man who was sworn to me, and for the gold that's yours to share.'

Gudrun, for her part, felt no blame for her father's choice of husband, and thought it likely that Sigurd had simply forgotten his vows because he'd found a better match. 'We can't settle this, so let's not speak of it again,' said Brynhild. But Gudrun could see that the betrayal of a valkyrie would not be settled by an exchange of words. Much misfortune was to come from that day of bathing in the Rhine.

Brynhild took to her bed that evening, and didn't get up to eat or drink. Her weeping and shouts of pain echoed throughout the halls of the Gjukungs. Sigurd tried to talk to her: he threw the bedclothes off the valkyrie and told her to wake up and face the sunshine. It would be so easy to return to the life that they had all enjoyed until so recently! Sigurd told her that he understood her pain – he loved her and had been deceived himself. But despite this, he felt content that they were all living as family in the halls of the Gjukungs, and he kept his sorrow buttoned up. He spoke to her of the accomplishments of her husband, of the honour that came from being married to the foremost prince of the Gjukung line. But nothing he said made any difference. 'The only thing that would make me happy would be to run a sword into your heart – then you'll feel my pain.' Sigurd had a feeling that her wish would soon be satisfied, but he warned the valkyrie that their fates were tied together – she wouldn't survive long after causing his death. 'Life is nothing to me,' was her reply. 'Vengeance for a broken vow is what consumes me now.' Sigurd made one final attempt to change the fate that was being set in motion. He offered himself as Brynhild's lover in the Gjukung halls. He would renounce Gudrun and marry her, and so fulfil his vow. Anything to stop this descent into destruction! His breast heaved so hard with emotion that the chainmail split. 'You have no grasp of my nature,' was her calm reply. 'You were the best of men, my oath was sacred, and this remedy comes too late. I will not betray my husband Gunnar, nor will I turn from my fate.' Sigurd reported only this to Gunnar: that his wife was now awake.

Brynhild Demands the Death of Sigurd

It wasn't long before Brynhild presented Gunnar with an ultimatum: 'Either kill Sigurd and avenge the wrong he has done to me, or lose me and die in his place.' Gunnar knew that no good could come from killing his sworn brother, but he valued Brynhild's love over everything else, and it seemed that the honour of the Gjukungs was now at stake. Gunnar and Hogni had both sworn oaths not to harm Sigurd themselves, but their younger brother Guttorm was not bound by any oath. The men built up the boy's courage by feeding him morsels of wolf meat and snake, and pressed him hard to carry out the deed for the honour of the family. After all their fighting talk, the youngster itched for violence: but twice he went into Sigurd's chamber to find the hero's eyes open and gleaming in the darkness, and lost his nerve. The third time, Guttorm found Sigurd asleep, and he stabbed him so hard with his sword that it ran Sigurd through and pinned him to the bed. Sigurd was fatally wounded and unable to raise himself up, but he always slept with Gram close to hand. He threw the old sword of the Volsungs at Guttorm as he backed away across the room, severing the boy in half. Gram's blade hadn't been dulled by the years.

Gudrun awoke from a troubled sleep to this scene of horror: the marriage-bed was drenched in blood, her brother lay dead on the flood, and the peace of the Gjukungs had been shattered. Sigurd tried to comfort Gudrun before he died, saying that he had no fear of death: he only regretted that he hadn't been waiting in his battle-gear to fight and die like a hero. Brynhild, for her part, simply laughed when she heard Gudrun weeping, but her cry of victory soon rang hollow, and it was hard for everyone to understand why she began to shed tears over the killing she had urged herself. The valkyrie no longer wanted to live: her face was ashen and she looked beyond men's eyes. A quick stab of a sword under her upheld arm was all it took to end her own life. She told Gunnar this truth before the blood drained from her body: that Sigurd had slept on one side of the sword and she on the other, and that he'd never broken his vows to his sworn brother: just to her. She then predicted the fate of the Gjukungs, the death and the violence that was to come, and the destruction of their line. She spoke as only a valkyrie could.

Brynhild's last request was to be laid on the funeral pyre alongside Sigurd, with a sword blade placed between them, as in life. Slaves and attendants and hunting hawks were to be sacrificed and laid beside them on the pyre. With that, the gash in her chest began to hiss and she faltered in her speech. Sigurd was placed on a great pyre, his infant son beside him, and when the fire reached its height, Brynhild used the last of her strength to walk into the flames and lie down at his side. So ended the lives of the valkyrie Brynhild and Sigurd, slayer of Fafnir, a man whose name will be remembered in the north for as long as there are people to remember.

It is said that Brynhild rode straight to Hel, and would let nothing delay her on the long road to Sigurd's side, not even a troll-woman who rose from the ground and blocked her way. 'Why do you come here looking for another woman's husband?' called the giant of the rock. 'Haven't you caused suffering enough?' But Brynhild had some choice words for the troll-woman, and sat proud at the reins. The valkyrie might have been denied the Volsung prince in life, but she wasn't about to be denied in death: no one would come between them.

Gudrun and Atli of the Huns

What now of the Gjukungs? Gunnar and Hogni inherited Andvari's gold, but Gudrun was mad with grief and fled into the forest. She wanted nothing more than to lose herself amongst the trees and to become a meal for the hungry wolves, but it was not her fate to die in this way. After months of wandering aimlessly along the tracks that animals take, she eventually found herself in the kingdom of the Danes, and was given refuge there by a noblewoman named Thora in the Kingdom of Half. Together, Gudrun and Thora wove a tapestry telling the life of Sigurd and the Volsungs. It gave colour to Gudrun's grief and helped to relieve her many pains. It took Gunnar and Hogni seven years to discover that their sister was alive, and when they did they quickly sent a delegation with red furs and gold to try to make amends for their treatment of her husband. Grimhild came too, and gave Gudrun a drink spiked with runes and bitter herbs to dull her grief. After this, Gudrun was more pliable. She consented to being married again, to Atli of the Huns, though even in her drugged state she realised that a match to heal long-held enmities was a terrible mistake. Gudrun was taken across the water and across the wide lands of the Huns to Atli's hall. The wedding feast was lavish, and Atli offered the marriage toast to his new wife, but though Gudrun wore a fixed smile on her face, her thoughts lay far from her new husband.

The marriage of Gudrun and Atli was loveless from the start, and Atli soon began to be troubled by ominous dreams. He saw sacred reeds pulled up from his ancestral lands, covered in blood, and offered at his table; he saw two hunting hawks which flew down from his hand to Hel; he saw pups crying out in pain and an unsavoury feast; he saw himself lying in his bed, unable to rise to meet his enemies. Gudrun did not beat around the bush when she interpreted Atli's dreams: there was little that was happy in her husband's fate.

As things between them grew sourer by the day, the leader of the Huns began to wonder what he had gained from this match with Sigurd's widow. He'd received no share of the dragon's hoard, beyond the ring of gold that his wife still wore. Gudrun's brothers had taken all of Sigurd's gold for the Gjukung tribe, when it was hers, and his, by rights. When he closed his eyes at night, Atli saw red gold behind his eyelids and felt the power it would bring. So Atli called together the leaders of his war-band, and they came up with a plan to win the ransomed gold with blood: they would invite the Gjukungs to a feast at Atli's hall, pretend to offer them honour as in-laws, and then sink in the knife.

A man named Vingi was selected to lead a delegation to the Rhine. He carried treasures to the Gjukungs as a sign of friendship, and invited them to a celebration in Atli's hall, but Gudrun managed to tie a wolf's hair round a gold ring as a warning. She wrote runes to her brothers, but these were found by Vingi and tampered with so that the Gjukungs were confused about their sister's message: was it a greeting or a warning? Hogni's wife Kostbera was better at deciphering runes than either of the brothers, and when the men lay snoring after drinking with their Hunnish guests, she sat pondering the runes by the firelight and caught a glimpse of what lay beneath the altered letters. In the morning, she shook her husband awake. 'I've seen what Gudrun was trying to write to you: there's danger in this invitation. You'd be mad to go.' But her wise words had the opposite effect on the Gjukungs. If Atli meant them harm . . . well, that was a challenge to their manhood that the heroes must accept! Kostbera shook her head.

Gunnar and Hogni Ride to Atli's Court

The brothers called for cups of the best wine to be brought to them, and ignoring the protests of their wives, announced that they would be travelling east to show the Huns what Gjukung men were made of. They would ride to whatever fate awaited them at Atli's court, but the gold would stay here on their side of the Rhine. Their retainers roared and cheered at their bravery. These were real men! The brothers rode out of the stronghold with a small band of warriors and the mad joy of war in their eyes, oblivious to the weeping of those they left behind. Vingi led them to the boats and the brothers rowed like Thor across the water, breaking the oar-locks and splitting the timbers in their eagerness to reach Atli and find out what treachery he'd planned. They didn't even bother to beach the boats when they reached land: the brothers did not expect they'd need a passage home.

When they reached Atli's stronghold they saw a host of men arrayed for battle, and Vingi now taunted the Gjukungs for their eagerness in accepting Atli's invitation. 'You'll soon be swinging from the gallows like Odin, and fattening the ravens,' he said, 'and you brought this on yourselves!' The brothers responded to the messenger with the blunt ends of their axes, beating Vingi to death beneath the walls before riding through the gates that swallowed them like a mouth.

Atli himself greeted the Gjukungs inside his stronghold and offered them peace, if they would only share with him the gold that Sigurd had won from Fafnir. The brothers were in no mood for ransoming their lives: Gunnar's reply was blunt. 'The Huns will never get their hands on the red gold whilst we live. But we've noticed that the eagles in Hunaland look half starved: why not stop the talking and give them a feed on real heroes' flesh?' The battle started with a shower of arrows falling like angry serpents on the shields of the Gjukungs. When Gudrun heard the sounds of battle, she emerged from the hall dressed in chainmail and carrying a sword. She pushed through the ranks of Atli's men and ran to her brothers' side, turning her sword against the Huns. She fought as strenuously as any man, cutting about her with a keen blade and meeting the onslaught head-on. The Gjukungs defended themselves so well that the battle raged for the best part of a day, and the enclosure grew slippery with the blood of fallen men. The fighting spilled into the hall itself, and Atli's own brothers were sent to Hel by Gjukung blades: when the cost was counted, the Huns could not rejoice in that day of fighting.

The siblings were eventually separated in battle. Gunnar was overpowered and taken prisoner, and Gudrun subdued. Hogni continued to fight in a wild last defence on the far side of the hall, leaving many men wounded before he was finally brought to heel. Atli, exhausted and red-eyed, ordered Hogni's heart to be cut from his chest, but an elder advised the king otherwise – better that they cut the heart from a slave, and persuade Gunnar that his brother had died squealing. Hogni tried to intercede on the slave's behalf, but the knives of the Huns made quick work of the deed, and the screams were horrible to hear. The heart was carried across the hall to Gunnar on a platter, but Gunnar simply laughed at the trembling organ. 'Bring me my brother's heart, not the timid heart of a slave!' he cried. 'The heart of a Gjukung would never tremble.' This time the Huns took Hogni himself, and the man laughed as they butchered him. It was a hard sound for heroes to forget. When Gunnar saw the heart standing proud on the platter, he was satisfied that it was his brother's, and he smiled. 'Now you've killed Hogni, I will die knowing that you'll never find where Sigurd's gold is hidden. It will serve the people of the Rhine, not be worn as trinkets on the arms of Atli's men.'

Atli ordered Gunnar to be thrown into a pit full of snakes with his arms bound behind his back. Gudrun could only help her brother by sending a harp down to him, and he struck the instrument so well with his toes that for a time the serpents were enchanted by the music. Only one serpent, an old and ugly adder, could not be charmed, and it was this creature that burrowed into Gunnar's chest and bit him near his heart: and so the last remaining son of Gjuki died.

The death of the Gjukungs had come at a great cost to Atli, and he was no closer to Sigurd's gold. Worse still, his own wife had fought against his men, and he could not resist taunting Gudrun about her brothers' grisly deaths: how did it feel to pick the losing side? Gudrun pretended to be chastened, and accepted the compensation he offered for her brothers' lives, but the daughter of Gjuki was just going through the motions. Her vengeance would come, and it would shake the kingdom to its core.

Gudrun's Terrible Revenge

Gudrun was at the centre of preparations for the victory feast, busily organising the servants and speaking pleasantly to the guests. Atli was pleased that she had grown so gentle after the killing of her brothers and the humbling of the Gjukung family. The feast was raucous and the wine flowed from bright cups. Gudrun saw that the time was ripe to shame her husband. She slipped away to the room where the princes – her own children with the king – were playing, and she gathered them in her arms. 'My little ones: this evening you have to die. I have a great thirst for revenge against your father which only your blood can quench.' There was no protest from the children, but they warned their mother that she'd get a bad name for killing them. Gudrun slit their throats.

Atli was drunk, and called for fresh sweetmeats and wine.

Gudrun served him dainty cuts of meat, watching as he swigged thirstily from the cup. As the king ate he wondered where his boys were and why he couldn't hear them playing. When Atli was finished, Gudrun told him a truth hard for anyone to hear: the wine was mixed with the blood of his children, and the sweetmeats were flesh of his flesh. A great groan came from the high-benches of the hall as her words sunk in. Gudrun leant in close to Atli: 'You'll never hold the boys on your lap again, or watch the little princes gilding spears and grooming horses in the yard. Can you feel my loss now, Atli? Can you understand the depth of my hatred for the Huns? No punishment is too great for a king as cruel as you.' Atli called the daughter of Gjuki a monster, and condemned her to be stoned to death, but his men were paralysed by the horror of it all. Atli sat and drank himself into a stupor, but there would be little sleep for that ring-giver. He woke to find Gudrun's sword buried in his chest and the bedclothes sucking at his blood. The king now saw the fullness of her revenge.

'I've suffered much as your wife: I've been caught up in the struggles at your court, provoked, and made to watch my brothers' deaths. But in truth, the thing that grieves me most is that I was once married to Sigurd, leader of men, and now I wake up every morning in the bed of a lesser hero. But I'll do you this last honour – I'll wrap your body in finery, and make this hall a pyre to your memory. That's the least that I can do.' Gudrun now woke the servants, shared out Atli's treasure, and set the hall ablaze with the warriors still sleeping on the benches. They woke to confusion and choking smoke, and hacked at each other as the flames spread. So Gudrun sent her brother's killers down to Hel and ended the conflict between the Gjukungs and the Huns.

Svanhild and Jormunrekk

Gudrun had waded so deep into killing that she didn't want to
live any longer, and she walked out into the sea, clutching rocks
to weigh her down. But the norns had other ideas, and the waves
carried her to the land of Jonakr, where she married the king
and had three sons. Her daughter with Sigurd, Svanhild, also
came to Jonakr's hall and was raised there in his household.
Svanhild had the snake-eyes of her father, and when Gudrun
decked her in Hunnish gold she glowed as brightly as the sun.

When it was time for Svanhild to be married, a delegation
came from King Jormunrekk of the Goths: he had sent his son
Randver to ask for Svanhild's hand on his behalf. Svanhild was
betrothed to Jormunrekk – Gudrun could find no support for
her misgivings – and the delegation left for home with Svanhild
sitting in the place of honour on the ship. The journey back to
the land of the Goths was not short, and during this time Randver and Svanhild became lovers. When the delegation arrived
home, Jormunrekk's ambitious retainer Biki was quick to tell
Jormunrekk about his son's intimacy with Sigurd's daughter,
and Jormunrekk flew into a rage. 'Hang him!' shouted the warlord. Before Randver climbed onto the gallows, he sent his father
a hunting hawk plucked clean of all its feathers, and when it was
passed into the king's hands he recognised the meaning of this
message: killing his own son was a great act of self-harm that
would leave his lineage in tatters. But the realisation came too
late: Biki had rushed through the sentence and Randver was
already swinging by his throat. Biki urged an even more shameful death for the bride-to-be. Seeing the shining woman
trampled by horses would be sure to satisfy the king's great
anger. Even wild horses would not go near Svanhild whilst she

stared at them with her piercing Volsung eyes, but once a bag was placed over her head, the horses lost their fear and their hooves left the daughter of Sigurd broken in the mud.

Gudrun's Final Retribution

When news of this reached Gudrun, she called the sons she'd had with Jonakr to her side. Their names were Hamdir, Sorli and Erp. She lashed out at them, accusing them of cowardice for not rushing to avenge their sister's death. Their uncles Gunnar and Hogni would not have thought twice about pursuing the family's cause. Hamdir recalled that Gudrun had been less admiring of her brothers when they plotted to have Sigurd killed, and that she herself had murdered the children of Atli in a rage: half-brothers who could have aided their family's cause against the Goths. 'You've lost your daughter Svanhild and now you're sending us to certain death: the last of all your sons. I doubt that it will bring you much relief.' But when all was said and done, the brothers leapt on their horses with the fire of battle kindled in their eyes. Gudrun had fashioned their mail in such a way that the blades of the Goths couldn't harm them, but she lost one son before the boys had even left the kingdom: the young Erp spoke in riddling ways about the help that he would give his older brothers, and they struck him dead, thinking he would be no help at all. For this reason, the sons of Gudrun arrived with their strength lessened and their wits dulled, and though they surprised Jormunrekk in his hall and hacked off his hands and feet, they left him alive when Erp would have silenced him for good.

Though fatally wounded, Jormunrekk had enough breath left to greet an old man with one eye who walked into his hall, seemingly oblivious to the fighting. The old man pulled back his hood and whispered to the dying king: and so Jormunrekk knew the secret to killing the Gjukung boys. With his last breath he ordered his men to stone the brothers, as iron would not harm them. Thus the brothers met their end in the hall of the Goths – Hamdir in one corner and Sorli in the other – and with them ended the Gjukung line, as Odin had determined.

Gudrun was now left as barren as a tree in winter, its leaves fallen one by one. She had achieved vengeance for the Gjukungs and bested all her enemies. But she'd also witnessed the fall of two great families, and none of it had brought Sigurd back or given her any relief from the pain of knowing what might have been. Now she would build a pyre and see if the norns would finally allow her to leave this world and be reunited with all those whom she'd lost. It was uncertain what welcome the daughter of Gjuki would receive.

7

Folk Heroes and Tricksters

Sigurd may be descended from Odin and raised above all other champions, but he is not the only Norse hero to claim a connection with the Father of the Gods. Ragnar Lodbrok and the warlike Aslaug; Starkad the giant, Hervor the shield-maiden and Heidrek the troublemaker; the Icelandic hero Egil Skallagrimsson: they all have their dealings with Odin and help promote his cause through their love of war and poetry, or their refusal to be afraid of the unknown. These legendary heroes even take on the characteristics of the one-eyed god: they are brave to a fault and handy in a battle, but also cruel and cunning, and quick with scornful words. Some of them will challenge the god at his own game: it's what he teaches them to do.

The Legend of Ragnar Lodbrok

Aslaug

Before Sigurd the Volsung married Gudrun and forgot his vows, he had a child with the valkyrie Brynhild. Their daughter's

name was Aslaug, and Brynhild's foster father Heimir raised her
as his own. When Sigurd and Brynhild burned together on the
pyre, Aslaug was three years old. Her foster father knew that
someone would come looking for the child, so he had an enormous harp made which was hollow inside: in this harp he hid
the best part of his fortune, along with the young Aslaug, and he
took to the road as a travelling musician. When the two of them
were far away from any settlement, Heimir let Aslaug run
around and play, but Aslaug knew she had to hide in the harp if
anyone came along the road towards them. When she was sad
about the life she'd left behind, Heimir played the harp beauti-
fully, and she soon stopped crying.

Life continued in this way for many months, until Heimir and
Aslaug had travelled all the way to Norway. One evening they
arrived at a remote farm owned by a sour old couple called Aki
and Grima. Heimir introduced himself as a poor musician, and
asked if he could stay there for the night. The old woman begrudg-
ingly agreed to let this weather-beaten visitor warm himself by
the fire until her husband came home. The firelight flickered on
the harp, and when the old woman looked closely she saw a rich
piece of cloth poking out of its base – leading her to suspect that
this travelling musician was not quite what he seemed.

Grima offered Heimir food, and seeing that he was ready to
fall asleep where he sat, she led him to the barn and offered him
a bed of straw. When her husband came home, the old woman
told him of her suspicions. 'I'm sure the man sleeping in our
barn was once a great hero with a fortune, but he's old and
asleep, and I'm sure you can deal with him, husband.' Grima's
words were persuasive, and Aki took his axe from above the
rafters, walked the short distance across the yard, and struck
Heimir in the head as he lay snoring. His death-throes almost

shook the barn out of its foundations, but Aki was safely cowering outside.

Now the old woman was eager to see what the harp contained, and when she broke it open she found not only a stash of gold coins and rich clothing, but also the child Aslaug. The girl would not speak a word. 'What do we do now?' asked her husband. 'I knew no good would come of this.' 'I'll tell you what we'll do,' replied Grima, 'we'll raise this little mute as our own. She'll be called Crow, and she'll be a help with all the hardest chores. We'll shave her head, and put tar on her scalp so that she looks ugly like us: no one will be any the wiser.'

Ragnar and the Dragon

Whilst Aslaug was being brought up in poverty, another noble daughter was being raised in Gotaland in Sweden with all the riches that her father, a powerful jarl, could lavish upon her. The child's name was Thora, and she was as beautiful as a doe. She lived in a small house next to her father's hall, and every day he sent her a new plaything. One day the jarl gave her a beautiful snake, which she kept in a chest of gold. Before long, this snake had grown into a dragon alongside the gold, and eventually became so large that it wrapped itself around the house; no one dared to approach it. The dragon had to be fed a whole bullock for every meal, and the jarl considered this to be an intolerable burden. He offered the gold hoard to anyone brave enough to kill it.

There wasn't a hero in all of Gotaland who was up to such a challenge, but in the land of the Danes there was a king called Sigurd Hring, who had a son called Ragnar – a prince who, despite his youth, had already made a name for himself as a Viking, and proved his wisdom as well as his strong arm. One day, Ragnar ordered a strange set of clothes to be made for himself: they were hairy all over, and boiled in pitch. He left to go raiding that summer with the clothes stowed away in a chest on board his ship. Before long, Ragnar's small fleet found itself sheltering from a storm in a fjord close to the house where Thora lived. Ragnar didn't tell anyone what his plans were, but he slipped away from his ship early in the morning with a large spear and his strange set of garments. Before leaving the beach he rolled in the sand, so that his pitch-soaked clothes were completely coated, and he removed the nail from the head of his spear so that it was loose on the shaft. Ragnar went straight to the enclosure where Thora lived, and he saw the dragon lying curled around the house. He wasted no time in thrusting the spear hard into the dragon's back, giving the shaft a powerful twist so that the spear-head broke off. The dragon writhed in pain and sprayed its corrosive blood around, but Ragnar had already turned his back, and was protected by his pitch-soaked clothes. Thora came out of the house at the sound of the terrible commotion, and Ragnar recited her a poem as she stood there in her night-clothes looking utterly astonished. The hero would come to be known as Ragnar Lodbrok after his pitch-soaked hairy breeches, but he didn't stand around to be congratulated, and continued on his way.

Thora learned from Ragnar's verse that he was only fifteen years old, but she knew nothing else about the man in the strange suit of clothes. Thora suggested that her father call an assembly and order all the men in the area to attend – she thought it likely that the dragon's killer would come for his reward, carrying the shaft that would fit the broken spear-head.

A great crowd gathered for the assembly, where the spear-head was passed to each man in turn, until it came to the young Ragnar – who'd been summoned from his ship like everybody else. The hero admitted it was his, and he carried the headless spear shaft to prove it. As a reward, Ragnar asked for Thora's hand in marriage, and the jarl was happy to see her married to such a brave man. Ragnar returned to Denmark with Thora that summer after a lavish wedding feast: they ruled together for many years, were devoted to each other, and had two strapping sons called Agnar and Eirik. But Thora was still young when she died suddenly of an illness, and Ragnar was so distraught at her death that he had no desire to rule without her. He took up his old habit of raiding, and found he hadn't lost his knack for it.

Ragnar and Aslaug

Ragnar's career as a Viking took him far and wide, and he never stayed in one place for long. One summer, he was visiting relatives in Norway and the wind was poor. He decided to anchor in a secluded harbour to take on provisions and wait for the conditions to improve, and he sent his servants off in search of a place to bake bread. They spotted smoke curling up from a house beyond the tree-line: it was the same farm where the old couple had been raising Aslaug as their daughter. Grima still called the young woman Crow, and forbade her to wash the grime off her face, or even comb her hair. Even so, it was hard to disguise her beauty, and when she saw the ships coming in to harbour, she cleaned herself up and ran home with her silky hair falling down to her ankles. The servants of Ragnar couldn't believe that this lovely woman was the daughter of such a rough old couple: they stared at Crow so often that they burned the bread they were baking, and Ragnar was not pleased when they returned to the ship. He said he would gauge for himself whether the girl was really so lovely, and sent men with a strange invitation. 'Tell her that if she's as beautiful as my first wife Thora, then I want to marry her and take her away from this hard life. But also tell her this,' he continued, 'that she's to call on me in this way: neither clothed nor naked, neither fed nor hungry, and neither alone nor in company. If she does so, I promise her my protection.'

Ragnar's men went to the farm of Aki and Grima: they were greeted by Crow, who was indeed as beautiful as the servants had said. They told her that the great hero Ragnar desired her company, and they repeated his riddle. 'He must be mad!' said Grima – but Crow told them that she'd think about what he'd requested, and visit on the following day. When she awoke next morning, Crow took her foster father's fishing-net and covered her naked body with it. 'Now I'm neither naked, nor dressed.' Next she ate an onion, reckoning that it wasn't a meal at all, though it would still take the edge off her hunger. Finally, she took her beloved dog as a companion: 'By doing so, I won't arrive alone, or in anyone's company.'

In this way, Crow came to the ship, and Ragnar was most impressed with the way she'd handled his riddle. Her hair shone like gold, and he couldn't deny that she was the most beautiful woman he'd seen. Ragnar bowed to her, and the dog bit his hand: his men strangled the poor animal for this insult, and although Crow had met her side of the bargain, Ragnar had already broken his promise of protection. Crow gave him short shrift when he proposed that she stay on the ship and marry him back in his kingdom. 'Sail north as you had planned, and if it still seems wise to take a peasant as a wife after you've cooled your head, then call back for me.' She wouldn't even accept a shirt threaded with gold that had once belonged to Thora. 'A gold shirt is not fitting for a woman called Crow, used to herding the goats.' She went home despite Ragnar's protests – and without her dog.

Ragnar sailed away, but he did not change his mind. He came back for this woman called Crow, and renewed his promise of marriage. This time Crow was more amenable. She gathered her few belongings, and took her leave of the old couple whilst they still lay in bed. 'I remember you murdering my foster father Heimir, and there's nobody who deserves punishment more than you – but I'll spare you death because of the long time we've lived in each other's pockets: you're almost the only people I know. But I will say this: every day from now on will be worse for you, and your last day will be your worst.' With that Crow left and never returned.

Crow would not give in to Ragnar's request to share a bed with him on the journey back to his kingdom: she refused to do so until they were properly married. And once their wedding feast had taken place, she asked that they wait three more nights and make a sacrifice to Odin before lying together; for, as she explained, 'I've had a premonition that if we do so earlier, I'll give birth to a child with no bones.' Ragnar ignored her misgivings, and slept with her anyway, and in nine months Crow gave birth to a child who was long and handsome, but who lacked bones – just as his mother had foreseen. The child was named Ivar the Boneless, and he would go on to great things despite his infirmity. The couple had other sons: Bjorn and Hvitserk and Rognvald; they were the best of warriors, and they always followed the advice of their older brother Ivar when they went to war. When they were of age, they left home with Ragnar's blessing and a troop of Vikings to seek glory and riches, and their stories have entered into legend.

But as for Aslaug, or Crow as she was known, she had not revealed who her parents were, and Ragnar still believed that his beautiful wife was the daughter of peasants. One summer, he was away visiting a powerful king of the Swedes by the name of Eystein who was holding a great feast at his hall in Uppsala. The two were fast friends, and it was not unnoticed that King Eystein had a fine-looking daughter called Ingibjorg who paid particular attention to Ragnar. After the feasting and drinking, Ragnar's men urged him to ask for Ingibjorg's hand: after all, it was more fitting for a king to have a noble for a wife than the daughter of a peasant. Ragnar agreed, but said that the marriage would have to wait for the following summer. When he was alone with his men on the long ride home, he told them not to mention a word to Crow about the arrangement: he'd wait for the right moment to tell her.

Crow greeted him with a strange look in her eye. 'What's the news from Sweden, husband?' she asked. 'Nothing worth telling,' was Ragnar's reply. His wife asked the same question all evening, and got the same answer. 'So you don't think it news,' she said eventually, 'that you have become engaged to another woman?' She'd heard all about it: not from his men, but from three birds who had been sitting in a nearby tree. Now Crow told him about her ancestry: 'My real parents are somewhat more famous than the old couple who raised me as their slave: I suppose you've heard the names of Sigurd of the Volsungs and Brynhild the valkyrie? My real name is Aslaug, and there's one way in which I can prove my ancestry. I'm pregnant with a child, and he'll have a mark that will distinguish him as Sigurd's grandson: there will be a little dragon in his eye. If this comes to pass, I want you to break off your engagement to Ingibjorg.' Ragnar was hardly in a position to argue: if Aslaug was the daughter of Sigurd, his match was a worthy one. And when the child was born, he did indeed have a mark that set him aside from other boys: there was the likeness of a brown serpent in his eye, and he turned away from the gold that Ragnar gave to him as a naming gift. He was known ever after as Sigurd Snake-in-the-Eye, grandson of the dragon-slayer and the descendant of Odin. Ragnar was true to his word, and broke off his engagement to the daughter of King Eystein.

When Ragnar did not turn up for the wedding feast, Eystein felt he'd been shamed, and declared that he was no longer a friend of the Danes. Ragnar's sons with his first wife, Eirik and Agnar, decided the time was ripe to go raiding in the land of the Swedes, and they had some success. But they had failed to take account of Eystein's enchantments, or of the sacred cow called Sibilja that ran in front of the troops and drove fighting men to distraction with her bellowing. When the Swedes intercepted the sons of Ragnar and their men, the cow bellowed so terrifyingly that the Vikings took to fighting amongst themselves: all except Agnar and Eirik. Both heroes fought bravely against the odds, but Agnar was killed, and Eirik captured: he chose for himself death on the point of a spear rather than Eystein's overtures of peace.

News came to Aslaug of the death of Ragnar's oldest sons whilst the king himself was abroad. She swiftly urged her own sons to avenge their stepbrothers, even though they had heard of the cow Sibilja, and were reluctant to face such sorcery. Aslaug led the troops over land, and each of the brothers gathered a fleet to sail to the country of the Swedes. Meanwhile, Eystein sent the arrow of war around his kingdom, gathering the fighting men into a mighty army. When the two sides came together, it seemed as though the outcome might be the same as before, with the cow Sibilja bellowing and driving the Danes mad. But Ivar had made ready, and was carrying a stout bow. The men carrying the litter of the boneless son of Ragnar saw him place two arrows in the bow at once, then shoot them straight into the eyes of the charging cow. The cow's anger only increased with her injuries, so Ivar had his men throw him on the back of the cow, where his weight crushed her like a stone. With Sibilja dead, the Danes stopped fighting amongst themselves and turned their attention to the Swedes, and Eystein's army was routed. Aslaug returned to tell this news to Ragnar, but her sons headed in a different direction to raid the rich cities of the south, where they had great success.

Ragnar's Death in England

With his sons' reputations increasing with each successful conquest, Ragnar worried that his fame might be eclipsed, so he decided to mount an expedition of his own, and ordered two huge ocean-going ships to be constructed. They were bigger than any ships seen before; the surrounding tribes saw that Ragnar Lodbrok was preparing for war, and they doubled the guard on the coast. But the hero meant to go further afield: across the sea to England. Aslaug thought he should take a larger fleet to improve his odds, but Ragnar insisted on just the two ships: for what would a woman know about winning fame in the west? Before he left, Aslaug gave him a shirt woven from a single grey hair, and told him that it was so enchanted that none of his blood would be spilled if he remembered to wear it. Ragnar took this gift – although he'd have done better to listen to her earlier advice.

Ragnar was driven by a gale on his voyage to England, and

though his forces were able to get ashore, clad in their war-gear, both his ships were wrecked and there was no going back. They raided farms and strongholds, and met little resistance. The most powerful man in England at that time was a king named Ælla, and when he heard about the Vikings running roughshod across his land, he gathered all the fighting men in his kingdom and marched to do battle with Ragnar. Ælla's army far outnumbered Ragnar's small band: but Ragnar did not shy away from the fray. Ælla had heard about Ragnar's famous sons and feared their retribution if their father was killed, so he ordered his men to capture the leader alive if they could. But Ragnar wore only the hair shirt given to him by his wife, and carried nothing that set him apart from his men. The battle was fierce, despite the difference in numbers, and Ragnar drove his spear into helmets and mail, cutting through the ranks of Ælla's men time and time again. But eventually, all his followers were killed, and Ragnar was hemmed in by a ring of shields and forced to yield to King Ælla. He refused to give his name, and King Ælla ordered that the captive be thrown into a snake-pit to see if that would loosen his tongue.

Ragnar sat surrounded by snakes, but none of them harmed him, and the wiser of Ælla's men wondered whether this man – who could not be marked by blades or bitten by serpents – was not the great Viking hero himself. But when the man still refused to talk, King Ælla ordered that they remove the captive's clothes to see if this would encourage the snakes. Without his hair shirt, Ragnar had little defence against the serpents, and they sank their fangs deep into his flesh. Ragnar looked up at the king from where he sat bleeding in the pit, and finally he spoke: 'The piglets will squeal when they hear how the old boar was treated.'

Ragnar recited a poem enumerating his battles and his

famous victories. When it was finished, the king suspected that the man dying in the snake-pit was none other than Ragnar; and his blood ran cold thinking of those war-hungry sons – descendants of Odin – setting sail to avenge their father. And King Ælla was right to look at the grey sea and to feel afraid, but that is another story and Ragnar's ends here.

Starkad

Starkad is a hero of a different mould: a giant of a man, destined to live for three lifetimes. It is said that he was born with six arms, and that Thor cut off four of them to make the hero less monstrous: he hated to see a giant become his father's champion. Starkad is an Odinic hero through and through, and is dedicated to the pursuit of glory in battle. He cares little for the other gods or for people of low birth: he cannot stand extravagance or frivolous men, and scorns the effeminacies of Freyr's cult. As well as excelling as a warrior, Starkad is also a poet with Odin's gift for words, and like the All-Father, he sometimes deceives those closest to him – despite holding others to the highest of standards. Even the greatest of heroes are flawed.

The Sacrifice of King Vikar

Starkad was the grandson of a giant who lived by a waterfall in the high mountains of Norway: legend has it that he took it upon himself to abduct a princess from Alfheim, and was killed by Thor in retribution. Starkad's father fared better in the household troop of Harald of Agder, but was burned in his house when Starkad was an infant, and Starkad himself was fostered by King Harald, and nursed alongside his son Vikar. When King

Herthjof usurped the throne from Harald, Starkad was put into the charge of a man named Grani Horse-Hair, who was really Odin in disguise. The big-boned boy was a layabout in his youth, and his foster brother had to drag him out of bed before he'd join him to avenge King Harald's death. When Vikar finally pulled Starkad to his feet, he was amazed at his foster brother's size, and by the fact that he already had a beard at twelve years old. It wasn't long before Starkad proved himself the bravest of men, and a worthy companion of Vikar: together, they overthrew Herthjof, subdued the surrounding tribes, and raided far to the east – where Starkad killed the king of Kiev, despite receiving wounds that would have felled a lesser warrior. King Vikar secured his rule and reputation as a war-leader, and Starkad was his champion and his right-hand man.

Things continued in this way for many years, with Vikar always having the victory and rewarding Starkad well, until one summer King Vikar decided to sail to Hordaland with his army, and the fleet found itself becalmed off a group of small islands. The king's advisors decided that to gain favourable winds, a man from the army should be sacrificed to Odin. They all drew lots, and King Vikar drew the lot marked for death. So they tried again, and still King Vikar was marked out for sacrifice. The men were very shaken by this, and opted to sleep on the matter before deciding what to do.

During the night, Starkad was woken by his foster father, Grani Horse-Hair, who beckoned the hero towards a rowing boat, and put out to one of the nearby islands. There, in a clearing in a wood, Starkad found that twelve thrones had been set up: one of them was empty, and Grani Horse-Hair went and sat on it himself. The assembled judges greeted Starkad's foster father by the name Odin.

'We are here to determine your fate, Starkad, and I'll start by predicting that you'll live an uncommonly long life: three life-spans, to be precise.' Another judge spoke up from the gloom: 'Then I promise that Starkad will commit a terrible deed in each one.' The speaker was Thor: he hated to see a man of giant stature blessed in this way. 'I also decree that he'll win victory and fame in every battle he fights,' said Odin. 'And I curse him to be wounded each time,' replied Thor. 'I will give him the art of poetry, and the ability to compose it as fast as any man can speak.' 'And I say he'll never remember any verse after it has left his mouth!' 'It is his fate to be praised and honoured by all nobles,' said Odin. 'And the common people will hate him!' replied Thor, getting increasingly animated.

With this, the judgement of Starkad was over, and his foster father escorted the hero from that sacred place. 'I've done you a service, foster son, in prolonging your life and granting you these gifts, and now I ask for something in return. You are to send me the warlike King Vikar in his prime. And this is how it will be done . . .'

Starkad returned to the ships before daybreak, and when the army awoke, they learned that Vikar's right-hand man had come up with a plan. 'We'll make a mock sacrifice of our king, since this is what Odin seems to want.' So they took King Vikar over to a nearby island and found a tree with high branches. Then Starkad took the entrails from a calf, slung the guts over a branch to make a noose, and asked the king to stand with the guts round his neck. 'I'll poke you with this reed, offer you to Odin, and the sacrifice will then be complete.' King Vikar agreed: it all looked harmless enough. But the reed had been given to Starkad by Odin, and it turned into a spear as he stabbed the king, and pierced right through his side. The calf guts tightened and turned to taut willow, and the bent branch swung upwards, pulling the hapless king into the air. So the sacrifice became real, and King Vikar went to join Odin. For this – the first of the infamous deeds predicted by Thor – Starkad became hated by all the common people who'd relied on Vikar as their protector.

The Life of a Champion

After the killing of King Vikar, Starkad joined a group of Vikings who raided far into Russia: when the Russians tried to check their advance by strewing the fields with nails, the Vikings put on wooden clogs to storm the stronghold of their enemies, and took so much plunder that it filled all their ships. Soon Starkad had become a man of some means, and when the leader of this band of Vikings was killed in battle, he took a break from raiding and spent seven years in Sweden with the sons of Freyr. Their cult had a temple at Uppsala, where they made sacrifices and performed outlandish rites to the tinkle of bells. Starkad grew to hate the dalliance and unmanly dancing of this fertility cult, so he cut his ties to them and joined another raiding party heading west to Ireland. He'd heard that the king in Dublin had a great fondness for actors and clowns, and that when he rewarded a warrior with a gift of new shoes, his notorious meanness led him to remove the laces. Small wonder that this king's men quickly abandoned the field when the Vikings attacked: however, it was Starkad's fate to be wounded in every battle he fought, and one brave champion split the giant hero's scalp in two, leaving a festering wound on Starkad's forehead. When the Vikings came to Dublin and looted its great wealth, Starkad made a point of gathering all the actors and fools outside the walls and having them insulted and beaten. He found their frivolous behaviour revolting.

What more to tell of Starkad's first span of life? He joined the Slavs to crush a rebellion in the east, and defeated a strongman in Russia by the name of Visin, said by some to be a sorcerer. In Byzantium he wrestled with an undefeated giant, throwing him to the ground; and later he was shipwrecked near Denmark and rescued by King Frothi – a man he would come to regard as the greatest and most generous of kings. As the champion of King Frothi, he fought with a Saxon called Hama, who was scornful of Starkad's age and came close to besting the hero in combat, knocking him to the floor with his powerful fist. But Starkad recovered quickly and split the Saxon in two with his sword: he won much glory for this deed, as well as a gift of Danish land and sixty slaves to work it.

Holding the Danes to High Standards

King Frothi was later killed by the treachery of a Saxon named Sverting, who burned the ruler of the Danes at a feast. The kingdom reverted to Frothi's son Ingeld, who thought to make peace with the Saxons and the sons of Sverting. Ingeld was a very different man to his father, and he gave himself over to a life of orgies and drunken feasts. His court was a court of vice, and Starkad would have none of it, so he left for Sweden, but he kept an eye on Frothi's family from afar and was not afraid to intervene in their affairs. One day, word came to him that Frothi's daughter Helga was having an affair with a goldsmith of low birth, and that Ingeld was doing nothing about it – so Starkad tracked the goldsmith down and entered his workshop disguised as a beggar – where he found the commoner asking the sister of the king to comb his pubic hair for lice and slipping his hands inside her gown. Helga blushed when she recognised the cloaked figure in the corner of the room as her father's old champion, and Starkad could contain himself no longer: he stabbed the goldsmith in his nether regions as he tried to flee the room, reasoning that such an injury was more humiliating than death for such a lecher.

Soon a more appropriate suitor came to ask for Helga's hand: his name was Helgi, and he had travelled from Norway in a ship with sails decked in purple and gold. The young man conducted himself well, but it was King Ingeld's whim to make him challenge the other suitors to combat. Helgi agreed, but didn't realise that he would have to face nine brothers one after the other: it didn't seem to be a fair fight to him, but what could he do? There was no backing out of it now. Helga recalled that Starkad had always been a friend to the family, and would have good advice, so she told her suitor Helgi to seek out the old champion in Sweden. Starkad soon agreed to come and help this noble cause. When he arrived at the court of Ingeld, the nine brothers were allowed to mock the old hero, and to grimace and snort like wild dogs; making Starkad all the more determined to teach them a lesson.

When the morning of the challenge came, Starkad left Helgi sleeping in Helga's bedchamber and made his own way to the site of the *holmgang* (as contests such as these were known): he liked to get an early start. Unlike the young Norwegian, the old warrior laid in wait in a snowdrift, buried up to the shoulders without any clothes. The nine brothers, meanwhile, had gathered round a fire at the battle site, shivering from the cold.

Day rode into the sky and the appointed time of the battle arrived, but the brothers could see no sign of Helgi, just this naked lump of a man lying in the snow. They demanded to know whether Starkad would fight them on Helgi's behalf, and if he'd rather face them one by one or all at once. 'I usually deal with snarling dogs as a pack,' was his reply, as he brushed the snow from his brutish arms.

Starkad killed six brothers at the first rush, but the last three were harder to deal with, and he received no less than seventeen wounds before he laid them low. The hero's guts were hanging out of his stomach, but as grave as his injuries were, Starkad refused the help of three passers-by: a passing bailiff, with whom he would have nothing to do; a carter, whom he mocked for marrying a slave-girl; and a servant, whom he told to run along to her snivelling children. It was only when an upright farmer offered assistance that he accepted a ride on his horse to Ingeld's palace from the site of the *holmgang*: toiling the earth was an acceptable profession in Starkad's eyes.

Back at Ingeld's court, Starkad had a score to settle: Helgi had not turned up at the contest he'd fought on the Norwegian's behalf. If there was one thing that angered Starkad more than cowardice, it was laziness: he smashed down the door of Helga's bedchamber, and demanded to know why Helgi had been love-making instead of fighting. Helga had warned Helgi to strike first if Starkad arrived in a rage, and the young man flew at the hulking figure in the doorway and stabbed him in the forehead with his sword. He would have followed up the thrust with another, but Helga intervened, holding a shield in front of the old man. Starkad nodded at this display, blood streaming into his eyes: this was a noble couple, not afraid of a fight, and he forgave them their misdemeanours.

He felt no such leniency towards Ingeld, who still ruled

Left: Odin, oldest and foremost of the gods (*Odin the Wanderer*, Georg van Rosen, 1886)

Below: A depiction of the Norse cosmos by Anne Schoerner (2018)

Left: Thor, holding his hammer aloft. (*Thor's Battle with the Giants*, Mårten Eskil Winge, 1872)

Above: A silver valkyrie figurine. Meaning 'chooser of the slain', these mythical women haunt the battlefield and select fallen warriors to carry to the feasting halls of Valhalla. From Tjürnehøj, Denmark

Left: Loki, the trickster and outsider: half-god, half-giant (*Loki finds Gullveig's Heart*, John Bauer, 1911)

Above: The giant girls Fenja and Menja at the mill. Illustration by Carl Larsson and Gunnar Forssell (1893)

Left: The fire-giant lord Surt, brandishing his flaming sword at Ragnarok (John Charles Dollman, 1909)

A panel from Hylestad Stave Church, Norway, (*c.* 1200), depicting Regin forging the sword Gram for Sigurd

Siegfried und Brunnhilde (Charles Ernest Butler, 1909), after the Middle High German version of the Sigurd legend, the *Nibelungenlied*

Left: The notorious rogue and saga hero Egil Skallagrimsson, as illustrated in the seventeenth-century Icelandic manuscript AM 426 fol.

Below: A depiction of Leif Erikson's first sight of Vinland (*Leif Erikson Discovering America*, Christian Krohg 1893)

A colourful depiction of the Rus' voyages in the East (*Guests from Overseas*, Nicholas Roerich, 1899)

The Varangian Guard, as depicted in a twelfth-century manuscript of Joannis Scylitza's eleventh-century *Synopsis Historiarum*

Above: Harald Hardrada, 'the last Viking', as depicted in a window in St Magnus' Cathedral, Kirkwall, Orkney

Left: A detail from the twelfth-century stave church at Urnes, Norway, which may depict Nidhog biting on the roots of Yggdrasil, one of the events which heralds Ragnarok

Above: A lively depiction of the apocalyptic final battle of Ragnarok by Johannes Gehrts

Left: The Norse myths continue to inspire new depictions and reinterpretations, like 2017's *Thor: Ragnarok*

Denmark as if it were a house of pleasure. It came to Starkad's attention that the son of Frothi had made a settlement with the Saxons, and – worse still – that he was entertaining the sons of his father's killer and had married a Saxon queen. Starkad knew spinelessness when he saw it, and resolved to remind the son of Frothi of his duty. He set off to do so with a bundle of charcoal on his back to show that he meant to stoke the fires of revenge, but when he arrived, the queen wouldn't let him sit on their benches for fear of getting soot on the furnishings. Starkad couldn't stand the dainty foreign foods that were being served on silver platters at the feast, and he thought marinated meat the height of decadence. He threw a gift of an expensive gold hair-braid back in the queen's face: was she trying to un-man him after her earlier insults? The music being played was sweet and soothing, but it had about as much effect on Starkad as it would on a stone: he threw a bone at the flautist and silenced him.

'What's your problem, old man? Is our hospitality not to your liking?' demanded Ingeld, belching from all the rich food. At this, Starkad could hold back no longer. He rose from his place, and with a face like a storm admonished Ingeld for all his indulgences. 'Have you forgotten the foremost duty of a son, to take revenge against his father's killers? You sit here entertaining with sweetmeats the very men that you should be putting to the sword.' It is said that the old man then recited a poem so scathing of Ingeld's behaviour that the Dane was moved to take up a sword and to cut down the Saxon princes where they sat. The son of Frothi finally found the courage of his forefathers, and showered the feasting tables with blood. The old hero Starkad was pleased with his day's work.

Starkad returned to Sweden, and the Danish throne passed from one ruler to another in the long twilight of his years. It was at this time that he was destined to commit his second infamous act: fleeing a battle between Danes and Swedes, caught up in the general panic of the troops. Starkad soon redeemed himself, of course, and though he was old and riddled with scars, he came to find an honoured place in the retinue of a Norwegian noble named Olo, and to take part in the epic battle of Bravellir on the side of the Swedes.

Conflict between the Swedes and the Danes had been brewing for some time, since Odin sowed the seeds of deceit between Sigurd Hring and his uncle Harald Wartooth. It is said by some that the old king found a pretext for war so that he could die with a sword in his hand and enter Valhalla. The run-up to the Battle of Bravellir was seven years in the making, and drew in tribes and mercenaries from across the seas who blackened the sky with their spears. Many heroes' names are remembered from that battle of battles, but Starkad fought at the front of the Swedes, and it is said that he slaughtered many of Harald's champions, as well as cutting off the hand of the shield-maiden who held the Danish banner. Another warrior-woman slashed Starkad's face so that he had to bite his beard to stop his chin from falling off, and the hero limped from the battle with a lung protruding from his chest, a deep gash in his neck, and a finger missing from his hand. Starkad's body was in pieces, and a great red mist floated across the battlefield from the steaming wounds of the slaughtered. Harald Wartooth was brought down by his charioteer in the midst of the battle, and beaten to death with his own club: some said this charioteer was Odin in disguise, taking one of his own to Valhalla. Sigurd Hring won the day, with no little help from Starkad.

Starkad's Death

The final infamous deed of Starkad's long life was perhaps his worst. During the Battle of Bravellir, Olo had commanded the fleet and fought in the vanguard, and he was appointed by Sigurd Hring to rule over Zealand. Starkad had been serving Olo for many years, and the old warrior was the most trusted of the king's household troop. But as king of the conquered Danes, Olo ruled harshly; and soon there was talk of rebellion. Twelve Danish chieftains got together and plotted the best way to overthrow the king, and they bribed Starkad to join their rebellion and to kill the king as soon as he had a chance. Starkad entered the king's room whilst Olo was in the bath, and the king's piercing gaze stopped Starkad in his tracks and left his giant limbs numb. It is said that one look from Olo could transfix the most daring of heroes, but he trusted his old friend Starkad so much that he covered his face with a cloth to hear what the old hero had to say. Once freed from Olo's gaze, Starkad overcame his scruples and plunged his sword into the naked man's throat. Although Starkad received a great sum of gold for carrying out this deed, he soon regretted this cowardly murder, and killed the leader of the plotters to help assuage his grief. He then tied the gold ransom in a pouch round his neck, and vowed to use it to pay for his own executioner.

So Starkad, now frail with age and with his sight failing, strapped two swords to his belt and set out on crutches to search for some way to bring about his death. On the way, he encountered a peasant who mocked the old man for having two swords: 'You can certainly spare one of them for me!' Starkad asked the peasant to come closer in order to receive the sword as a gift, and then promptly ran him through: he was never a man to suffer impertinence. Some hunters on horseback then decided it would be amusing to run at this frail old man and to scare him to death: but Starkad used his crutches to throw them from their steeds, and killed them where they lay. Their companion, a man named Hather, rode towards Starkad and recognised him for the grizzled hero that he was.

The two exchanged verses: Starkad recounting his glory days, as old men so often do; and Hather insulting the once-mighty hero and his diminished physique. Eventually, Starkad realised that he was dealing with a man of noble birth and a passable poet. So he offered his sword to the young man and asked to be killed: 'It's only right that young saplings should be nourished, and ancient trees cut down.' The old man helped Hather to strike by reminding him that he'd killed his own father not long ago: 'So take pleasure, boy, in ending my life, and if you manage to sever my head and jump between it and my body before it hits the ground, you'll gain a new skill – you'll become impervious to weapons.' Hather did as he asked and severed the old man's head from his neck, but he didn't attempt to jump under the body; and this was fortunate, as Starkad's giant torso came crashing to the ground with such force that it would have crushed him to death, just as Starkad intended. It is said that the old hero's head snapped at the grass with its teeth, as savage in death as the man had been in life. And so ended the three life-spans of the hero Starkad, a man who'd outlived whole dynasties in the service of Odin, and who let no offence go unpunished: even his own.

Hervor and Heidrek

The Enchanted Sword Tyrfing

Thor's hammer, Mjolnir; Freyr's burnished boar; Odin's spear Gungnir; Sif's golden hair . . . all these things were made by the dwarves, whose skill with metals is known across the worlds. The dwarves also made a sword for a king in Midgard, and this sword's name was Tyrfing. Tyrfing was the sharpest of all swords, and when it was drawn from the scabbard it shone like a sunbeam breaking from a cloud. But Tyrfing had this special attribute: if it was drawn, it would always cause a wound; and that wound would always be the death of the person who received it. Tyrfing also granted victory in every battle, but it had to be sheathed whilst the blood was still warm on its blade.

Tyrfing passed to a great Viking named Angrim, who settled on the island of Bolm. Angrim had twelve sons, and they were all berserkers of the fiercest kind. The eldest was Angantyr, and he led the brothers into battle as they gnashed their teeth and chewed on their shields. The brothers were always victorious, and had such a fierce reputation that no one would go against them. They took what they wanted, and one brother wanted a woman named Ingibjorg, princess of the Swedes. He declared his intention to marry her in front of her father the king, but another man jumped up from his seat: his name was Hjalmar the Big-Hearted. 'Don't give away your daughter to this troublemaker,' he pleaded, 'whatever threats he makes. Give her to me, your loyal retainer – I've had my heart set on Ingibjorg for many years.' The king faced a dilemma, and he gave the choice to his daughter. She preferred Hjalmar to a berserker as a husband, but the brothers would not bear this shame without a fight. They challenged Hjalmar to *holmgang* on the island of Samso: the winner would take all.

Hjalmar sailed to Samso on the appointed day with his sworn brother Orvar-Odd, and they set out at once to search the island, leaving their men to guard the ships. While they were gone, Angantyr and his berserker brothers arrived and attacked the ships in a frenzy: they howled as they cut the Vikings with heavy blows that no shield could resist. After they'd butchered all of Hjalmar's men, the rage left the berserkers, and they were standing slouched over their swords when Hjalmar and Odd appeared on the horizon. The two heroes swooped down on the exhausted berserkers, even though it was far from clear whether they or the twelve brothers would be joining Odin in Valhalla that night. Odd fought with eleven of the brothers in turn, and defeated each one, but Hjalmar had a harder time with Angantyr: the oldest brother had unsheathed the shining sword Tyrfing, and even though Hjalmar killed Angantyr he was wounded sixteen times – and just one wound from Tyrfing would have been enough. Odd bid farewell to his dying friend, and he did right by the berserkers: he had them buried in a mound with all their weapons. Angantyr still clutched hold of Tyrfing.

Hervor the Shield-maiden

Angantyr left behind a widow named Svafa, daughter of Jarl Bjarmar who ruled the lands round Lake Lagoda. She was pregnant, and soon gave birth to a beautiful girl named Hervor. Hervor refused to play the courteous princess: she preferred training with a sword and bow to sitting at needlework. The jarl tried to rein her in, but whenever she was prevented from fighting, Hervor would just run away to the forest and cause even more harm by ambushing travellers. When she learned that her father had been none other than the great hero Angantyr, and that he was buried on the island of Samso, there was no holding her back. She joined a raiding party, travelled west, clad in the gear of a warrior, and soon became the leader of this Viking band and commanded the fighting men in battle.

Eventually Hervor reached Denmark with her ships, and put in at the island of Samso. The men were reluctant to set foot in that place, as it was rumoured to be haunted by evil creatures: but Hervor insisted on dropping anchor within sight of the burial barrows. She rowed ashore at sunset on her own, and asked a shepherd which was the burial mound of her father Angantyr. His reply was ominous: 'I'd advise you to leave, lady of Vikings, before the earth opens up and the flames light the homes of the dead. This is no place to be after dark.' But Hervor feared no mound-dweller, and she set off towards the flickering light of the farthest cairn.

Hervor passed many mounds lit up by the light of red gold before she came to the mound of Angantyr and his brothers. She was not alarmed by the fire that flared up on the headland, and spoke a poem summoning her father from his grave: 'Wake up, Angantyr, from the mouldering earth and the close embrace of roots! Ghosts have no need of costly mail and helmet, or of the sword forged by Dvalin the dwarf.'

The mound opened at her words, and flames leapt into the sky. 'Why do you call me from the grave, daughter? Hel's gate is open, and the whole island is on fire. I'd flee to your ships if I were you: there's nothing for you here.'

But Hervor stood with her hands on her hips, and stared down at her father. Her eyes flickered with the flames of the underworld. 'I want your sword Tyrfing, Father, and I'm not leaving till I get it.' 'You are a fool, daughter. I know no woman on earth who would dare to wield the bane of Hjalmar, and you are evil to ask for it: it will be the ruin of all of our family.'

Nevertheless, Angantyr could not refuse Hervor her request – for there was no doubting that this fierce woman was his daughter, and that the sword belonged to her. The two parted: Angantyr back to the grave and his long years of rest; Hervor to the ships through the fires in the darkness, where she found that her stout-hearted men had all fled.

Heidrek the Troublemaker

Hervor continued her raiding for a time, serving in the retinue of King Gudmund of the Glittering Plains. Eventually she found her way back to her foster father and gave up the life of a Viking. She married King Gudmund's son Hofund, and together they had two sons: one was named Angantyr after her father, and the other was called Heidrek. Angantyr grew up to be a pleasant man to deal with: Heidrek was the opposite, though his mother had a soft spot for her unruly second child. When the brothers were of age, a feast was held and Heidrek wasn't invited – but he came anyway. He caused all kinds of trouble there, and though his brother stood up for him, he was asked to leave the celebrations. Heidrek had more mischief in mind: he lingered in the shadows outside the hall, and hurled a stone at some figures he saw talking under the eaves. When he went to see what damage his stone had caused, he recognised his brother Angantyr lying dead on the ground. Heidrek was forced to leave the kingdom for this savage deed, but before he left, his mother gave him the sword Tyrfing, and told him of its power. His father had some advice for his teenage son before he was banished: he told the young hero not to assist a man who has committed murder; not to let his wife visit her family too often; and not to foster the son of a more important man. Heidrek decided, there and then, to do exactly the opposite of what his father advised – he was a teenager, after all. He started by giving his gold away to two murderers he met on the road. That would teach the old man a lesson!

Heidrek soon travelled abroad, and took up with an old king in the land of the Goths. The king's hold over his kingdom had weakened with his advancing years, and he was troubled by two rebellious jarls. Heidrek led an expedition to punish the rebels and killed both the jarls with his own sword. He returned, victorious, to the king, and was rewarded with land and followers. He married the king's daughter, and they had a son named Angantyr, after his uncle and his great-grandfather. When the boy was still young, a great famine came over the kingdom, and a powerful sorceress determined that a sacrifice must be made to Odin of the highest-born boy in the land: it was the only way to appease such a demanding god. There were two choices: either Heidrek's son was the highest-born, or the old king's. Heidrek's father tried again to intervene: he advised Heidrek to offer his own son, but to demand the allegiance of every second man at the assembly in return for this sacrifice. Heidrek still wasn't ready to follow his father's advice: he demanded the allegiance of every second man, but as soon as he had secured their oaths, he rallied them and turned on the old king. There was a great battle, and Heidrek was victorious: instead of sacrificing his son, he dedicated the whole host of the fallen to Odin. His Gothic wife hanged herself in the hall of the Disir.

Heidrek extended his kingdom through war on the Huns, and took the daughter of a Saxon king as his new wife. She was taken home to Heidrek's court, but often wanted to return to stay with her father, and Heidrek allowed her to do so – merely because his own father had warned him not to. But Heidrek couldn't deny his growing suspicions: his wife was spending a very long time with her family, and he decided to find out for himself what was drawing her back so often to the land of the Saxons. He took his fleet south, and when night fell, he travelled under cover of darkness to the royal apartments where his wife was staying: she was lying in bed there, and next to her was a man with a shock of blond hair. Rather than killing this adulterer in his sleep, Heidrek cut a large piece of hair from his fringe so that he would know that he'd been caught in the act. The next morning he announced his arrival and called everyone to a feast by his ships. He walked around the Saxon nobles, eyeing up their hair, but it was clear that the lock he'd cut off the night before didn't belong to any of them. He had the buildings scoured by his men, and finally a slave was dragged out of the kitchen wearing a cloth wrapped around his head: underneath was a shock of blond hair with a gap in its fringe. 'Here's the low-born man your princess prefers to take to bed!' Heidrek announced to the Saxons. He left her there in shame, and returned to his kingdom without a wife.

During his raids that summer, Heidrek captured the daughter of a Hunnish king – her name was Sifka – and took her home as his concubine. She bore him a healthy son, but did not show the loyalty that Heidrek demanded of his mistresses. At that time, he had decided to go against the last of his father's good counsels by offering to foster the son of the king of Gardariki. The king granted Heidrek this honour because of his fear of invasion by the Goths, but he suspected Heidrek was after something more – the hand of his daughter in marriage, something that he vowed he would never give to such a troublemaker. Heidrek brought up the boy well, and he was very loyal to his stepfather. When the lad was a little older, they went back to his family in Gardariki, where they took part in entertainments and went hunting. Whilst they were riding through the forest on one of these hunts, Heidrek told the boy to hide himself at a farm they were passing, and only return to the city when he was sent for. Heidrek pretended to be sad when he rode home – he confided in his concubine Sifka that he'd drawn his sword Tyrfing to cut some apples, and that he'd killed the boy by accident. Sifka couldn't keep this information to herself, and quickly told their hosts the news. Heidrek was seized, chained up, and sentenced to a public execution, but he got word out to his foster son, and before anyone could be persuaded to carry out the execution of such a formidable chieftain from the north, the boy turned up alive and well. Out of shame over the treatment of Heidrek, the king of Gardariki offered the trickster his daughter in marriage, and so Heidrek got what he'd wanted all along. As for Sifka, she had proved herself a gossip – and once they were back home in the north, Heidrek killed her by breaking her back in a fast-flowing river and letting her body float downstream.

Riddles with Odin

Heidrek returned to his kingdom, where he ruled more sensibly than he had before. He began to favour Freyr as his god of choice, and, like Freyr, he kept a great boar with golden-hued bristles that he used for swearing oaths: he would lay his hand upon the boar, and make it known that any man who had done him wrong could redeem himself by posing a riddle that he hadn't heard and couldn't solve.

There was a powerful man named Gestumblindi who had got on the wrong side of Heidrek, and when he was summoned to judgement, the man made sacrifices to Odin, hoping to obtain his help. That night a stranger arrived at the door, calling himself Gestumblindi. They exchanged clothes, and the next morning, this stranger set off for Heidrek's court in the real Gestumblindi's place. No one was any the wiser. When the imposter came before the king, he was given the same choice as every man: he could subject himself to the king's judgement, or he could enter into a riddle contest. If he asked a riddle that the king couldn't answer, he would save his neck.

The man chose riddles, and started by asking for ale 'that gives speech but also makes speech harder'. Heidrek called for some ale for the visitor, and the contest continued. Gestumblindi began with simple riddles: he talked of a place he'd walked where birds could pass under his feet and over his head. The king guessed a bridge. He told of an object with a piercing voice that gave kisses to gold. The king guessed a goldsmith's hammer. He talked of creatures he'd seen outside the god Delling's door: one of them turned its head down to Hel, with its feet searching for the sun. The king guessed a leek. Now the riddles became harder. A swan's egg used as a casket; a dead snake on an ice-flow; a game of *tafl* played between a god and a giant; the waves seeking their father Ægir. But Heidrek was a match for every riddle, and he was never long in finding the solution.

'What home is protected by swords that bite grass, and roofed by a rock used for drink?' 'A nest built between the jaw-bones of a great horned ox,' was the king's answer. The man's riddles turned stranger still. 'What did I see outside the door of this hall: a creature with ten tongues, twenty eyes and forty feet?' The king thought he knew the answer. He had a pregnant sow brought inside and cut open; inside, there were nine piglets. The atmosphere in the room had suddenly grown cold, as if a shadow had passed across the sun, and the king began to suspect that this man was not who he seemed. 'What are the names of those two who run on ten feet together, but have only three eyes?' Heidrek paused and looked hard at the man who called himself Gestumblindi before giving his answer: it was only then he noticed that the man's grey hair fell down over one eye. 'The answer to your riddle is one-eyed Odin, riding on Sleipnir.' The stranger and the king stared at each other. 'Then answer me this, great king, if you're wiser than all others and a match for the gods. What did Odin whisper in the ear of Baldr before placing him on the funeral pyre?' Now Heidrek knew who he'd been testing his wits against. 'Only you know the answer to that, old greybeard,' he replied, and he pulled Tyrfing from its sheath and slashed at the figure in front of him: but Odin had already turned himself into a hawk, and the blow only clipped his feathers as he flew away.

Odin perched on the door-post before bidding Heidrek farewell: for this insult, the king would be condemned to death at the hands of his own slaves. It wasn't long before Odin's prediction came true. King Heidrek, son of Hervor the shield-maiden, was murdered in bed by a group of slaves, and Tyrfing was stolen from his bloody corpse. It is not wise to contend with Odin, even if you happen to be a hero as bold and as stubborn as Heidrek.

Egil Skallagrimsson

The last of the folk heroes and followers of Odin to be mentioned (and there are many more) is an Icelander called Egil Skallagrimsson, the most famous warrior-poet of the settlement age – with a bone-headedness to rival any legendary hero, and a gift with words to match.

Settling in Iceland

Egil's grandfather was called 'Evening-Wolf' because of his tempers, which tended to come on at the end of the day: he was rumoured to be a shape-shifter. His sons were Thorolf and Skallagrim, Egil's father: Thorolf inherited Evening-Wolf's best qualities, but Skallagrim was ugly and prone to their family's dark moods. Both were handy around the farm on the west coast of Norway, and they were no slouches when it came to raiding in the summer. Like many men of standing, Evening-Wolf eventually clashed with Harald of the tangled locks, who had vowed not to cut his hair until he'd brought the whole of Norway under his control. Thorolf was killed in a skirmish with Harald and his men, and Evening-Wolf had no desire to accept compensation for his son, or to submit to such a power-hungry king. The family decided to settle in Iceland, where they'd heard there was good land for the taking, and preferred the prospect of living as independent farmers to that of hard rule at home. Evening-Wolf and Skallagrim ambushed and butchered a ship full of Harald's men – father and son fighting like wolves – and then they set sail for Iceland in the ship they had captured. Evening-Wolf died from exhaustion on the journey, but his coffin floated to shore, and Skallagrim knew that he should settle in the bay close to where it washed up. He established a farm and called it Borg, and was an industrious man. He had two daughters and two sons with his wife Bera: the eldest son was handsome and good-natured, and was named after his uncle Thorolf. But the younger brother took after his father and grandfather, and it soon became clear that he would grow into an unsightly and difficult child. They named him Egil, and the local boys knew not to cross him.

Egil Skallagrimsson developed two talents at a very early age: a way with words, and a gift for causing trouble even when he was sober. When Skallagrim left his infant son at home to go to a feast, Egil stole a horse and followed the grown-ups across the moors. On his arrival at the gathering, he recited a poem to the room of ale-drunk men, and received a reward of shells. He was three years old. At the age of seven he killed for the first time, burying an axe in the head of an older boy who tackled him too hard in the winter games. Skallagrim pretended indifference to Egil's unruly behaviour, but his mother praised him: 'He has the makings of a true Viking, this one.' When he was twelve, Egil was playing ball with his father; during the game, he provoked Skallagrim into such a rage that he threw Egil's friend (who was standing nearby) to the floor and killed him. That evening Egil calmly walked up to Skallagrim's table and buried a sword in the chest of his father's favourite farm-hand. Father and son barely spoke that winter, and the following year Egil pressed his older brother to take him to Norway.

Egil's Feud with Eric Bloodaxe

By that time, Harald's son was ruling over the west coast of Norway: his name was Eric Bloodaxe. Eric tried to make amends with Skallagrim by sending him the gift of an axe inlaid with gold, which in Skallagrim's eyes only added insult to injury. Thorolf entered Eric's service and did his best to smooth over the feud between their fathers, but Egil was not so keen on reconciliation.

Soon after bringing his younger brother to Norway, Thorolf decided to marry a woman called Asgerd, who had grown up alongside them in Iceland, and whose father owned good land in Norway. Egil also desired this girl, and he pleaded sickness to avoid the wedding. He was left to recover with a friend of the family.

Egil quickly grew bored in that quiet place, and when he heard that a man named Olvir was heading off to collect rents in the area, he asked to accompany him. They sailed down the coast, but were forced to take shelter from a storm on the island of Atloy, where they approached a landowner named Bard, asking for his hospitality. Bard was a surly man, but he agreed to put the men up in an outbuilding, feeding them curds – as he claimed to have nothing better to drink. But in truth, Bard was saving his ale for more important guests: King Eric Bloodaxe and his wife Gunnhild were touring the lands they owned, and Bard was hosting a lavish feast to celebrate a sacrifice they'd made. Egil and Olvir left their beds and joined the celebrations: everyone got very drunk, and some men were throwing up. Bard took particular pains to fill Egil's horn again and again, but the Icelander downed all the ale that was offered to him, and returned the gift by reciting insulting poetry. After one of these verses, the queen advised Bard to spike this unruly Icelander's drink with poison – which might have worked if Egil hadn't known runes of protection. He smeared blood onto the poisoned horn and it burst apart.

It was now clear to Egil that the time had come to leave the party. He manhandled the stupefied Olvir towards the door, only to find Bard waiting for them with a horn full of ale, insisting that they should drink once more before leaving. Egil recited a slanderous verse through his beer-soaked beard, and then stabbed Bard in the stomach with his sword. The host slipped to the floor in a pool of his own blood, and Olvir began vomiting in the doorway. Egil sped away from the farm and swam to a nearby island, where he made good his escape after killing some of Eric Bloodaxe's men. That was the beginning of Egil's feud with the great Viking war-leader and his fierce wife Gunnhild.

Egil took part in Viking raids in the Baltic on that first trip abroad, plundering and killing, and burning whole households even when his companions advised him against it. He didn't mend his relations with Eric, and though Thorolf admired his brother's bravery, he saw that Egil had inherited his fore-fathers' fondness for reckless behaviour. When Egil attacked and defeated a friend of King Eric's during a battle in Jutland, the brothers thought it wise to avoid Norway that autumn, and they headed off to England instead.

The king in England at that time was Athelstan, and there was trouble brewing in his kingdom. The Scots, the Strathclyde Welsh, and the Vikings of Dublin were banding together to rebel against Athelstan's rule. The king had need of good fighting men, so Egil and Thorolf went with their followers and signed up as mercenaries. They proved their worth to the king, but in the great battle that followed, Athelstan kept Egil and Thorolf in different parts of his army, and in the press of the fighting Thorolf died, even as the invading army fled. Egil came to Athelstan's victory feast, but he glowered at the king across the room with eyebrows like thunder. Eventually the Anglo-Saxon king approached the Icelander with his sword drawn: he slid a weighty silver arm-ring onto the sword-tip and held it out to Egil, who lifted his own sword and took the ring onto his blade. In this way, Athelstan paid the first compensation owed for Thorolf's death; two chests of English silver would follow. Egil recited a verse to mark the occasion: his bristling eyebrows returned to their place.

Egil had always been attracted to his brother's widow, Asgerd. He married her on his return to Norway, and then equipped a merchant ship to sail home to Iceland. He had been absent for twelve years, and Skallagrim was very happy to see at least one of his sons again. Egil farmed the land for several winters, and his looks did not improve: he was balder than ever, with a thick neck and heavy forehead. Though he abandoned the life of a Viking for a time, he was still on the lookout for trouble, and when he heard his father-in-law had died, it gave him an excuse to set out again for Norway in order to lay claim to his wife's inheritance. On his arrival, early in spring, Egil was bold enough to make his grievances heard at the local assembly in front of Eric Bloodaxe himself. But he only succeeded in enraging the king even further, and was lucky to escape from that place of sanctuary alive. Egil was now declared an outlaw throughout the whole of Norway. Before he left for Iceland, he hunted down the man who'd fleeced his wife of her inheritance, and dealt him his death blow. 'I've dressed Odin's wife Earth in a new cloak of blood,' was his reply when his men asked where he'd been. On top of this, Egil killed Eric's son Rognvald, boarding his painted warship and cutting him down; and to add insult to injury, he raised a scorn-pole to Eric and Gunnhild: he set a horse's head on top of the pole and carved it with a curse on the family and all their descendants. It called upon the spirits of the land never to leave them in peace.

Eric's rule over Norway didn't last long: he was deposed by his half-brother Hakon the Good. Meanwhile, Skallagrim died of old age, and Egil inherited his father's lands and turned his hand to farming once more. News of Eric Bloodaxe's change of fortune hadn't reached Iceland, nor had the fact that the warrior-king had fled across the sea to become the king of Viking York.

Egil quickly grew restless with the settled life in Borg, and he decided to sail again to England, meet with King Athelstan, and see if he could collect the rest of the reward he'd been promised for his service. But Egil delayed his departure until late in the year, when the weather had grown severe. The Icelanders' ship skirted the Orkneys and sailed down the east coast of Scotland, but strong winds drove them ashore at the Humber, and the men were forced to beach the vessel and salvage their provisions. It was only then that Egil heard the unwelcome news: Eric and Gunnhild were now ruling in Northumbria, and their loyal followers were all around. There was only one thing for Egil to do: go to his enemy and face his fate head-on.

The next morning, Egil walked into the hall of Eric Bloodaxe in York, kissed the astonished king's foot, and offered his arch-enemy his head. Eric was minded to kill the Icelander immediately, as was his wife, and it was only through the intervention of Egil's life-long friend Arinbjorn that he was granted a stay of execution till the morning. Arinbjorn's plan was for Egil to write a poem in praise of the king, and to save his neck by doing so. The poem Egil composed was called 'Head-Ransom', and its words seemed to do so much honour to the king in front of all his hardened warriors that Eric had little option but to let his enemy go. However, when people recalled the poem later, they had doubts about exactly who was being praised: was it the king or the poet? Such was Egil's skill with verse: they say he carried Odin's mead in his mouth to English lands. This was the last of Egil's encounters with Eric Bloodaxe, who died soon afterwards raiding in Britain: a Viking to the very end.

Egil Settles His Scores in Norway

Egil made his way to Athelstan, and after serving that winter in the household of the king, returned to Norway to pursue his inheritance claims with Eric's half-brother Hakon. King Hakon received the Icelander in peace, and granted Egil the right to pursue his claims according to the laws of the land, but the injuries done to his family made full reconciliation impossible. Egil resolved to settle his affairs in Norway and to return to his farm in Iceland. According to the ancient custom, he challenged Atli the Short to a duel to resolve his property claim once and for all: and he managed to prevail, despite Atli's sorcery. He fought a second duel on behalf of a farmer who gave him good hospitality: this duel was with a berserker, and was fought according to the old rules of *holmgang*. A circle of stones was laid out, and within it the two men took up their shields and swords. Though the berserker started off howling and fighting with all the savagery of a man possessed, Egil's blows soon took their toll, and the fierce man tired. The upshot was that Egil knocked him to the ground and severed his leg: that was the end of the contest. Little more of note happened on that visit to Norway. Egil had won his wife's inheritance, and returned to Iceland with his reputation greater than ever.

Egil's restless spirit took him abroad one final time before he settled in Iceland for good. He'd heard news that his great friend Arinbjorn had reclaimed all his old lands in Norway, so the time seemed right to travel there and spend the winter in his company. The two exchanged rich gifts at the Yule celebrations, and Arinbjorn even paid Egil compensation for lands won from the berserker, after the Icelander's claims to them were rejected by the king. Egil was visibly moved. 'Much time will pass before we see another man of your nobility,' was all he said.

The two friends went raiding together in Frisia that summer, and plundered many villages on that low-lying coast. On one of these expeditions Egil was separated from his men whilst pursuing fleeing villagers across the dykes. The villagers turned on him, but Egil fought his way through them and made his way back to the ships that were now under attack by the rallying Frisians. Egil's men were loading the ships under protection of a shield-wall, and had given him up for dead, but the Icelander came charging at the rear of the Frisian lines, and broke through with great swings of his halberd. That was a good day of plunder.

Egil now parted from Arinbjorn and sailed back to Norway to spend the winter with Arinbjorn's nephew, Thorstein. Thorstein was out of favour with King Hakon, and the king asked him to prove his loyalty by going to collect the revenues due to him from the restive province of Varmland: previous expeditions had all come to gory ends. Egil agreed to go in Thorstein's place as a favour to the family, and the group set off over the snow. On their way, they spent the night with a farmer named Armod Beard, who was not a good host: first he served Egil and his men nothing but curds; and then gave the guests such a strong brew that it made them sick. Egil had to drink the ale poured for his men to stop them keeling over, and concluded that these toasts were not being made with their good health in mind. Without warning, he rose from the table, pinned their host up against the wall, and threw up all over the shocked man's face. The vomit poured into Armod's nostrils and into his open mouth, so that he was choking and drowning under the deluge. Egil followed this up by reciting a poem, returned to his seat, and called for more drink from the farmer's wife. He stayed drinking long into the night.

The next morning, Egil woke early, took his weapons and walked into the room where Armod was sleeping. He grabbed the farmer by the beard, and dragged him to the edge of the bed. It was only due to the pleading of his wife and daughter – who'd been more hospitable than the men of the house – that Egil spared his life; although he did gouge out one of Armod's eyes (inspired, no doubt, by devotion to Odin), and cut off the man's famous beard before leaving. On that same trip through Varmland, Egil cured a sick woman of fever using his skill with runes, saw off an ambush from Armod's men, and took tribute from the Earl of Varmland. He even defeated the earl's men on the way home, against odds that did not look good, even for a man of Egil's stature. The collectors returned safely from Varmland bearing the king's tribute, and a long list of the earl's treacheries. Thorstein was reconciled with King Hakon thanks to Egil's expedition, and they parted in great friendship.

Egil's Old Age

Egil was a different man back in Iceland: he was not known for starting feuds or duelling, though few dared to test him. He had three sons and two daughters with Asgerd, and these children were now fully grown. His daughter Thorgerd was very close to him, and though she was strong-willed like her father, she was more peaceful than he had been in his youth. Egil's son Bodvar was a very handsome and promising man, and Egil had great affection for him. One day, when Bodvar was rowing timber across the fjord to the farm, a storm blew up and capsized the boat, and Bodvar was drowned. His brother Gunnar had died shortly before this, from fever. Egil was more distressed at the loss of his sons than anyone had ever known him to be, and he locked himself away in his room, refusing to eat or drink. No one dared to approach him, until Egil's daughter Thorgerd came to the old warrior and lay down next to him. 'I want what you want, father: to starve to death. There's no other way to stop this grief. But I'd like to keep you alive long enough to compose a poem to Bodvar's memory. Afterwards, we'll both die, if you wish.' Egil was persuaded to write the long poem called 'The Loss of My Sons', lamenting the fact that Ægir had taken Bodvar from him, and that Odin had given him nothing but poetry to lessen his grief. But writing the poem did the trick – Thorgerd persuaded her father to rise from his bed.

Egil also composed a poem in praise of his life-long friend Arinbjorn when he heard of his continued successes in Norway, but he did not return again to the lands he'd spent so long disputing. The old warrior was now resolved to making poems about great events rather than taking part himself. He eventually handed over the farm at Borg to his son Thorstein, even though the two didn't see eye to eye: Thorstein was too mild and likeable by half. Thorstein Egilsson was an upright man, and not afraid to defend his claims in Iceland with the strength of his arm, but did not share his father's delight in conflict.

Egil took part in an assembly as arbitrator of his son's dispute with a neighbour, and he was more cantankerous than ever when it came to his dealings with others, but the once great Viking grew increasingly frail. Women mocked Egil when they saw him lose his footing around the farm, and the servants were fed up with this half-blind man getting in their way. He lamented his frailty in verse, but few people were listening. Even in his feeble state, Egil dreamed of riding to the assembly and throwing his hoard of English silver to the crowds, simply to cause a scene, but no one would agree to help him with this mischief. So he took two slaves and headed out from his step-daughter's farm at Mosfell up into the hills. On his horse were the chests full of Athelstan's silver. When he came back to the farm, he was alone and without his chests; and nobody ever saw the slaves or the silver again. Egil died from illness later that year, and was buried in a mound with his weapons and a suit of fine clothes.

Some say that silver coins from England wash up in the creek after floods, but the hoard of Egil Skallagrimsson has never been found, and only Odin knows the truth about where it is hidden.

8

Exploration in the North Atlantic

Odin is a finder of ways. He travels to the farthest reaches of Midgard, and he's not afraid to visit Jotunheim or to take the road to Hel. On every journey, Odin learns a little more about the world. Even if there's no stopping Ragnarok, he hopes he'll learn enough to buy the gods some breathing room and delay the inevitable destruction. The legendary heroes whose stories we've heard share Odin's restless energy, and their exploits teach humankind a valuable lesson: you don't gain much by sitting on your chair at home.

The Norse peoples spread out from their Scandinavian home-lands like the roots of the World-Tree, following the water. In the east, the river networks opened up trade routes to the Black Sea and Byzantium, and to silver from the Caliphate; in the south, Norse seafarers followed the Iberian coast to North Africa, and crossed into the Mediterranean – raiding, slaving, and serving in the courts of powerful kings. In the west, Vikings sailed up the Seine to sack Paris, turned York and Dublin into great trading hubs, and settled in great swathes of Ireland, England and France, carving up old kingdoms and helping shape the countries that exist today. But these way-finders had the most lasting impact in the North Atlantic, where they broke new ground. They settled the remote Faroe Islands, turned Iceland and Greenland into thriving communities of farmers, and even pushed on to explore lands farther to the west.

This much is history. But there are also stories that the Norse peoples told themselves about their great age of exploration, full of characters as colourful as the legendary heroes, and set in a landscape as remarkable as anything in Jotunheim.

The First Steps

The Scandinavian homelands of Norway, Denmark and Sweden have long coastlines, and the Norse peoples knew how to travel Ægir's meadows in their ships. Viking ships were clinker-built, with a single sail and steering oar on the starboard side, and by the end of the Viking Age there were as many different vessels as there were reasons for taking to the sea – from small coastal craft for ferrying goods and people across the fjords of Norway, to warships with more than thirty pairs of oars, bright sails and decorated stems: these beautiful sea-creatures were given names like Grey-Goose, Crane, and Long-Serpent. The ships used for raiding were fast and light, with shallow keels that allowed for quick beaching when the Vikings sailed them up estuaries: they were built to bring warriors across the sea, and they needed a powerful chieftain as a backer, and many hands to sail them. These are the vessels most closely associated with the Viking Age, but they weren't the ones used to bring families to settle Iceland, or to carry goods, slaves and animals between the remote outposts of the Norse world. Merchant ships were broader and more stable in high seas, with plenty of room for carrying cargo, and they served as the workhorses of this age of exploration. They may not have been decorated like the ship Hringhorni on which Baldr was cremated, and couldn't be folded and carried in the pocket like Freyr's Skidbladnir, but they transported people and their animals to the remote outposts of the North Atlantic, and further west to the edge of the encircling sea.

The Norse expansion west didn't begin with a great leap across the North Atlantic. Soon after the Viking raid on Lindisfarne in 793 – an event which has itself passed into legend – there were reports that pirates had rounded Scotland and sacked the holy islands of Iona and Skye; and before long, these seaborne raids started to gather pace. The Norse pirates found easy pickings on the coasts, and islands were particularly vulnerable. They would sail from Norway in the early summer, when the seas were calm and the days long, and return to their farms with wealth and slaves. We are used to calling these people Vikings, but for the Norse seafarers who raided England the word 'Viking' referred to what they did, not who they were: at home, these pirates were farmers, landowners, the hearth-companions of local kings.

To reach Ireland and the west coast of Britain, Norwegian Vikings could make use of islands, just as they did when sailing down the broken Norwegian coast: first to Shetland, then Orkney, through the Western Isles of Scotland past Iona and Islay, then through the North Channel to the Irish Sea. Whilst the first Vikings came to raid, others saw good land on these islands, and staging posts for further attacks along the coast. Shetland, Orkney, Lewis, the Isle of Man . . . all eventually became Norse colonies, and stepping stones across the North Atlantic. In Ireland, Vikings began to winter on the mainland in protected camps with easy access to their ships. In time, Norse trading centres developed on these rivers: Dublin by a dark pool on the Liffey, Limerick on King's Island in the Shannon, Waterford beside the Suir, and Cork on the island mudflats of the Lee. Caithness in Scotland came under Norse control, as did the lands along the upper Seine that became Normandy; and England was invaded by a great army of Danes intent on conquest.

The Vikings who sailed to the Scottish Isles may have come from Norway, but Norway was a country of warring kings and tribes, and different bands of Vikings often fought each other for control of sea routes and bases in the west. It is said that when Harald of the Tangled Hair finally won his kingdom, he sent out a fleet to subdue the Norse colonies in the Scottish Isles, as he feared Viking raids himself. Harald established a powerful earldom in the Orkneys to bring them under Norwegian control: other kings in Europe gave Vikings land with the promise that they would keep rival bands of pirates away, or hired their fleets as mercenaries in their wars. The fortunes of Norse colonies waxed and waned as power shifted throughout Scandinavia and the British Isles. When one possibility for raiding dried up, or Vikings were expelled from lands they had acquired, they took their ships and moved on. Odin's example must have taught these seafarers to be bold and ruthless, but crucially, it would also teach them to adapt. Over time, that would also mean abandoning the old gods for the ascendant Christ.

The Faroe Islands lay off the main routes towards the British Isles, and they were settled by a man named Grimr Kamban, if the saga accounts are to be believed. Kamban is an Irish name, and Grimr may have been a Norse settler from Ireland or the Western Isles: Irish monks had been to these remote islands well before Grimr, and perhaps it was these religious men who

pointed him the way. Unlike the islands to the south settled by
the Norsemen, the Faroe Islands weren't inhabited; and the settlers were not here for plunder or conquest, but to break new
ground. Whole households came from Norway and the Norse
colonies with the intent of farming this uninhabited land, and
their descendants are still there today. With them came the old
gods, and they named the bay on Streymoy, where they held
their assemblies, 'Thor's Harbour'. Many followed Grimr to the
Faroe Islands, halfway between Norway and an as yet unsettled
island even further to the west.

The Settlement of Iceland

The First Explorers

According to the Book of Settlements, Norse explorers were not
the first to visit Iceland. Before Ingolfr and the settlers arrived,
men called *papar* sailed to this remote place to spend their summers in seclusion from the world. They didn't stay long after the
Norse settlers arrived. It is said that the *papar* left bells and
books behind, and by this, it was known that they were Irish
monks.

The Book of Settlements tells us that Norse seafarers first
came to Iceland by chance. A man named Naddod was sailing
from Norway to the Faroe Islands when he was blown off course.
He sighted land, and sailed into a bay backed by high mountains. Naddod climbed one of them to get the lie of the land, but
could see nothing to suggest that there were people living there.
As he climbed back on board his ship, snow began to fall, even
though winter had passed some time ago. Naddod named this
vast place 'Snowland', and brought the news of his discovery

back to the Norse colonies: he was full of praise for this new land, despite the weather.

The next man to reach Iceland was Gardar the Swede. Some accounts say that he was guided there by his mother's second sight; others that he was driven out into the sea by a storm that blew up in the Pentland Firth. Gardar took it upon himself to sail around the coast: he proved it was an island, and built a shelter in the north at a place now known as Husavik: the bay of houses. He spent the winter there, and put out to sea again in the spring. But before he sailed out of sight of the coast, the boat they were towing broke loose, with a man named Nattfari and two slaves on board. They made land in a bay that still carries the name Nattfaravik, but little is known about their fate. Gardar was not a man afraid of self-promotion: he named the island 'Gardar's Isle' on his return, and reported that it was covered in trees all the way from the mountains to the shoreline.

News of this new land came to a man named Raven-Floki: he was a great Viking and an adventurer. He sailed from Norway to Shetland with his followers and his daughter, intending to seek out Gardar's Isle: his daughter drowned whilst they were staying in Shetland, but he pressed on north into the emptiness of the sea. Floki took three ravens with him on board. The first raven he set free flew over the stern of the ship, back to Shetland, and Floki sailed on. The second raven he set free circled the ship, and then settled on the mast. Floki continued on his course. The third raven he released flew over the prow and disappeared – and then Floki knew that he must be close to this mysterious new land. He sailed round Reykjanes and Snæfellsnes and on into the West Fjords. There was such good fishing that the crew forgot to gather hay, and many of the animals they had brought with them died that winter: Gardar had not been wrong about the snow. In the spring, Floki climbed a mountain to the north, and when he looked out he saw a fjord still choked with drift-ice. He complained that they were living in a land of ice, and this name stuck. Floki and his men prepared to leave, but hadn't got the ship ready until late in the season, and when they tried to tack around the Reykjanes peninsula, they were driven back into the bay, and the tow-boat broke loose with a man named Herjolf at the oars: the two boats quickly drifted apart and lost each other in the clouds. The Norwegians were forced to winter there again in two different camps. In the spring, Raven-Floki found Herjolf, and finally sailed back to Norway the following summer. Raven-Floki had little good to say about the place he called Iceland, but Herjolf had a better opinion of the land, and their companion Thorolf liked to tell people that the grazing was so good that butter was dripping from every blade of grass. From then on, he was known as Thorolf Butter.

Ingolfr Arnarson

Ingolfr Arnarson was a man of standing from Fjalar in Norway. He had a blood-brother called Leif, and the two of them regularly went raiding together. On one Viking expedition, they teamed up with the sons of Earl Atli the Slender, but fell out with these fierce men, and killed two of the brothers in a skirmish. Earl Atli would only accept compensation on the following terms: that all the lands of Ingolfr and Leif would now belong to him.

Ingolfr and Leif found a large ship, and set out to explore this place that people were calling Iceland: they spent a winter in the Eastfjords. After exploring the country, it seemed to them that the south of Iceland was better than the north, and most suitable for settlement. When they returned to Norway, Ingolfr gathered all his possessions to leave for this new land, whilst Leif went raiding in Ireland and won a great deal of plunder, as well as many Irish slaves. On this raid, Leif entered an earth-house and saw a flash from a sword in the darkness. He killed the man holding it and took the sword: from then on he was known as Leif Sword, or Hjorleif. The two men stayed in Norway that winter, and Ingolfr made a sacrifice to the gods to discover what they had in store for their expedition. For his part, Hjorleif never sacrificed, and he didn't see the need to do so now. The two men left in the spring with everything they owned.

As soon as Ingolfr neared the coast of Iceland he threw his family's high-seat pillars overboard, and vowed to settle wherever the gods brought them to shore. It would be several years before he found out where they were. In the meantime, Ingolfr and his household set up camp where they made land on the south coast. Hjorleif drifted for some time with his fresh water running low, and made land further along the coast. He built two houses there, and in the spring he wanted to plough and plant grain. He only had one ox, so he yoked his Irish slaves to the plough. The slaves did not take well to being treated like animals, so they killed Leif's ox, and told the Norwegians that a bear had attacked it. The slaves then picked off Hjorleif and his men one by one as they spread out to search for the wild animal – they didn't know that bears have never lived in Iceland. The slaves took the dead men's wives and possessions, as well as their boats, and rowed across to some small islands they'd seen off the coast. Their leader was a man called Dufthak.

Meanwhile, Ingolfr had sent out his own slaves in search of the high-seat pillars, and they came across the unburied bodies of Hjorleif and his men. Ingolfr took the news badly. 'That's what happens when you refuse to sacrifice, blood-brother,' he mused as he prepared Hjorleif's body for burial, 'but don't worry: I won't let your shameful death go unavenged.' Ingolfr had seen the islands off the coast, and guessed that this was where the slaves had fled: he wasn't wrong. Ingolfr and his men surprised the Irish slaves whilst they were eating a meal, and they scattered in all directions. There weren't many places to run, except up the steep valley sides to where the puffins nest. Ingolfr hunted down the Irishmen one by one: some jumped off the cliffs to avoid capture, and Dufthak was killed at the place that's now called Dufthak's Precipice. The Irish were known as West-men, and these islands have been called the Westman Islands ever since.

As for Ingolfr, he returned to the mainland, and when his high-seat pillars were found in a bay named Reykjavik, after the ground which seemed to smoke, he moved his farm there. This was where he believed the gods intended him to settle. He claimed all the land in the area in the first land-take. Two of his slaves also set up their own farms: one a freed-man and one a runaway. Ingolfr built a hall, and his high-seat pillars could be seen many years later in that same spot.

Ingolfr is known as the first person to settle in Iceland permanently, but many followed his example, coming from Norway or from the Scottish Isles and Ireland with their slaves. There was no ruler to oversee the settlement, and the independent farmers who arrived organised their own affairs: they took what land seemed most auspicious, and it is said that within three generations all the farming land in Iceland had been claimed. The names of those larger-than-life pioneers are still remembered: Ingolfr's son, Thorstein, who helped to establish the Althing (parliament); his son Thorkel Moon, law-speaker at that gathering of free men; Aud the Deep-Minded; Helgi the

Lean and Ketilbjorn the Old; Hrollaugr, who named Hrollaug's Islands; Evening Wolf and Thorbjorn the Black; Hall the Godless, who refused to sacrifice to the Æsir and trusted only in his strength; Thorunn, who owned land next to Thurid the Priestess; and Grim, who was told where to settle by a merman. Each of these pioneers had a story, and many of them are remembered in the sagas.

Aud the Deep-Minded

Aud the Deep-Minded was one of the foremost of the early settlers. She was the daughter of a man named Ketil Flat-Nose, who had been sent by King Harald to lead the conquest of the Hebrides. Ketil Flat-Nose succeeded in gaining control of these islands, but after he had done so he refused to pay the king tribute. His sons were expelled from their ancestral lands in Norway, and headed straight for the new colony in Iceland.

At this time, Aud was married to a man named Olaf the White, who was King of Dublin and leader of the Dublin Vikings. When he died in battle, Aud left Ireland with their son Thorstein the Red and his followers. Thorstein was a great Viking and tried to conquer Scotland with his war-band, but he died whilst Aud was staying in Caithness. News of her son's death reached her at the same time that she learned of her father's death in the Hebrides. Aud concluded that fortune was not favouring her in Scotland. She ordered a large boat to be made in secret, and left Caithness with a great number of followers and a large part of her family's wealth. She first sailed to the Orkneys, where she arranged the marriage of her granddaughter to a powerful earl. Then she headed for the Faroe

Islands to the north, and married off another of her grand-daughters: the Gotuskeggi clan are all descended from her. Aud then left to search for Iceland.

The crossing itself was uneventful, but when Aud tried to navigate the southern coast she was caught by unfamiliar currents, and her ship was wrecked. Everyone scrambled out alive, and they managed to salvage most of their possessions. Aud set off at once in search of her brother Helgi, with twenty followers in tow. Helgi welcomed her, and offered to put up half her followers if the rest would find their own place to stay. Aud was not impressed at this half-hearted gesture, and set off to find her other brother, Bjorn. Bjorn was much more accommodating: he knew that his sister liked to live in style, and he invited Aud to stay for the winter, along with all the followers she cared to bring along. Aud was happy that at least one of her brothers knew what it meant to be generous.

Brother and sister spent a comfortable winter together, and in the spring Aud set sail across Breidafjord, claiming whatever land she took a fancy to, and naming the coastline as she went: one promontory is called Kambsness, after she lost a comb there; another 'Breakfast Point' because it was where she stopped for a meal. Aud eventually found her high-seat pillars at the head of Breidafjord, and settled where they'd washed ashore. She set up a farm at Hvamm, and gifted plots of the land she'd claimed to many later settlers. It is also said that she rewarded her slaves by making them free men, and that from her all the people of Breidafjord can trace their descent. Aud the Deep-Minded managed her estates in Iceland throughout an advanced old age, and bore herself with poise even on the day of her death.

Onund Tree-Foot

Iceland has been called the retirement home of Vikings, and some of the early settlers came to this colony with their scars proudly on display. Onund was the name of a man of good standing from Norway, and there is no doubting his prowess as a Viking. He sailed west in a fleet of five ships and raided in the Hebrides, fighting a king called Kjarval in the Barra Isles, and using these islands as a base from which to raid the coasts of Ireland and Scotland on three successive summers. They were profitable years.

Onund returned home to Norway during Harald Tangle-Hair's push to extend his power in the west, and the Viking soon became caught up in the conflict, fighting against the king at the Battle of Hafrsfjord where Harald crushed the chieftains who opposed him. Onund fought bravely in the prow of his ship, stepping up onto the bulwark to deliver hard blows against Harald's forces: but as he pressed forward, his leg was cut off below the knee, and he had to be dragged onto another vessel for safety. From then on, Onund walked with a wooden leg, and was known as Onund Tree-Foot. People said it hardly slowed him down.

Onund fled west after the battle to escape Harald's retribution, and he joined the many Norwegian refugees who'd regrouped in the western isles. Word had spread about the land that was still there for the taking in Iceland, and several of his companions cut their losses and sailed that same summer. However, Onund Tree-Foot wasn't quite ready to leave. He took to sea again, and ambushed a group of Vikings who'd made the Hebrides their base. During this battle, which took place in a narrow fjord, Onund wedged a log under his stump to keep his footing firm, and the Hebridean Vikings soon regretted their earlier taunting of him. Onund spent some time in Ireland with Eyvind the Norwegian, who had been appointed to defend the Irish coast, and he saw more of his companions leave in ships to settle Iceland. But Onund went east again, to Norway: there, he stayed with relatives who kept him concealed from King Harald, but urged him repeatedly to leave with whatever property he could carry away before Harald's men caught up with him. So Onund set his affairs in order: he killed the man who'd taken over his farm, burned the buildings to the ground, and in the spring he loaded up his ship with riches that he'd won from the settling of scores, and made the crossing to Iceland. It wasn't his wooden leg that made it hard for him to step on board.

Onund took one ship, his friend Asmund another, and they made the crossing to Iceland together. The seas were very rough, with winds blowing strongly from the south, and they almost shot right past Iceland. They first sighted land in the north-east of the country, at Langanes, and tacked to the west; but before they had made much progress along the northern coast, a gale blew up from the south, and they decided to make for the safety of a nearby fjord. Asmund managed to get into the lee of an island in the mouth of the fjord, but when Onund tried to tack into the fjord the yard came loose, and the crew were forced to lower the sail.

For two days they were driven out to sea by the strong winds, but then the wind suddenly turned and blew them back to a large bay in northern Iceland called Strandafloi. A boat rowed out to them from the nearby settlement: the news was that there was very little land in that part of the bay that hadn't been claimed. Onund consulted his men, and they decided to sail further west. They anchored in a small estuary and rowed ashore, where they were greeted by a wealthy man named Eirik

Snare who'd claimed all the country thereabouts. He offered Onund whatever land he needed to establish a farm there, as almost everything else had already been taken. Onund wanted to see what kind of land it was, so Eirik accompanied him further into the bay and pointed out the place that he was offering. Behind the river rose a steep ridge of snow-topped mountains called Kaldbak. Onund surveyed the scene.

'My land and my power have drifted away like a ship on the sea. I've left my friends and exchanged my home-fields for this: the cold mountainside!' he remarked. Eirik Snare nodded his head and followed Onund's gaze towards the mountains. 'Many people have lost so much in Norway that it can't be mended. But I'd advise you to take what I offer, as there's little else left for newcomers to claim.'

Onund took the land with its three streams, and established a large household. He was later given more land by Eirik, and the great Viking became a settler. He was said to be the most able one-legged man who ever came to Iceland.

Erik the Red and the Norse Discovery of Greenland

The Norse peoples had settled all the northern isles from Iceland to the Hebrides, but the encircling sea stretched off further to the west. No one would have expected to find the pastures of Iceland up here in the expanse of the North Atlantic – so perhaps there were further lands to be discovered? Wouldn't Thor, who rowed out to find the Midgard Serpent, have pushed on even further into these unknown seas? The discoveries the Norse seafarers made were not always by design, but who was guiding their ships to these new coasts – if not Odin, Thor and the sea-god Njord?

Erik the Red came to Iceland after his father killed some men in Norway. Erik inherited lands in Haukadal, where he established a farm; but he wasn't to settle there for long. His slaves started a landslide that destroyed a neighbour's farm, and the conflict escalated to the point where Erik killed some men of note. He was banished from Haukadal, and moved his household to a nearby island in the fjord. But he gave his family's decorated timbers to another neighbour for safekeeping, and when they were not returned, he fought and killed this man. Erik was finally outlawed from Iceland for this act. He escaped capture, and boarded a ship that he'd already provisioned: he'd heard about a sailor called Gunnbjorn who'd sighted land when he'd been blown out into the ocean. The plan was to sail to the west with his followers, and see what he could find.

Erik put out to sea past Snæfellsnes with a good wind behind him. After several days of sailing west, he sighted land beneath a large glacier, and changed course to the south to see whether this coastline was habitable. He and his followers rounded Cape Farewell, and spent the first winter at a place called Erik's Island. They sailed up the fjord in the spring and decided it would be a good spot to establish a base: there were good pastures, and the fjord was free of ice throughout the summer months. Erik spent the next summers exploring the surrounding fjords and naming landmarks as he went: it is said that he discovered the remains of some skin boats and several stone tools, and understood that people had passed through that place before; but there were no signs that they'd settled there. After three years of exploring this new land, Erik sailed back to Iceland and came to a settlement with the men who wanted him dead: but he was not planning to stay there long, farming his meagre plot of land. Erik wanted to put down roots in the high fjords he'd discovered to the west.

He called this new territory Greenland, as he thought the name would attract others to settle there. And he wasn't wrong.

It is said that twenty-five ships set out from Iceland with Erik on that first wave of settlement, but that only fourteen of them arrived. Many of those who made it settled in the fjords surrounding Erik's lands in Brattahlid; some went further north to found a second settlement. Their houses had thick turf walls against the cold, and long communal hearths: the best of them were lined with driftwood and hung with tapestries. The settlers found that there was good pasture along the fjords for sheep and cattle, and the hunting wasn't bad: walrus ivory and furs could be traded, and occasionally a polar bear was sent back live to Norway. But as tough and self-sufficient as these farmer-settlers were, there were some things that only the Norse homelands could provide, and trading ships regularly ploughed the North Atlantic between these far-flung coasts: bringing timber, grain and metal; and heading back with more exotic goods. It is said that narwhale tusks were greatly wondered at by people who hadn't seen the animal itself.

Sailors were at the mercy of Ran and her daughters on that long crossing from Iceland through unpredictable seas. In the early years of the settlement, a friend of Erik's called Thorbjorn sold his lands and set out to Greenland with his daughter Gudrid the Far-Travelled and thirty followers. They soon ran into difficulty, and the storms and contrary winds made progress so slow that disease broke out, and half the men and women on board died from illness and exposure. Thorbjorn and Gudrid finally made land at the start of winter, and were only saved by the hospitality of Herjolf and his family, who'd established a farm at the southern tip of Greenland.

A man called Bjarni also set out to Greenland following his

relatives, but he drifted far to the south, and when he emerged from the fog that had enveloped his ship, he found he'd reached a place that looked nothing like the descriptions he'd been given. This was a land of dense forests, not steep-sided fjords, and he made his way north along a coastline covered in great slabs of rock. When he reached a shore with ice-caps on the mountains he thought the land looked worthless, and that they had probably sailed too far. A strong gale took them back out to sea, and eventually he came across a coast that looked more like the Greenland that had been described to him. They made landfall at dusk, and received a warm welcome at Bjarni's father's farm, but people thought it a shame that he hadn't visited the lands he'd seen from his ship: it showed a great lack of curiosity.

People who know these things say that Iceland's eastern coast is seven days' sailing from Norway; that with good winds it takes four days to reach Greenland from Snæfellsnes in Iceland; and that Slyne Head on the west coast of Ireland is five days' sailing to the south. If traders want to sail from Bergen in Norway directly to Greenland, they should first pass out of the channel by Hernar Island, and then head west. They should keep just north of Shetland so that it can be seen when visibility is good, and close enough to the Faroe Islands that the sea-swell passes halfway up the mountains on the horizon. The ship should sail to a point far enough south of Iceland to enable sightings of whales as well as birds. The next land reached will be the Greenland coast.

Leif Erikson Discovers Vinland

Erik had two sons: Thorstein and Leif. Thorstein spent the best part of his life in Greenland and farmed the land there until he

died, but Leif was not content with a settled life. He sailed to
Norway, and served in the army of the Christian king Olaf
Tryggvason. Olaf asked Leif if he planned to go back to Greenland in the summer, and Leif replied that he did. 'Well,' said the
king, 'if you must leave my service, I have a task for you: to take
Christianity back home, and preach it in my name.' Leif thought
it would be a hard task to convince the stubborn settlers to
abandon their old gods, but he agreed to try.

He set out from Norway, but the journey did not go as
planned; and when he sighted land, it was not the land he had
been expecting to see: instead of the misty peaks and glaciers of
Greenland, he saw fields of wild wheat and maple trees. Leif
sailed into a bay and set up a small camp, sending men out to
explore the surrounding area. They reported that the rivers were
teeming with fish, and that the grass was lush: it seemed to them
that the climate must be kind. Amongst Leif's crew was a German by the name of Tyrkir. One day this man went missing
from the camp, and Leif sent out a search party. They found
Tyrkir walking home with an unsteady gait. He seemed to be
very pleased with himself, and was babbling away in German.
His lips and fingers were stained by grape juice: it turned out
that he'd found vines growing wild near the bay, and filled up
on fermented fruit. Leif decided to name this land Vinland after
the vines, and he made sure to stock up on grapes, wood and
wild wheat before heading back to his father's settlement.

On the way back to Greenland, Leif came across some shipwrecked sailors stranded on a reef. Because of the slim chance of
spotting a shipwreck in this great expanse of ocean, Leif was
known from then on as Leif the Lucky; and news of his discovery of Vinland spread.

Once back in Greenland, Leif preached the Christian faith,

and his mother Thjodhild converted and had a small church built. After this, she wouldn't live with Erik the Red, and this annoyed the old warrior: he would remain a follower of the old gods until his dying day. Erik's spirit of adventure was still strong, and one summer, he set out with an expedition to see for himself this place called Vinland that his son was always talking about. But Erik wasn't destined to reach the land to the west, and his journey began badly when he fell from his horse and broke several of his ribs. Once at sea, his ship was carried to within sight of Iceland, and so far south that he could hear the call of seabirds from the Irish coast, but he didn't catch an easterly wind until late in the season. He returned to Greenland, exhausted but happy to be alive: the gods meant to leave the discovery of new lands to someone else.

Karlsefni's Expedition

One winter, a merchant called Karlsefni came from Iceland with a large cargo of grain and ale to trade. Erik the Red offered him hospitality, and they spent the season together cheerfully: there was much talk of the lands to the west that Leif had found.

Karlsefni asked for the hand of Gudrid the Far-Travelled, who was born in Iceland and would later travel all the way to Rome. Their wedding feast was held at Brattahlid, and soon after the celebrations were over, Gudrid began to talk about Vinland and the possibilities that awaited them across the sea. Karlsefni agreed to mount an expedition: not just to explore, but to settle if the land was as good as he'd been told. Several men and women of note went with Karlsefni: Erik's daughter Freydis and his son-in-law Thorvald; a brute of a man by the name of Thorhall; a Scottish couple gifted to Leif by Olaf Tryggvason; and, not least, Gudrid herself. In all, one hundred and sixty people set out on that expedition.

Karlsefni sailed from Greenland with a good wind, and after two days they came to a land covered with great slabs of rock, just as Bjarni had described. There were many foxes there. He named that place Helluland after the slabs of rock, and sailed south. Next they came to a place that was unlike Greenland because it was thickly forested, and Karlsefni named it Markland – which means 'Forest Land'. He continued down the coast and past a large promontory where they saw the keel of a shipwrecked boat, and then continued along a stretch of sandy coast that seemed endless. Eventually, the Greenlanders pulled into a bay and dropped anchor. Karlsefni now called upon the Scottish couple loaned to him by Leif Erikson: they could run without tiring, and Karlsefni told them to set off and explore as much of the land as they could in three days. The couple set off at a good pace, wearing hooded shirts open at the sides, and nothing else. When they arrived back, three days later, they carried wild wheat and vines. Karlsefni thought that Vinland must be close.

The settlers sailed a little further down the coast and entered a fjord, past an island screaming with birds. They set up a winter camp, where Karlsefni and Gudrid's son was born: his name was Snorri, and he was the first Norse child to be born in this new land. The rest of the settlers were so busy exploring the coast and admiring the scenery that they failed to prepare for winter – which, when it came, turned out to be exceptionally harsh. The hunting was poor, and food ran scarce. Thorhall the Hunter prayed to Thor for assistance: when a whale washed up on the coast, his prayers seemed to have been answered, but its meat ended up making them all ill. Many of the crew thought it better to ask for Christ's help after that, and Thorhall the Hunter cursed the expedition. 'I didn't come all the way here to survive on water and rotten whale-flesh: where's the wine for my trouble?' he complained, to anyone who'd listen. Thorhall wanted to search for Vinland to the north and put out to sea with a handful of men, but a westerly wind drove their ship all the way to Ireland, where they were enslaved and eventually died. They never found their vines.

The Norse Explorers Meet the Skrælings

As for Karlsefni, he led the small fleet south, and after several days he took the settlers into a tidal lake: the land around was abundant with wheat and vines, the streams were well stocked with fish, and the forest was full of animals to hunt. It seemed that they were alone in that land, but early one morning, as the settlers went about the first chores of the day, a group of men approached the camp across the lake in nine skin boats. The men in the boats were swinging wooden flails over their heads in the direction that the sun passes through the sky. Karlsefni thought that this might be a sign of peace, so the Greenlanders put out a white shield, and waved the strangers closer to the shore. The Norse settlers were amazed at the appearance of these people, who had large eyes and wide cheekbones: they thought them evil-looking, and called them Skrælings. The native men looked back with as much amazement at the Norse settlers, and didn't stop staring until they'd rowed on past the headland. Karlsefni and his followers were more cautious now: they built their homes on a slope above the lake, and stayed there for the winter without being troubled. The grass was so good that the livestock hardly needed tending to at all.

Spring arrived – and with it, the Skrælings returned. This time, so many skin boats rounded the headland that from a distance it looked as though the lake was covered in charcoal. The native tribe wanted to trade with the newcomers, and what they sought most was red cloth, which they tied around their heads and exchanged for pelts: the Greenlanders traded all the cloth they had, in smaller and smaller pieces. Karlsefni would not agree to sell the Skrælings spears or swords. The trade only ceased when a bull came charging from the settlers' fields, startling the natives back to their boats and away across the lake.

Three weeks of peace followed this encounter. And then the boats appeared again in the lake – but this time the flails were being waved against the sun, and the Skrælings were sending up a terrible war cry. The Norse men took up their weapons and prepared hastily for battle. The native warriors had catapults, and flints rained down on Karlsefni and his men, as well as a strange sphere which flew over their heads and struck the ground with an otherworldly din. This was all too much for the Greenlanders, and they turned and ran for the safety of the cliffs. But not Freydis, daughter of Erik the Red. She came out of her house when she heard the sound of the retreating warriors, and wasn't slow to call them cowards. 'I'd put up a better show than you if I had a weapon to hand! You should be killing them like cattle, not running for the hills!' she cried, but her taunts fell on deaf ears. She followed the men, heckling them in this way, but she could not keep up, because she was heavily pregnant. The Skrælings were still firing their catapults as they chased the settlers, and Freydis stepped over the body of a man who'd been killed as he ran. He had dropped his sword, which Freydis stooped awkwardly to pick up. She turned round to defend herself, and when the warriors charged up the slope towards her she uncovered one of her breasts, beating the flat of the sword against it. The native warriors were so astounded by this display that they broke off their attack and ran back to their ships. Freydis showed the men the meaning of courage that day.

Only two of the settlers and four of the native warriors had been killed, despite the fierce assault. It is said that the Skrælings took the axe out of the hand of a dying settler and struck it against a rock: it broke, so they did not think to value these strangers' weapons, which were weaker than stone.

Karlsefni decided that the threat of attack from the lake made it too dangerous to settle in that place, so the Norse settlers packed up their ships. Their next meetings with the Skrælings were not happy. On the way up the coast they found five skin-clad Skrælings asleep on a rock next to a bowl of deer marrow mixed with blood. Karlsefni's men thought they must be outlaws from their tribe, and killed them all. In Markland they captured two native boys in an ambush and took them as slaves; and whilst their vessels were pulling in for supplies, a one-legged creature came out of the bushes and fired an arrow at Erik's son-in-law Thorvald, who was sitting at the helm of his ship. Thorvald pulled the arrow from his groin, with a great hunk of fat wobbling on its barb: 'This must be a rich land we've found: I'm clearly well fed!' he quipped, though the wound later killed him. The settlers spent the third winter of their voyage near where they had first camped: it was another hard season, with the unmarried men in particular getting restive after three years on the move. Karlsefni decided it was time to cut their losses and head for home, and that summer they arrived back in Greenland, where they were welcomed by Erik the Red.

Karlsefni and Gudrid would later return to Iceland as farmers, having spent three years of their life living in what later

explorers would come to call the New World. Vinland does
not seem to have been found again by Norse explorers, but
Markland – the place of trees – was visited for timber; and the
land to the west, so far from the Norse homelands, was never
quite forgotten.

9

Expeditions to the East and the South

The Norse expansion in the North Atlantic is well known, and when we think of Vikings we tend to imagine fleets crossing the North Sea to raid the monasteries of England, Ireland and France. But Vikings from Sweden were active in the Baltic long before the famous raid on Lindisfarne, and there were no fiery dragons seen in the sky to mark the coming of these Norsemen. In the Viking Age, the followers of Odin in the east just did more of what they'd done before. They raided and forged alliances with neighbouring tribes, traded and settled, and exploited the Baltic's access to Central Europe and beyond. But whereas accounts of the Norse expansion in the west are dominated by Viking raids and the settlement of new lands, in the east the stories celebrate the river trade and the great quantities of Arabic silver bought home along these routes. Norse seafarers took their ships south to Constantinople and to the shores of the Caspian; they served as bodyguards to the Byzantine Emperor; and traders from the north rode camels through the desert to the slave-markets of Baghdad. Like Norse explorers in the west, these were a people pushing at the limits of the world.

The Baltic

The Baltic Sea is almost land-locked: only the narrow straits around the Danish islands allow ships to sail to the Kattegat and the North Sea beyond. It is said that the goddess Gefjon created the largest of these islands in the neck of the Baltic by tricking a king named Gylfi: as a reward for entertaining him, he allowed the goddess to take as much land in his kingdom as she could plough in a day and a night with four oxen. But the 'oxen' were Gefjon's giant sons – and she ploughed up the land itself, dragging it from Sweden to set it in the sound where Sjælland now lies. The hollow she left behind flooded with the water from the Baltic, and became Lake Mälaren in Sweden.

There was a trading centre on the small island of Birka on Lake Mälaren from early in the Viking Age. Merchants returning from the eastern Baltic offloaded their wares at the harbour-side – bringing silks and pottery, exotic jewellery and sometimes silver coins – and amongst the closely crowded houses, craftspeople worked antlers and metals, and preserved furs for sale to the markets in the south. For a merchant setting out by ship from Birka, it was less than a week's sailing across the Baltic to the trading centres of Wolin on the River Oder or Truso by the Vistula, or Staraja Ladoga on the River Volkhov. A rune-stone raised in memory of a merchant named Svein says that he often sailed his beloved cargo-ship round the dangerous headland of Domesnäs into the Gulf of Riga, and from there to the rivers of Latvia. His wife, who raised the stone, doesn't say if he made it home.

The Scandinavians soon became a permanent fixture in the Baltic trading towns: Staraja Ladoga could be reached from the Gulf of Finland by sailing up the wide River Neva to Lake

Ladoga, and it lay on the main route to the river systems leading east to the Volga and eventually the Caspian Sea, where Arabian silver would be paid for furs and slaves. Other river systems could be reached by heading south to join the Dniester and the Dnieper which flowed to the Black Sea. This network of waterways and portages was known in Old Norse as Austrvegr: the way to the east.

The conditions in the Baltic may not have been as unpredictable as those that Vikings faced in the North Atlantic, but no sea-crossing was without risk, and several Swedish rune-stones speak of men who died. Ingibjorg commemorates her husband whose ship sank to the bottom of the Gulf of Finland: she says that only three men came out of that disaster alive. Other rune-stones speak about war and violent deaths: the killing of Otrygg in Finland and Onund in Estonia, and the death of a warrior named Egil on a military expedition which passed through the south of Finland and on to lands further to the east. It was led by a chieftain named Freygeir, and the brother who had the stone commissioned claims to have carried Freygeir's battle-standard himself.

At times throughout the Viking Age, both the Swedes and Danes made more concerted efforts to impose Scandinavian control on the lands around the Baltic Sea: Olaf, King of Birka, made a successful invasion of the Courlanders in Latvia, to bring the town of Grobin back under Scandinavian control: it had been settled by people from the island of Gotland many generations before. The Danish King Gudfred defeated his Slavic neighbours, and forced the merchants to move from the thriving town of Reric to Hedeby, where he could ensure tribute from their trade.

The brotherhood of Jomsvikings were said to operate from a

base on the Polish coast: they were staunchly loyal to the Norse gods and to each other, but they would sell their swords to the highest bidder: all heroic deaths served Odin's cause. The Baltic did not escape raids from the Jomsvikings and other bands of Vikings, but whereas the silver hoarded in the undefended monasteries of England and Ireland made raiding a profitable business in the North Sea, here in the less populated regions of the east it didn't make sense simply to loot the silver trickling down the rivers to the Baltic markets. The trade to the east was a source of wealth that could be tapped.

Travellers to the Baltic

The Danish settlement of Hedeby was a thriving centre of Baltic trade, which attracted bought visitors from far away. Not all of them, though, were impressed with what they found. Ibrahim al-Tartushi was an emissary from Islamic Spain who passed through Hedeby. He was shocked by the state of this Baltic trading hub: the one thing it seemed to have in abundance was fish, which the merchants ate for almost every meal. The people living there had strange customs, which included throwing unwanted babies into the sea to save the cost of bringing them up, and hanging sacrificed animals on poles outside their homes to satisfy their gods. Wives were able to divorce their husbands whenever they liked, and both men and women used eye makeup to make themselves more beautiful. And they were the worst singers that he'd ever heard: more like barking dogs than humans.

Seafarers also travelled to the Baltic from the west, and returned home with valuable knowledge about the lands and cultures they encountered. One such man came to the court of

King Alfred of Wessex. His name was Wulfstan, and he was well acquainted with the eastern Baltic and its sailing routes: the information he provided was valuable enough to be written onto vellum. Perhaps Alfred was curious to learn about the source of the exotic goods that Wulfstan carried, or perhaps he hoped to learn more about the sailing routes of those Vikings that had brought his kingdom to its knees.

Wulfstan began his journey in the trading town of Hedeby, and had nothing to say about its singers or its fish. From there, he travelled under full sail for several days through Danish waters and on into the Baltic, passing the island of Bornholm which has its own king. He then sailed – with the lands of the Swedes to his north and the lands of the Wends to the south – all the way to Truso in the Vistula Delta. The River Vistula struck Wulfstan as being very large, and was known to separate Wend-land from the lands of the Baltic tribes known as the Este – who have many different kings and are often at war. Wulfstan noted that in the vast lands of the Este there is such an abundance of honey that it is the poor folk and slaves who drink sweet mead: the wealthy people drink mare's milk.

It is the custom of these Baltic tribes, he reported, that when a man dies, he is left indoors with his relatives for a month or more: the higher the rank, the longer his body remains in his home. One of these tribes knows how to bring about cold: they can make a container of beer freeze over in the summer, and chill a body to prevent it rotting. During the time that the cold body lies at home, there is a great deal of drinking and gam-bling, and when it finally comes to the day of the funeral pyre, men race horses to claim shares of the inheritance. The largest portion of the deceased's wealth is placed farthest away from the family home, and smaller piles are made at intervals along the way, with the very smallest placed at the doors of the house itself. The race begins six miles from the home of the dead man, and the first rider to reach a pile of property can take it away, even if they are a stranger. For this reason, the Baltic tribes prize good horses above most things.

Russia and the Road to the East

The Finns had a word in their language for the Swedes: the Ruotsi. It referred to a people who rowed the eastern Baltic and its rivers in their boats – which is probably how the Swedish warrior-merchants also saw themselves. At some point, the East Slavs borrowed the word from their Finnish neighbours and began to call these people the Rus'. Over time, the Scandinavians merged with the local tribes, and Rus' came to refer to a dynasty which dominated the river routes from Novgorod to Kiev in the south. Eventually the Rus' would give their name to Russia.

The Russian Chronicles have their own story about the way the Scandinavians came to populate this vast kingdom in the east. Here it is said that a people came from beyond the sea, and took tribute from many tribes round Novgorod before they were eventually driven back to their homeland. But after shaking off their overlords, the Slavic tribes found that they were unable to govern themselves, or agree on common laws. So they took a desperate measure, and sent an emissary across the sea to invite the Scandinavians back. Three brothers returned to rule over the warring tribes, and brought their people with them to settle in the tribal lands of the Finns and Slavs. This people from across the sea were called the Rus', and the eldest of the brothers was named Rurik: he established himself at Novgorod. Within two years Rurik's brothers were dead, and Rurik had assumed control of all the tribes.

Accompanying Rurik on this expedition were two Rus' nobles called Askold and Dir, who sought Rurik's permission to push further south along the river routes to Constantinople. Sailing down the Dnieper, they saw a small town on a hill, and asked who owned it. They were told that three brothers – one of them named Kiy – had founded the settlement, but that since their deaths it had become a tributary town of the Khazars. Askold and Dir decided to cut short their journey to Constantinople and to stay here, at this town so well positioned above the river; and they sent word to other Rus' families to join them. Soon, they seized control of the surrounding territory, and this town would grow in stature to become the foremost city of the Rus'. It would be known as Kiev, or Konugard to the people from the north.

Askold and Dir were not content with controlling the Dnieper from Kiev: they remembered their initial boast that they would take their ships to Constantinople and introduce the Byzantines to the axes of the Rus'. The Chronicles tell how a fleet of Rus' ships, led by the rulers of Kiev, sailed into the Black Sea like a storm of hail, and crossed to the high walls of the city they called Miklagard. They'd picked the perfect time for their attack: the emperor had taken his troops east to repel the advance of the Abbasid army, and the city was not expecting an incursion from the north. The Rus' broke through the defences of the Bosphorus, and their army rampaged through the suburbs of the city, pillaging monasteries and homes, and slaughtering everyone they found. The emperor rushed back from his campaign against the Abbasids, and prayed all night for the city's deliverance. The next day it seemed his prayers had been answered, as a fierce storm blew up and scattered the Rus' fleet. Some ships were wrecked on the shore, and the survivors sailed back the way they'd come.

Constantinople was left reeling from the sudden arrival of the Rus'. 'A people has stolen down from the far north,' recorded Photius the Patriarch. 'Nations from the ends of the earth have been stirred up like wasps, vicious and showing no mercy. Their voices roar like the sea.'

It is said that some fifty years after that first attack, a fleet of two thousand Rus' ships sailed with Prince Oleg from Kiev, and that the Byzantines surrendered to the terms of this fierce northern army. The emperor agreed to pay a sum of silver to each ship's crew, but more lucrative still was the right the Rus' secured to trade on their own terms. All merchants were to be provided with food and shelter for six months whilst carrying out their business in the city, and given assistance to make their ships ready for the journey home. These men would not arm themselves within the city limits, and would refrain from making trouble, but they would also pay no taxes to the emperor. This was Black Sea trade ratified by treaties, but backed up by the long-handled axes of the Rus'.

The Rus' River Routes

After these incursions from the north, the Byzantine emperors took a special interest in the routes the Rus' took down the River Dnieper, and one emperor had the information written down. In his account, it is the Slavs who make dug-out boats during the winter – and, once the lakes thaw, bring them down the waterways to Kiev; there, they sell them to the Rus', who fit them out with rowlocks and oars. In June, the Rus' merchants set out from Kiev to the tributary city of Vitichev, where they gather all the boats together in a convoy before heading further south. When they come to a barrage in the river Dnieper – falls or a stretch of rapids, of which there are seven on this stretch of the river – they disembark the crews, and several sure-footed men strip and guide the boats along the bank or between the rocks, as the rapids swirl on either side. The first barrage is called 'Don't nap!', and is punctured by jagged rocks over which the water rushes with a great roar; others are called River Roaring or the Gulper, and the largest of the barrages is named after the pelicans which nest in the rocks at its centre. At this point, the boats and all the goods need to be carried overland, and to make things worse, this is a stretch of the river where Turkic tribes often attack, and so one group of the Rus' stays to guard the boats beached at the head of the barrage, whilst the other group carries the goods under armed guard for six miles to the end of the falls. The slaves have to walk this distance in their chains. Next, the boats are brought along the same route, dragged part of the way, and shouldered for the rest of that long six miles. Once all the boats have been transported, they are loaded up again, and the convoy sails onwards.

At the ford which makes up the final barrage on this stretch of the Dnieper, the convoy is most at risk from attack, as this is the river crossing used by the Pechenegs, and it is perfect for an ambush. The Rus' need to keep their wits about them as they cross the ford, but once the convoy is through, it isn't far to a safe resting place on an island in the Dnieper. Here, the Rus' sacrifice live cockerels at a great oak tree, giving offerings of food and arrows to their gods. They are now free from the threat of the Pechenegs, and it is four days' plain sailing to the mouth of the Dnieper and on to the Black Sea island of Berezany.

Here, they rest again for several days and make their ships seaworthy, before beginning the final stretch of sailing down the Black Sea coast to the great city they call Miklagard, and we call Constantinople.

Constantinople and the Varangians

Trade in amber, furs and slaves drew many Norse merchants down the Baltic river routes, but there was another reason for making the long journey to Gardariki and on to Miklagard. Both the Rus' and the Byzantine emperors had need of mercenary soldiers, and the war-like Scandinavians with their long-handled axes and Frankish swords came to be particularly prized. Men called Varangians – perhaps from the Old Norse word for 'pledge' – entered the employ of the Byzantines soon after the Rus' raids on Constantinople, and some of them formed an elite group of bodyguards for the emperor himself. Unlike the Rus', whose leaders kept Norse names but had assimilated into the culture of the Slavic tribes, the Varangians were more often Scandinavian than not: from Sweden, but also from Denmark, Norway and as far away as Iceland. Varangians had a reputation for loyalty and honouring their oaths, and the emperors rewarded these pledge-makers well for their service. They even had the right to help themselves to treasure from the palace when one emperor died, and before another took his place. Joining the Varangian guard was a way for a fighting man to make his fortune: particularly if there was trouble back at home he needed to escape from – and there was often trouble back at home. Many of these Varangians fought in campaigns around the Empire, and they were among the most travelled people of their day.

Some of the Norse warriors who served in the Varangian guard were commemorated back at home on rune-stones recording their service in the south, or in sagas written long after the events. A few of these mercenaries also carved runes whilst they were in the south. A white-marble lion, now keeping watch over the Venetian Arsenal, once stood proudly at Piraeus harbour in Athens: a monument to Greek power and mastery of the seas. But sometime late in the Viking Age, a group of Scandinavians added their own story to the lion's side, carved in runes within a serpent design. The names of these adventurers have faded almost to vanishing point, but there's a good chance that the rune-writers were Varangians recording their exploits. The Scandinavians may have been serving the Byzantine Emperor, but it is hard to see the Greeks approving of this strange addition to their lion.

Another piece of Norse graffiti was carved at the centre of Constantinople itself, in the gallery of the Hagia Sophia. The man who left his mark under the vast dome of the cathedral was named Halfdan: perhaps he was a bored Varangian watching over a ceremony that he only half understood, thinking of his own traditions and his distant home.

Harald the Hard-Ruler

Harald Hardrada is best known for his unsuccessful invasion of England in 1066, but in his younger days he led the Varangian guard, and he is the most famous of the many Norsemen who served in the east.

Harald was just fifteen when he fought at the Battle of Stiklestad where his half-brother King Olaf was killed. The teenager was smuggled out of Norway, first receiving sanctuary in

Sweden, and then getting passage on a ship that was sailing across the Baltic and down the river routes to Russia. In the Rus' capital of Kiev – or Konugard as Harald would have known it – he was put in charge of the Varangian troops defending the city, and served King Jarizleif well for several winters. But the young Norwegian was not content with travelling halfway along the Viking route to Miklagard: the great city was calling, and there was silver and fame to be won.

Harald took many followers with him on the passage south. His warships were hung with bright shields, and it was clear to the watchmen guarding the Bosphorus that this seafarer was not there to trade trinkets. From where Harald stood on the prow of the leading ship, shielding his eyes, he saw the glint of sunlight on metal roofs – and soon the ramparts of the city towered into view.

Queen Zoe the Great ruled over the Byzantine Empire at that time, and Harald went straight up the paved streets to the palace, where he offered his service as a mercenary in the Varangian guard. The young Norwegian was assigned to the Byzantine fleet, and commanded a company of his own men as they scoured the Eastern Mediterranean in pursuit of pirates. The leader of the Varangian guard at that time was a relative of the queen – a Greek called Gygir – but more and more of the men of the north began to follow Harald as he proved himself the bolder man in battle. The two leaders almost came to blows over whether the Greeks or Varangians would have the first choice of mooring and camp: Harald got his way in this, as in most things, and eventually Gygir left with the Greek forces to return to Constantinople, whilst the Scandinavians and Normans and a few ambitious Greeks threw in their lot with the young Norwegian.

Harald led his army of Varangians to North Africa and the lands the Norse called Serkland: the poets say that he took eighty cities on that campaign in Muslim lands, some surrendering, and some taken by force. Harald fought as if he had no fear of death, and won great quantities of flame-red gold across the desert lands. After enriching his men in this campaign, he took the fleet to the Emirate of Sicily. There was one city on that island that had such high walls that Harald was not certain he could lead a successful assault against it. He sat contemplating the ramparts from the Varangian siege-lines, and saw some small birds that nested in the city flying to the forest for food. With a cruel cunning worthy of Odin himself, Harald ordered nets to be used to catch the birds. His men covered the creatures with wax and shavings of pine, and set these flying candles alight. The birds made straight for their nests under the thatched roofs of the town, and soon house after house was bursting into flames. The inhabitants surrendered and threw themselves on the mercy of Harald, who this time spared their lives.

Harald plundered many other cities, using his wits when force would not suffice. He gained great wealth from these adventures, and returned to Constantinople with news of his boldness travelling ahead of him. The Holy Land was next in Harald's sights, and all the cities along the way to Jerusalem submitted to the Varangians he led. After washing himself in the River Jordan as pilgrims used to do, he gave a great quantity of riches to the Church of the Holy Sepulchre, and rid the pilgrim routes of cutthroats and thieves.

Now, after years of hard campaigning in the south, Harald was keen to head back to reclaim his lands in Norway. But there was a problem: Queen Zoe had grown so fond of her commander from the north that she wouldn't hear of him leaving the Varangian Guard and setting off north with all his followers. She accused him of holding on to more of the wealth he'd gained in raiding the Empire's enemies than was proper, and at her insistence the emperor had Harald locked away. Harald had gone from leading the mercenary army to languishing in a deep dungeon, and most men would have lost all hope at this point: but in the darkness Harald saw a vision of his brother Olaf, and he knew that help was on its way. A rope was lowered down into the dungeon and Harald made his escape. He went straight to his loyal Varangians, who had joined in a revolt against the emperor, and broke into the royal apartments with his men. Harald used to boast that he was the one who took hold of the emperor in his sanctuary and gouged out both his eyes. His revenge complete, Harald headed for the docks with Queen Zoe's niece as a captive, and put out into the Bosphorus that same night in two ships belonging to the Varangian guard.

At that time, the passage from the harbour to the Bosphorus was protected by an iron chain that would rip the hull out of any boat. Harald ordered his men to pull hard at the oars and build up speed as they approached. Once the ship was gliding like a porpoise through the water, he had all the men who weren't rowing grab their gear and run to the stern of the ship, so that its prow reared up in the water. The keel scraped against the heavy chain as the ship shot forward and mounted the barrage. As soon as they came to a stop, Harald ordered his men to scramble over the rowing benches back towards the prow. The ship groaned mightily as it pivoted on the chain, but with a great heave of the oars they freed themselves and escaped the last defences of the city. The other vessel was not so fortunate: the keel split in two and many Varangians drowned as they scrambled to abandon ship. Harald now had the open water in front of him, but before he sailed north, he dropped Queen Zoe's niece ashore and had her escorted back to Miklagard. Harald had abducted her to show the queen that a Varangian of his stature could take whatever prize he claimed. The dawn was rising over the Black Sea as the sails filled and Harald the Hard-Ruler set his bearing north for home.

The Traveller Returns

Men and women arriving back from expeditions to the east made quite an impression, not least Bolli Bollason, who returned to his home in Iceland after travelling to Miklagard and serving as a loyal member of the Varangian guard. Bolli had always had a reputation as a stylish man, and during his time with the emperor he not only made his fortune, but also became a follower of imperial fashion. He cut quite a dash as he disembarked from his ship in Iceland, dressed as he was in a scarlet cloak and a suit of silk brocade – a gift from the emperor himself – and carrying a sword at his belt which he'd had inlaid with copious amounts of gold. He wore a gilded helmet, and carried a red shield with the image of a rider painted in gold. Even his bearing had changed, and he held a lance in his hand as he rode, as they tend to do in foreign parts. When Bolli passed between farms on his way back home, the women couldn't take their eyes off him, or his well-dressed followers. It is said that after he came back from his adventures in the east, Bolli wouldn't be seen dead in anything other than clothes of silk or scarlet cloth, and he became known throughout the country as Bolli the Elegant.

An Expedition to the Mediterranean

The Mediterranean could be reached from Scandinavia by two
different routes: via the rivers leading to the Black Sea and the
Bosphorus (the route that Harald and the Varangians took), or
down the west coast of Iberia in sturdy, ocean-going craft. This
might have been the fastest route to the south, but the Vikings
had to sail through the straits of Gibraltar and test the sea power
of Al-Andalus (Muslim Spain) – and even Bjorn Ironside's
famous raid into the Mediterranean was a campaign of mixed
success.

Vikings first tested the defences of Spain in 844, moving from
their base in the Loire to look for pickings further south. They
raided in the Bay of Biscay before being beaten by an Asturian
army near the Tower of Hercules and forced back to their ships.
The same fleet went on to capture the town of Lisbon, to raid the
southern coast, and to capture Seville deep within the Emirate
of Al-Andalus, though here they were put to flight for good by
the rallying Arab forces. Hundreds of the Vikings were captured
and hanged from palm trees in the city, and it would be some
years before the Norse seafarers returned.

The Viking attacks had caught the Emirate by surprise, and
in response the sea defences were improved, and a delegation
was dispatched from Al-Andalus to the leader of these fierce
people. A man named al-Ghazal sailed north to what was probably Denmark and comported himself well before the king,
offering rich gifts and a letter from the Sultan. He later described
the Vikings as living on a great island in a sea of islands, and said
that some of them had already given up their old beliefs and settled for the Christian faith, though many to the north were still
worshippers of fire. The Vikings were full of curiosity about this

emissary from Al-Andalus, but none more so than the Queen. It seems al-Ghazal was quite taken with her too. He learned that Norse women stayed with their husbands of their own free will, and were allowed to be familiar with other men. He dyed his hair to cover up the grey at her suggestion, and wrote poems in praise of her beauty, the like of which he hadn't seen before.

Whatever agreements were made between the emissary of Al-Andalus and the Norse kingdom that he visited, it was to be over a decade before the next serious expedition to the south: the famous raid into the Mediterranean led by Bjorn Ironside and a Viking chieftain named Hastein. Bjorn was said to be the son of the legendary Ragnar Lodbrok, and he had the ambition of his father. It is told that the two men left with a fleet of sixty-two ships, and that they intended to take the western route to the Mediterranean and to raid Rome itself, the greatest city of them all. Bjorn and Hastein were in high spirits setting out from their base in the Loire, but they found the north of Spain a hard nut to crack: both the Christian kingdoms and the Emirate had learned from the raids of 844, and they put up a much better defence. The fortunes of the Vikings only improved when they sailed through the Strait of Gibraltar and plundered the town of Algeciras off the southern coast, before crossing the sea to raid al-Mazimma in Morocco. After working their way up the Mediterranean coasts of Spain and France and raiding the Balearic Islands, the fleet took refuge in the mouth of the River Rhône, and set up camp. It must have been a kinder winter than the northerners were used to, there amongst the wetlands of the Camargue.

In the spring, Bjorn and Hastein took their fleet up the Rhône to raid Nimes, and then along the French coast to Italy – where they raided Pisa, and a town with high walls that Bjorn guessed was Rome. The small force of Vikings couldn't hope to breach the walls, so Hastein pretended to be dying from illness and had his stretcher brought to the city gates. 'I don't want to die a heathen!' he cried. 'Show mercy, and lead me to your church to be baptised.' The inhabitants took pity, and allowed Hastein's stretcher to be brought inside the city walls: but as soon as they were inside, Hastein jumped from his death-bed and hacked his way back to the gates, letting in Bjorn with the rest of their men. The Vikings took great glee in sacking that city, but Bjorn was not happy when he found out that the place he'd assumed was Rome was no more than a provincial town called Luna.

Bjorn was all for hurrying on to sack the real Rome, but an old man they met in Luna persuaded him of just how far away the Eternal City really was. The old man had a pair of dilapidated shoes hanging from his pack, and the ones on his feet were not in a much better state. He told the Vikings that when he'd set out from Rome, both these pairs of shoes had been brand new. Bjorn looked at the old man's toes poking through the leather, and decided Rome would be a step too far for his exhausted men.

It's said that Bjorn and Hastein were intercepted on their way home by the fleet of Al-Andalus, and that many ships were lost. Bjorn's much depleted force raided Pamplona on the way back to their base in the Loire, and the men returned home fabulously wealthy, but with only a third of their ships. Bjorn and Hastein had secured their places amongst the legendary figures of their age, but the cost of this campaign would not be forgotten, and it was to be a century before Vikings would return to Spain in force.

Though the Vikings were called majus in Arabic – fire-worshipping heathens – and were feared enough for defences to be organised and fleets deployed against them, they left little trace of their sporadic raids. A small whalebone box, carved in a distinctive interlace design, is one of the only objects reminding us that the Norse travelled these sea-routes to the south, and it tells a different story to the accounts of Viking raids: one of traders and artisans. The box – used as a reliquary (a container for the bones and other relics of saints) for many years – is kept in the treasury of San Isidoro in León, perhaps brought there by a pilgrim or an emissary from the north. In the Mediterranean, at least, the fear of the Vikings was more potent than their occasional attacks.

Silver from the Caliphate

Contacts between Norse seafarers and the Arabs of Al-Andalus may have been limited to the occasional raid, but in the east, it was trade with the Caliphate that drove the Norse expansion. Transporting slaves and furs along the Volga river system and on to the Caspian Sea was a profitable business, and it was Arabic silver, mined east of Baghdad, that first drew the Scandinavians along the river routes. Many of these silver coins were melted down, but thousands of dirhams also found their way back to Scandinavia, and some were even worn as jewellery. The Norse settler in Lincolnshire who wore a coin minted in Afghanistan may have been flaunting her access to the trade routes of the east without knowing that the Arabic coin legend proclaimed the holy creed, 'There is no god but Allah.'

The lands around the lower Volga were not controlled by the Rus', but even if tribute had to be paid along the way, there was great wealth to be made in the markets of the Bulgars and the Khazars, where Baltic trade met the flow of silver from the east. Rus' merchants may have undertaken this long journey with their whole families in tow, travelling in small convoys for protection, and encountering unfamiliar landscapes and peoples along the way. Some of the merchants went even farther afield, to trade directly with the Abbasid Caliphate which was centred on Baghdad. To get to the capital, they sailed from the Khazar town of Itil south across the Caspian Sea, and loaded up camels in the harbour of Gorgan for the long trek through the mountains and the desert. In the bazaars of Baghdad they sold beaver and fox pelts, amber, Frankish swords and slaves – passing themselves off as Christians, and using enslaved Rus' as interpreters to haggle for silver. In the markets of the east, Scandinavians would have found goods from as far away as China and India that had arrived on the Silk Road. Perhaps some of these bold people travelled even further east themselves.

Ibn Fadlan's Encounter with the Rus'

The Scandinavians were not the only ones to travel long distances: the Abbasid Caliphate stretched from the Mediterranean to the Arabian Sea, and being an emissary of the Caliph meant travelling to lands on the border of the known world. Ibn Fadlan had already seen more than most people would believe by the time he arrived at the upper reaches of the Volga, on his latest mission as secretary and advisor to the ambassador. But it was here, in the territory of the Volga Bulgars, that he met a people whose like he had never come across before. These merchants called themselves the Rus', and Ibn Fadlan recorded in his journal that he had never seen such perfect specimens:

'They resemble date-palms in their stature, and they have fair hair and reddish skin, which they tattoo from the toes to the neck with dark green outlines of trees and other figures. The men wear a cloak which leaves the sword-arm free, and they have an axe, Frankish sword and knife about them at all times. The women have gold and silver bands around their necks and metal discs above each breast, and the higher their husband's worth, the more valuable the metal. They also carry knives hanging from these discs, and they prize dark green beads of glass for their necklaces.

'These Rus' are a striking people to look at, but there's no denying that they are the filthiest of all of Allah's creatures. They don't wash after sex, or after excreting, and it is small surprise that they don't clean themselves after eating their food either. When they do wash, it is in a communal bowl of water which a slave-girl passes from man to man: each one blowing his nose and spitting in the water after washing his face and hair. They live together in wooden houses they build next to the river-bank where their boats are docked, and in these houses they hump their slave-girls in front of each other: sometimes when a merchant comes to buy a slave he has to stand around waiting until the owner is done.

'When the Rus' arrive here from their own territory on their ships, they go straight to a wooden idol carved with the face of a man, and make an offering of food and alcohol, thinking that these empty prayers will help them get the prices they want for their goods. They ask to meet with merchants with pockets full of dirhams who don't like to haggle hard, and if it all goes well, they kill an animal and offer its meat to the wooden figures as a mark of thanks.

'When one of the Rus' falls ill, the invalid is thrown into a tent pitched far from their camp with some bread and water, and left there until they either recover or die from their illness. Slaves who die are left to be eaten by the dogs, but better men are buried or cremated in a small boat. Chieftains are given an even more elaborate funeral, and whilst I was on my embassy to the Bulgars, a great man died and was burned on his ship. I was there to witness the funeral, and it is something I will never forget.

'The Rus' first gave their leader a quick burial whilst they made preparations for the funeral itself. A third of his possessions were used to buy his rich funeral clothes, a third given to his family, and a third reserved for the purchase of great quantities of alcohol. I've noticed that these people drink at all times of the day and night: some of them even die with a full cup in their hand! The drink flowed freely in the run-up to the funeral, and one woman drank more than the rest and sang cheerful songs: I learned that she was a slave-girl who had volunteered to be cremated with her master. Two other slaves were appointed to care for her over the coming days, and to wash her feet with their own hands. Even if she changed her mind, there would be no backing out.

'On the day of the funeral, I arrived at the river to find that the chieftain's ship had been pulled up onto the river-bank, and that a scaffolding of wood had been built around it. The Rus' were processing around the ship, speaking words I didn't understand. An old and severe-looking woman appeared, whom the Rus' call the Angel of Death: she was in charge of the proceedings. She laid rich silk coverings on a divan on board the ship, and prepared it for the arrival of the chieftain's body, which the Rus' now exhumed: his corpse had grown black from the cold of the earth, but to my surprise, it hadn't yet begun to stink. They dressed this man in rich clothes and a silk caftan with buttons of gold and a hat of fur: the Angel of Death was the one who sewed him into his funeral suit. Next, they carried his body to the divan, and propped him up on cushions within a tent-like structure made of wood. They surrounded him with food and herbs and alcohol, and laid his weapons next to him on board the ship. A dog was cut in two and thrown up to him, and two horses were made to gallop until they had worked up a sweat: then they were butchered, along with two cows, a cock and hen, and all of these sacrificed animals were thrown on board alongside the chieftain.

'As this was happening, I saw the slave-girl. She was passing from tent to tent, and having intercourse with the owner of each one: when he was finished, he would say, "Tell your master that I have only done this out of love for him." Around the time of evening prayers they led the slave-girl to a frame they had constructed there on the beach. She stood on the men's hands and they raised her head above the frame. She spoke words I didn't understand, and I turned to my interpreter. "Behold, I see my father and mother," was what she said the first time she was raised, then "I see all of my dead relatives." When she was lifted a third time, she was held up for a longer look. "Behold, I see my master seated in the afterlife. It is a beautiful land, and green. His men and slaves are with him, and now he summons me. Send me to him."

'She was carried to the ship, where she removed her bracelets and anklets and passed them to the Angel of Death. The slave-girl took a cup of strong alcohol and chanted over it, bidding farewell to her female companions. She was given another cup, but by now she seemed to be unsure of what was happening, and the Angel of Death had to drag her into the wooden tent where her master lay. The men began to bang on their shields so that her struggle and screams would be drowned out: they didn't want to put the other slave-girls off making the same sacrifice when their time came. Six men climbed on board the ship, and each of them had intercourse with her in turn before lying her beside her master and holding her down by her hands and feet. The Angel of Death wound a rope round her neck and passed it to two of the men, and while they strangled her, the old woman stabbed her again and again between the ribs.

'The next of kin had the honour of starting the cremation fire. He was naked, and walked backwards with a burning brand in one hand and his other hand covering his anus, never taking his eyes off the crowd of faces gathered in front of him. After he had thrown his torch onto the pyre, the rest of the onlookers advanced with lighted sticks, and the wooden scaffolding soon blazed up in a great inferno, the wind whipping hot flames and smoke across the beach. Within an hour, the boat, the chieftain and the slave-girl had all been burned to ash. The Rus' built a small mound over the site of the cremation and erected a birch log at its middle, carved with the name of the deceased.

'Such a spectacle I am certain I will never see again.'

Ingvar the Far-Travelled

Although it was trade that drove contact with the Abbasid Caliphate, the Rus' made several raids into the lands around the Caspian Sea: one fleet was said to boast five hundred ships, and to have caused great destruction before being ambushed on the way back up the Volga by an army of Khazars. Following one raid on the town of Barda'a in Azerbaijan, the Rus' buried their dead with their weapons, as was their custom: after the Rus' left for their ships, the locals plundered the graves to retrieve their Frankish swords, which were greatly prized.

It wasn't only the Rus' who sent their warships this far east:

Vikings from Sweden undertook at least one major expedition into the Caliphate, though this last great venture under Ingvar the Far-Travelled ended in disaster. Ingvar set out with his fleet following the river routes to Serkland: the Swedes had come to make their mark on the lands around the Caspian Sea, but the sagas say that only one ship of survivors made it home. Rumours spread back up the trade routes that disaster had befallen Ingvar and his men. Around Lake Mälaren in Sweden, many rune-stones were raised to commemorate lost fathers, brothers and sons. A rune-stone from Gripsholm raised in memory of Harald, Ingvar's brother, includes this short poem which tells of this fateful expedition to the east, and what drove the men who joined it.

> *'As bold men they travelled*
> *far for gold*
> *and in the east*
> *gave food to the eagle.*
> *They died in the south*
> *in Serkland.'*

10

Kings in the North

It was usual for the great dynasties of the Viking Age to trace their family line back to the Norse gods. We've heard how the legendary Sigurd was the descendant of Odin, and how the Father of the Gods intervened directly in the Volsung family's affairs. For heroes of a later age, the chain of connections was a little longer. The Norwegian kings in the line of Harald Fairhair were known as the Ynglings, and they traced their line back to Sweden and the Norse god Yngvi-Freyr. The great Icelandic historiographer Snorri writes of these legendary kings in his *Ynglinga saga*, compiled from genealogies and interspersed with skaldic verse, and the names of some of these figures – such as the Swedish kings buried in the great mounds at Uppsala – were remembered long after their histories had been forgotten.

The old kings had a cultic role as well as earthly power, and even later in the Viking Age they presided over feasts and sacrifices in honour of their preferred gods. For Jarl Hakon, who ruled Norway from the pagan heartlands in the west, honouring

Odin was a family matter, as he traced his ancestry back to Sæmingr, the son of Odin and Skadi. Even in Christian Anglo-Saxon England, royal houses looked back to Odin – Woden – as their forefather. When the Norse kings began to adopt Christianity themselves, it helped to centralise the power of the throne and increase the influence of Scandinavian royalty abroad, but it didn't represent a sea-change in the way that kingship worked. The great missionary kings like Olaf Tryggvason were as ruthless in their raiding as their pagan ancestors, and the prerequisites for kingship stayed the same: reputation, wealth in silver, and a strong war-band at your back. Succession was often fought over, and being the eldest son of a strong ruler was no guarantee that the throne would come to you.

It took some time for the idea of petty kings and chieftains with their local cults to be replaced by the idea of consolidated rule over the countries in Scandinavia that exist today, and the power of regional families was a constant challenge to the kings in the north. But by the late Viking Age, rulers had emerged who dominated affairs across the whole of Scandinavia, and who projected their power to the west: not only through small-scale Viking raids and settlement, but through conquest at the head of splendid fleets. Cnut was the epitome of this expanding idea of kingship – he not only conquered England and took control of Denmark, but added Norway and parts of Sweden to his North Sea empire. He was a Christian king, but also the leader of brutal Viking raids; a patron of the Church, but praised in skaldic verse as 'the Freyr of battle'. The story of kingship in the Viking Age is one in which the old gods give way to Christianity, and legend gives way to history, but neither is quite lost.

The Sons of Ragnar

The sons of Ragnar Lodbrok mark the point where the shadowy figures of the legendary sagas enter the historical record, and their names are synonymous with the first great conquests of the Vikings. Whilst Bjorn Ironside is famed for leading the Viking expedition to the Mediterranean with the aim of sacking Rome, and Sigurd Snake-in-the-Eye appears as a shadowy figure in the line of Danish kings, his brothers Ivar the Boneless, Halfdan Ragnarsson and Ubba were leaders of the Great Heathen Army that terrorised the Anglo-Saxons and brought England to its knees. According to legend, it was the killing of Ragnar in King Ælla's snake pit that brought his fierce sons to England. In this account, the brothers were led by Ivar the Boneless, a man who was carried into battle on a litter and who was always at the centre of the fighting, despite not having the use of his legs: after all, Tyr's lack of a hand never held him back, nor did Odin's single eye. One version of events says that Ivar pretended to seek reconciliation with Ælla of Northumbria by claiming, as compensation for his father's death, only as much territory as he could cover with a single ox-hide. However, Ivar had the hide stretched and cut into such thin strands that he was able to claim an area big enough for both a city and a fortress; and from this foothold in the kingdom, he began to prepare the ground for his brothers to invade. It is said that when the sons of Ragnar defeated Ælla at York, they carved a blood eagle on his back by ripping out his lungs through severed ribs – or that they left his body to be bloodied by the bird of prey. Either way, the eagle got his food.

There's a gap, of course, between the legendary sagas and the historical realities of the Great Heathen Army that came to the shores of England in 865. The *Anglo-Saxon Chronicle* records that in this year the Great Army overwintered for the first time in East Anglia. It probably arrived from Francia, and amongst its ranks were many Danish Vikings seasoned from years of campaigning on the continent. This was not to be a hit-and-run raid of the sort that the Anglo-Saxons had weathered since the attack on Lindisfarne in 793: the Great Heathen Army under Ivar was a force intent on conquest. The kingdom of East Anglia managed to avoid being overrun by supplying their unwanted guests with horses, which the Danes then used in the spring to advance into the kingdom of Northumbria. But the policy of bribing the Great Heathen Army with silver did little more than buy the Anglo-Saxons time, as the Danes moved quickly between kingdoms, occupying strategic towns and reneging on promises of peace. Whether or not King Ælla had killed the legendary Ragnar Lodbrok, it was his divided kingdom of Northumbria that fell first to Ivar and Halfdan: York would become the centre of Norse rule in the north. East Anglia under King Edmund was the next kingdom to fall: the captured king was killed by being shot full of arrows after he refused to renounce his Christian faith. Edmund was later declared a saint, and it was said that a wolf sat guard over his severed head until it was discovered by his followers.

At this point Ivar the Boneless disappears – or at least his name is lost amongst the comings and goings of that Great Heathen Army with its own internal factions. Ivar may be the same person as Ímar, who turns up in Ireland before and after Ivar's time at the head of the Great Army, and who made war on the Irish kings. His dynasty, the Uí Ímair, came to dominate the Irish Sea, ruling a Norse empire from the powerful trading axis of Dublin and York. Even if this was not Ivar the Boneless, son of Ragnar Lodbrok, this was still an age where famous Vikings carved out kingdoms and made legends of themselves.

Back in England, Mercia would hold out against Halfdan Ragnarsson and the Great Army for a time, with the assistance of Wessex and the payment of tributes, but was eventually to fall as well. The Vikings overwintered at the royal seat of Repton and installed a puppet king, held to their will with hostages. The Great Army had been reinforced by another fleet of Vikings under a chieftain called Guthrum, and a decade after the Ragnarssons first arrived in England, Wessex was the only Anglo-Saxon kingdom that wasn't subject to the Danes. Whilst part of the Great Army moved north under Halfdan to occupy and farm the lands they'd conquered in Northumbria, Guthrum had his eyes set on Wessex. The defence of this last kingdom was now left to the youngest of five brothers, a man in his early twenties whose name means 'Elf-Council', and who would come to be known as Alfred the Great.

The next years saw a game of cat-and-mouse between Guthrum and King Alfred. In 876, Guthrum struck deep into the heartlands of Wessex, occupying Wareham near the Dorset coast. Alfred managed to besiege the Danes here with his own forces, but this confrontation ended in a stalemate: the two sides exchanged hostages and made peace – only for Guthrum to kill the hostages and lead his army away by night to seize Exeter and continue the offensive. In the following year, shortly after Twelfth Night, Guthrum and the Great Army crossed again from Mercia in force, and this time Alfred was outmanoeuvred; forced to retreat into the Somerset marshes whilst his kingdom was overrun. This winter must have been the bleakest of times for Alfred and his household, but there were glimmers of hope: a Viking faction led by Ubba Ragnarsson was defeated by the *fyrd* of Devon; their famous raven banner is said to have been taken in that skirmish, and Ubba killed. More importantly for Alfred, the security of the Somerset marshes and his stronghold at Athelney offered some time to regroup and to muster the *fyrd* from three shires into a formidable force. The *Anglo-Saxon Chronicle* tells how the men of Somerset, Wiltshire and part of Hampshire met at Ecgberht's Stone, and marched to face the Great Heathen Army at Edington, where they fought a battle as important as any in the Viking Age. Alfred won a decisive victory, besieged the remnants of Guthrum's army, and forced them to come to terms. Great oaths and important hostages were given by the Vikings, and Guthrum himself was baptised as part of the agreement. A border was established at the old Roman road of Watling Street and along the Thames, dividing Anglo-Saxon England from the lands beyond that were controlled and settled by the Danes: this territory would be called the Danelaw, and this new political reality was the great legacy of that army that first came to England under Ivar.

In the following decades, Alfred's descendants in the only kingdom to hold out against the Vikings would slowly bring the Danelaw under their control: Alfred's eldest daughter Æthelflæd – who'd probably hidden from the Vikings in the marshes of Somerset as a child – would play a central role in driving the Viking forces from the midlands as *de facto* ruler of the Mercians, and Alfred's son Edward the Elder would add the former kingdom of East Anglia to this growing territory under the rule of the Wessex royal house. The map of Anglo-Saxon England had been redrawn: from the south, a single 'Kingdom of the Angles and the Saxons' was beginning to emerge, whilst the creation of the Danelaw embedded Norse language, law and culture into the fabric of England. The Great Heathen Army may have sailed out of legend with the sons of Ragnar, but its impact on the British Isles lasts until this day.

Harald Fairhair

In the early Viking Age, the name 'Norway' didn't refer to a kingdom or people, but to the sailing route north up a convoluted coast, and it was not a landscape that lent itself to centralised control: Norway was a land of petty kings and local strongmen holding sway over their ancestral lands. Harald Fairhair was the Norse king who began to change this. His family's lands were in Vestfold bordering the Oslo-fjord, and when he inherited from his father aged ten, he styled himself king like many other rulers of that time. His kingdom was soon under threat from the neighbouring chieftains around the Olso-fjord, but with the help of his maternal uncle Guthorm, Harald defeated them all in skirmishes, and added their lands to the patchwork of his realm. One anecdote told by Snorri charts his rise: a landowner named Aki invited both Harald of the Tangled Locks and King Eirik Eymundarson of the Swedes to a feast at his farm; each king had claimed the surrounding territory as his own. Aki owned two halls: both were large and very fine, but one was ancient, and the other still smelled of freshly felled timber. He hosted King Eirik in the old hall, and served him with ancient tableware, finely decorated, but chipped and worn with age. King Harald was hosted in the new hall, and the gilded horns and serving bowls were polished so they shone like glass. Harald was very pleased with the entertainment, and promised Aki that his friendship would be rewarded. King Eirik of the Swedes was not in such good humour, and left abruptly. Aki escorted him away from the farm. 'Why did you serve Harald in a new hall with all the newest plates and horns?' asked the king of the Swedes. 'Have you forgotten that you are my subject, here in Varmland, and that you owe allegiance to me?' Aki replied, 'I served you with the ancient tableware, which was fine in its day, because you're a rather old king. I served Harald in the new hall with the new tableware, because he's a young ruler, with everything ahead of him.' At this, Eirik drew his sword and killed Aki: but the farmer was right. Harald was on the rise, and Eirik of the Swedes could do little more than chew his beard as the young king pressed his claim to Varmland.

Harald had become a powerful regional ruler, but the kings in the west of Norway did not see any reason to bow their heads towards the east. One of the foremost of these west-coast kings ruled a territory called Hordaland: he had a beautiful daughter called Gyda, and Harald asked for her hand in marriage. Marriages were power-plays as well as overtures of peace, so when Gyda refused to marry Harald until he was king over the whole of Norway, it was more than a personal affront. The sagas say that when Harald was told about Gyda's reply, he didn't react with anger like the emissaries he'd sent: he simply made a vow that he would not cut or comb his hair until he'd done as she requested and made the whole of Norway his. He would be known as Harald of the Tangled Hair: a tyrant to the chieftains he came to dispossess, but the greatest of kings to those who followed him.

Harald's campaign to bring Norway under his control lasted ten years – during which the war-leader's locks must have become very tangled indeed as he toppled Viking chieftains one by one, and suppressed rebellions from all sides. The skalds say he fought in the thick of it from his dragon-prowed ship, his sword ringing against shields and making red wounds spit blood, as around him the arrows rained down with the shriek of valkyries.

The decisive battle of Harald's campaign took place at Hafrs-fjord, against a confederacy of southern and western kingdoms led by King Eirik of Hordaland, the father of that same Gyda who'd rebuffed Harald all those years ago. It was fought at sea, like so many of the decisive battles of the Viking Age, and Harald's ship was manned by a troop of hardened warriors known as berserkers. Berserkers were said to be Odin's men: they fought without armour, dressed in wolf-skins, and they were strong as bears and mad as dogs. Before battle they would bite their shields, and neither iron nor fire was able to touch them. With these elite troops at his shoulder, and his fleet arrayed on either side, Harald waited in Hafrsfjord for the rebel kings with their war-hardened Vikings to arrive. The berserkers started to howl and rattle their weapons as the enemy drew close, and Frankish blades were soon hammering against white shields. The battle was fierce and long, and the fighting spilled between ships, their decks slippery with blood. Eirik of Horda-land was killed there, along with the King of Rogaland and many leading men, and the survivors fled the battle by land and sea, covering their backs with their shields and cowering in the bilges as missiles rained down from Harald's ships. Harald of the Tangled Hair watched his enemies scattering, and he knew that he'd broken the last resistance to his rule. Some of the powerful families would flee abroad, to the Scottish Isles and to Iceland, and his enemies would continue to raid Norway from these Viking bases to the west. But there would be no serious challenge to his kingship, and Harald must have felt that he'd achieved the victory he'd promised. When he cut and combed his locks he was no longer known as the tangle-haired king, but as Harald Fairhair: King of Norway.

The realm that Harald won does not quite resemble the

Norway of today – he held little sway over the north, and the powerful Jarls of Lade did little more than nod to the authority of the man and continue as they were – but Harald Fairhair's achievement was to turn a land of petty kings and chieftains into something more like the kingdoms to the south. The next centuries would see his successors struggle to emulate this feat.

Eric Bloodaxe

Eric Bloodaxe, eldest son of Harald Fairhair, is a shadowy figure, presented as the villain of the sagas – a king who bloodied his axe in Viking raids and ruthlessly killed his half-brothers to help secure his claims to his father's lands. His wife, queen Gunnhild, is the evil power behind the throne in these accounts, using her beauty and the magic arts to manipulate the men around her and pursue a personal feud against the Icelandic hero Egil Skallagrimsson. The sagas tell us that Eric and Gunnhild were the short-lived rulers of Norway after the death of Eric's father, but Eric emerges more clearly from legend as the last Viking king in Northumbria – a proud but hard-pressed pagan ruler contending with both the resurgent kings of Wessex and the Dublin Vikings to the east. Coins were minted in York for 'Eric Rex', complete with sword: a fitting symbol for this warlike king. Between the legend and the fragments of history lies one of the most intriguing figures of the Viking Age.

Eric, we're told, cut his teeth on Viking raids at the tender age of twelve, and his career as a pirate took him almost from one end of the Viking world to the other: he raided the Baltic coasts, the British Isles, Ireland and France, and travelled to the Sami lands that bordered the White Sea, sailing up the Northern Dvina deep into Russia to sack the settlement of Permina.

Harald Fairhair was an old king by this time, with many sons; and whether or not he gave his eldest one his blessing as successor, Eric must have been preparing for a fight. It's no surprise that he moved quickly against his half-brothers: legend has it that he killed all of them except Hakon, who had been fostered to King Athelstan of England; and it was the one brother he left alive who eventually deposed him. It's also no surprise that Eric's rule is remembered for its severity: the petty kingdoms did not recognise the unity of Norway, but only Harald Fairhair's strong-man rule, and Eric took their tribute by force. What is more surprising is that when Eric's half-brother Hakon arrived with a fleet from England and rallied his supporters to seize the throne, the great Viking appears to have abandoned Norway without a fight. Seeing the weakness of his position, Eric had decided his prospects were better in the west.

Eric and his wife Gunnhild headed first to the Viking staging post of Orkney, but it wasn't long before Eric was back on the offensive and had installed himself as the King of Viking York. He may have been allowed to rule Northumbria with the blessing of the English king as a protection against the Scots and the Dublin Vikings: raids on Scotland and Ireland would have been an extra source of income for this seasoned pirate, who, like every Viking leader, needed silver to keep his war-band firmly on his side. It was during this time that Egil Skallagrimsson was shipwrecked on the coast of England and came into his arch-enemy's hands, saving himself with the skaldic poem 'Head-Ransom'. Winning silver with his sword-arm was the means to earthly power, but poetry was the way to gain eternal fame.

Eric was driven out of York by Olaf Guthfrithson of Dublin, backed by the new king of the Anglo-Saxons who was less keen on Eric as a neighbour. When Eric regrouped and returned to

England with his fleet, it was not as a vassal to an Anglo-Saxon king: he came to claim Northumbria for himself, and it seems the Northumbrians were happy to take Eric as their king and drive Olaf back across the Irish Sea. It was during this time that Eric's sword-coins were minted as an expression of his independent rule in York: but for all this, Eric would only rule Northumbria – in defiance of both the Anglo-Saxon King Eadred, and Ivar's descendants in Dublin – for two years. The sources say that Eric was killed in battle along with five Norse kings, ambushed at Stainmore against forces mustered from the Irish Sea. Eric was able to call upon the earls of Orkney and the kings of the Hebrides to fight his cause: even if Norway had eluded him, and the fight against powerful rivals to every side had proved too much, Eric Bloodaxe was a major player in this turbulent age.

Eric's widow Gunnhild returned to Orkney, and later to her father in Denmark; and the sons she raised with Eric – the so-called wolf-pack – would be as ferocious as their father. Gunnhild commissioned a poem praising Eric's achievements that has survived to this day: in it the cups are rinsed and the drink prepared to welcome a warrior king to Odin's hall. All the Einherjar are raised from their benches, and the sound of Eric's arrival is like the return of Baldr himself to his father's side. The heroes Sigmund and Sinfjotli are sent to greet this Eric Bloodaxe, a warrior from the world of men who reddened his sword in many lands, and who will be needed in the fight against the mighty wolf.

Hakon the Good

Eric's half-brother Hakon was raised a Christian in the court of King Athelstan, but he soon dropped his plans to convert the

Norwegians: the situation back home was fragile enough without stirring up this hornets' nest. In fact, it may have been Hakon's flexibility and concessions to the heathen chieftains that allowed him to succeed where Eric's stubbornness and bloodied axe had not. He quickly won over the powerful men in the west with promises that their lands would not be taxed: they may have had scruples about Hakon's Christian upbringing, but what matter, so long as he let them keep their dues, and observed the sacrifices to their ancestral gods? The last would be a sticking point for Hakon. During local sacrificial feasts, at least as Snorri understood it, animals were slaughtered, including horses, and twigs used to spatter the altar, the temple walls, and all the onlookers with blood. The meat was cooked and blessed by the king, who drank a cup of ale first to Odin, then to Njord, and finally to Freyr for prosperity and peace in the coming year. One story tells how at one such feast, King Hakon made the Sign of the Cross over the cup, and almost caused a breach of the peace: his quick-thinking Jarl told the horrified farmers that Hakon had made the sign of Thor's hammer over the horn because he trusted in the strength of this god most of all. The muttering subsided; but Hakon would still not eat the horseflesh that was served.

Hakon's reign in Norway was constantly challenged by the sons of Eric Bloodaxe, who were far more active than their father in pursuing their claims to the Norwegian throne. Hakon fought them first near the royal seat of Avaldsnes: he had the victory, and Eric's son Guttorm was cut down in that battle. This would set a pattern for the years that followed – the sons of Eric throwing themselves like waves against Hakon's defences in the west, and being constantly beaten back. For their part, the brothers had found refuge in the court of King Gorm the Old of

Denmark, who furnished them with troops to strike at his northern rival and pursue their claims: but the poets say that Hakon always had the upper hand. When the sons of Eric sailed up the west coast of Norway with a large force of Danish Vikings, word reached Hakon late that the land was under attack: but he refused to give quarter, and invited the invaders to meet him at the island battle-site of Rastarkalv. Hakon only had time to raise a small force, but to make the army appear larger than it really was, the battle standards were spread out in a long line across the ridge: when the Danes arrived, they wavered at the approach of what looked to be a mighty troop, and were cut down by Hakon's small force as they retreated to their ships. Another son of Eric was killed as he tried to mount a last-ditch defence, and a burial mound still stands to mark the site of that victory at Rastarkalv.

The sons of Eric were repulsed again two years later when Hakon steered his fleet of sail-bearers to the south, and again in 961, when they surprised Hakon at his royal residence in Fitjar. Once more, Hakon mustered a quick defence that saw off the attackers, but though the golden-helmed warrior was victorious, he'd rushed into battle without his mail, and his arm was pierced by an arrow. The wolf-pack had finally landed a bite, and Hakon the Good would later die from the wound that he'd received. Though his reign was far from peaceful, Hakon was remembered as a just king who established law and allowed the land to prosper under its protective gods. He was buried with his weapons and armour in a high mound, and sent to join the heroes in Valhalla alongside his pagan brothers: no matter that his own faith once lay with the White Christ (as the Christian God was sometimes called by the Vikings). The skald Eyvind the Plagiarist wrote a eulogy that expresses the mood of the followers he left behind: 'Not until the realms of man are laid waste by the unbound Fenrir will the equal of such a king be seen again.'

Olaf Tryggvason

In a time of warrior kings and almost constant warfare in the north, Olaf Tryggvason stands out as the most distinctive of Viking rulers. It's no contradiction that this warrior king was also a convert to Christianity – perhaps the faith was forced upon him after a botched raid on London. After all, Christ meant many things to the Norse converts, and accepting the ascendancy of the new religion did not mean renouncing the life of a Viking. Olaf's life is told in Snorri's history of the kings of Norway, and it is a colourful account.

Olaf was the son of the petty king Tryggvi, and it's said he was born, on an island in a lake, shortly after his mother escaped the murder of her family by the sons of Eric Bloodaxe. The infant Olaf was raised in hiding until he was three years old, and then spirited away east, like so many refugees of Scandinavia's internecine wars. The aim was to get passage on a merchant ship to the Rus' court where Olaf's uncle held a position of rank, but the ship was captured by Vikings from Estonia: Olaf's elderly guardian Thorolf Louse-beard was considered useless and killed, while Olaf found himself sold first for the price of a goat, and later for the price of a fine cloak. He was a slave in Estonia for six years, until his uncle happened to pass through the area collecting taxes for the Rus' king, and recognised the boy for the noble that he was. The two Norwegians were reunited, and Olaf continued his journey south.

Olaf was nine when he came to Gardariki and spotted the

slaver who had captured and killed his companions, and he almost caused a riot when he buried an axe in the slaver's head in the middle of the market. After all, the slave trade – from Dublin in the west to the Bulgar markets in the east – was a profitable business that had to be protected. It was only through the refuge given by the queen and the payment of a substantial fine that Olaf escaped being hanged for that act of revenge against his captor. He grew to be a strapping man in the court of the Rus': handsome, strong, and the best of all Norwegians at sport.

When Olaf reached maturity, he set off with a ship to cut his teeth raiding in the Baltic, heading first to the island of Bornholm and gaining much plunder. He married a princess of the Wends and ruled lands in the southern Baltic for a time, but when his wife died he took up the life of a Viking once more, raiding the Low Countries and the Saxon coast, and feeding the ravens with the flesh of Frisians. Next in his sights were the rich islands to the west, and we're told he made a grand tour of Viking hunting grounds, from Scotland to the Isle of Man, ending up with raids on Ireland, Wales and the Scilly Isles. Olaf was probably the leader of the Viking fleet that fought at the Battle of Maldon, and he won great sums of Danegeld from the English. After a failed attack on London, Olaf agreed to take a large tribute on the understanding he would not raid in English lands again: as part of this pact, he took baptism, with King Æthelred as his sponsor, though some sources say he'd already been converted by a hermit in the Scilly Isles. Either way, Olaf was now spectacularly rich and at least nominally Christian, married to a princess of Viking Dublin (if Snorri is to be believed), and with a dog called Vigi, picked up in Ireland, who could sort sheep and cattle by their markings, and who was always at his side. More importantly, Olaf's legend was growing, and he now had the reputation that would rally mercenaries to his cause. The time was ripe for this career Viking to return to his homeland and make a bid for the throne itself.

The powerful Jarl Hakon was ruling Norway at that time from his ancestral lands in the west. He was a dedicated follower of the Norse gods, and traced his family's descent from Odin, so he had not taken kindly to the baptism forced on him by the Danish king after an unhappy expedition to the south. It was well known that Jarl Hakon had sent the missionaries ashore as soon as his fleet was ready to sail, and that he'd held a large sacrifice to Odin on an island off the coast of Sweden, at which two ravens appeared and cawed loudly to show the god's approval. This was a man the poets called the Tyr of the sacrificial blood-bowl, and the Njord of fleeing enemies: they say that he sent nine men of royal blood to sit with Odin in Valhalla, and his victories were known to have been granted by his kinship with the gods. But though the pagan Jarl Hakon may have had the favour of Odin and the pagan credentials to match his subjects in the west, he fell out with the old Tronder families; and Olaf Tryggvason, when he arrived from Ireland with his fleet, quickly won the support of powerful men. As Snorri tells it, Jarl Hakon – that loyal follower of the old gods – was murdered by his own slave whilst hiding in a pigsty, and Olaf became king of the land from which he'd been banished all those years before.

It is said that Olaf extended his power over most of Norway, and that he promoted Christianity to a population not yet enamoured of the faith, using the same stubbornness that had enabled him to rise as a leader of a Viking war-band, and bend reluctant chieftains to his will. We're told he toppled the idols in the temple of Trondheim in a public show of defiance to the Norse gods – striking Thor with his own weapon, and sending him tumbling to the floor. He killed those who refused to convert in ways that would discourage others from resisting: one powerful farmer in the north had a snake forced down his throat to eat its way out of his insides; and he burned practitioners of the witchcraft known as *seidr* alive as they feasted in his hall. It is even said that a one-eyed traveller gained a private audience with the king and kept him talking late into the night with tales of the ancestors, and that this man was Odin, attempting to move Olaf from his course and stop him going to Mass: the stranger could not be found the next day, and Olaf vowed to send him packing if he came again. Perhaps it was Olaf's stubbornness in his pursuit of his preferred faith that eventually led to his undoing: an engagement to a Swedish princess broke down when she would not abandon the old gods, and he made a powerful enemy when he called her a heathen dog and struck her with his glove. And pursuing claims on Wendish land from his first marriage led him on the expedition to the south of the Baltic that gave his enemies the opportunity they'd been waiting for: the great Viking was ambushed as he sailed home with just eleven ships.

Olaf fought valiantly in this final battle at Svolder, lashing his small fleet together to form a floating fortress with his ship Long-Serpent at the centre. Long-Serpent was the largest longship of its day, and its gilded prow protruded far out from the Norwegian battle-line, giving Olaf a clear view of his enemies arranged on all sides: he scorned the fleets of the Danes and Swedes, but the exiled Eirik Hakonarson was Norwegian, and Olaf knew that he'd get no quarter from those battle-hardened men. Olaf's ships were overrun, one by one, with the help of Eirik's flagship, Iron Ram, until only Long-Serpent was left. In a last-ditch attempt to turn the tide, one of Olaf's loyal retainers fired two arrows at Jarl Eirik which struck the tiller next to the jarl's head and the padding of his seat before the great bow broke. 'What was that I just heard breaking with a mighty crack?' shouted Olaf over the din of the battle. 'That was Norway, breaking from your hands!' was his loyal man's reply. The sagas say that once he saw the battle was lost, Olaf jumped from his longship in his mail to sink to the bottom of the sound: a fitting end for this extraordinary Viking king, who some believed would later return when Norway was in need of his strong arm.

Harald Bluetooth

Harald Bluetooth was not the first king of what is now Denmark – that title is usually given to his father, Gorm the Old – but if his own claims are to be believed, Harald also extended his control over Norway and made the Danes Christian. One thing that's clear is that Harald Bluetooth understood the role of self-promotion. His father had raised a modest rune-stone at the royal seat of Jelling to honour his accomplished wife Thyra, 'the adornment of Denmark', but Harald had a much larger stone raised nearby and carved with intricate designs. The inscription is offered in memory of his mother and father, but rather than celebrating their achievements, Harald makes reference to his own. On one side of Harald Bluetooth's rune-stone there is a depiction of Christ accompanying the claim that Harald brought Christianity to his subjects, but it is a very curious image. The figure doesn't hang on a cross, but is suspended in coils like Odin on the World-Tree. Perhaps this was a symbol of continuity between the old gods and the new – Odin's sacrifice to gain knowledge of runes upstaged by Christ's sacrifice to redeem the whole of humankind. Harald Bluetooth also built a church in the Jelling complex, and moved his parents' remains from the great burial mounds into the church's sacred ground: this re-interment would have been a great spectacle, and a signal to the Danes that though the official religion had changed, the royal line had not.

Harald's mother, Queen Thyra, is remembered in the Danish tradition for overseeing the extension of the Danevirke – a line of defences on the southern border of the realm – and Harald continued this ambitious building programme: in addition to his overhaul of the Jelling complex, he constructed ring forts in a line across his kingdom with Arhus at the centre. Each of these large forts was protected by a circular earth rampart faced with wood, and they had gates to the north, south, east and west out of which the mustered troops could ride. Harald is also credited with founding the Viking fortress of the Jomsvikings on the Baltic coast, and for constructing the Ravning Bridge across water-meadows near Jelling: this oak bridge was wide enough to allow traders to pass in both directions, and provided a quick route for his war-parties to speed towards the defences to the south.

How well these defences worked in practice is a subject of debate. Harald Bluetooth's bold claims that he made the Danes Christian may have been a condition of King Otto's victory over Danish forces when the Germans breached the Danevirke. Harald's campaigns in Norway, in support of his nephews – the sons of Eric Bloodaxe and Gunnhild – did not go all his way, and Denmark itself was raided several times by fleets from the north. Harald's influence extended into the south and east of Norway, and the powerful Jarl Hakon paid him tribute for a time, but the Danish king was never able to extend the reach of Christianity far into Norway. Snorri tells us that a fleet of Danes and Joms-vikings he sent to chastise the rebellious Jarl Hakon was routed in a sea-battle and sent limping back to Denmark. The Danish forces had more success late in Harald's reign when they allied with the Wends and drove the Germans back past the Dane-virke defences, but King Harald Bluetooth did not lead this campaign: it was his son, the rising star Svein, who rode at the front of the war-band, and it was his son who finally ended the rule of the old warrior-king. One account tells that Harald was defeated in battle against an army of disgruntled Danes led by Svein, and that he fled, wounded, to Wendland where he died. It was a miserable end for such an industrious king, whose lasting legacy was to secure Denmark for his ambitious son. One of the more unusual ways Harald Bluetooth's own ambitions are remembered is through computing and the short-range wireless technology that bears his name. The symbol for Bluetooth is a combination of the runic characters H and B, recognising Harald's reputation as a well-connected, outward-looking king.

Svein Forkbeard

Svein Forkbeard followed the route of his father Harald Blue-tooth in promoting Christianity, but there was little to distinguish him from the Viking kings of old. He did not forget the Danish claims in Norway, and entered into an alliance with King Olof of Sweden and the exiled Norwegian jarl Eirik Hakonarson to depose King Olaf Tryggvason. After the famous sea battle at Svolder, King Svein claimed the eastern lands around the Oslo fjord for himself. Jarl Eirik and his brother governed the rest of Norway between them, but they owed tribute to Svein Fork-beard: he'd brought the north back under Danish control.

Viking raids exploited the rise and fall in fortunes of the rich kingdoms to the south, and any show of weakness provided pirates with an opportunity. After years of relative security, the rule over England and the Danelaw had passed to a twelve-year-old called Æthelred, who was dubbed the 'ill-advised', and whom history remembers as an ineffective king. Vikings from Denmark began to probe the coast of England early in his reign, and in 991 a large Viking army under Olaf Tryggvason attacked the east coast and defeated an Anglo-Saxon levy at Maldon. Their spirited defence under the elderly Byrhtnoth is immortalised in a famous Old English poem, but resistance to these Viking raids was soon replaced by a policy of bribery with silver. Such payments must have encouraged further raids, probably by veterans of the previous extortions bolstered by settlers from the Danelaw keen to cash in. So began a demoralising cycle of Viking incursions, and ever greater payments to the Danes.

In the year 1002, King Æthelred made perhaps the worst move of his misguided reign. It seems to have been frustration at his inability to counter Viking attacks effectively that led him to order the Danes living in the kingdom to be uprooted 'like weeds growing in the wheat'. Their massacre would take place on Saint Brice's Day: in Oxford, a band of young Danes – all fighting men under the age of twenty-five – were attacked by Anglo-Saxon townspeople. One account tells how the Danes sought refuge in the church of St Frithuswith, only for it to be set on fire by the angry mob. The mutilated bodies of some thirty-five Danes were thrown into a ditch outside the city walls, on land that now forms part of St John's College. Similar revenge attacks must have happened in towns across the south of England, and though in Oxford it seems to have been fighting men who were targeted, tradition has it that settled populations and hostages from the Danelaw were also caught up in the killing, including a noble woman named Gunnhild. She was the daughter of Harald Bluetooth and sister of Svein Forkbeard, and this gave Svein the pretext he needed to escalate Viking raids into a campaign of conquest and revenge.

Svein attacked the following year with a Viking army that harried the coast of England and sacked Exeter, Salisbury and Norwich: a successful defence led by an Anglo-Scandinavian named Ulfkell outside Thetford caused them to retreat, but the only means of resistance for the English against the incursions of 1005 seems, ironically, to have been the famine that left no food for hungry Viking troops. Nevertheless, Svein kept up the pressure on England, with the Danes often using the Isle of Wight or Normandy as a base of operations: sometimes the local Anglo-Saxon levies were raised in defence, but more often than not the Danes were paid to leave after sacking towns and laying waste to the countryside. Svein may have been Christian, but this didn't stop the Danes plundering without scruples: the Archbishop of Canterbury refused to be ransomed, and met a gruesome death – pelted with bones by a drunken mob, and bludgeoned with the back of an axe, despite the protestations of the Viking chieftain Thorkell the Tall. In 1013, after a decade of intensive attacks and a steady flow of English silver back to Denmark, Svein Forkbeard led the full-scale invasion that would finally bring England under the rule of a Norse king.

Svein's army headed first for the Danelaw, where he could expect support: East Anglia and Northumbria quickly submitted to him, as did the Five Boroughs in Mercia. He then left his hostages and a garrison with his son Cnut in the north, and took the main force south to Oxford, Winchester and London. Only London put up much resistance – amongst their forces was the former Viking leader Thorkell the Tall, who'd entered the service of King Æthelred after witnessing the horrific treatment of the Archbishop – but he, too, submitted in the end, and Æthelred fled to Normandy, following his sons and his Norman wife Queen Emma. On Christmas Day, after a short campaign, Svein was declared King of England.

Svein had little time to enjoy his new title and his conquered lands: he died just five weeks afterwards. His empire was divided: his eldest son Harald took over the Danish kingdom, whilst Cnut became the leader of Svein's army in England. His reign over the English, when it came, would last for almost twenty years.

Cnut

Knut, or Cnut as he is known in England, grandson of Harald Bluetooth, was perhaps the most successful Norse ruler of the Viking Age, and his empire encompassed England, Denmark and Norway, as well as parts of Sweden. Cnut didn't inherit England on the back of his father's conquest: when Svein Forkbeard died, the Anglo-Saxon nobles were only too happy to give the hapless Æthelred a second chance, and he quickly returned from Normandy to take the throne. The only region loyal to Cnut was Lincolnshire, but with the odds looking so poor, the Norse prince deserted his allies in the Danelaw and sailed away to muster forces in Denmark, now under the rule of his older brother Harald.

Cnut returned with an imposing fleet – it is said that the ships shone with precious metals as they approached the coast, and that it looked as though all the nations of the earth were bearing down on England. The Danes began by harrying the southern coast, and this marked the start of a brutal campaign to recapture the country that had submitted to Svein only a year before. The English response to Cnut's invasion was hampered by defections and the divided loyalties of the Danelaw, as well as the mobility of Cnut's sea-borne army. The fortunes of the Anglo-Saxons improved once Edmund Ironside succeeded his father to the throne, and there were even some victories for the Anglo-Saxon *fyrd* against the Danes: London was besieged but not taken, and Edmund drove Cnut's forces back to their ships on more than one occasion. It was at the Battle of Assandun that the *fyrd* was finally broken: the *Anglo-Saxon Chronicle* says that the treacherous Ealdorman of Mercia, Eadric Streona, withdrew his troops from the battle and left the remaining forces under Edmund to their fate. Edmund himself was wounded but escaped west to Gloucester, and here the two kings came together and made peace: Edmund Ironside would rule over Wessex and London, and Cnut over all of England north of the Thames: the proviso was that Cnut would inherit the whole kingdom in the event of Edmund's death – and Edmund duly obliged by dying within the month.

Cnut dealt with his rivals ruthlessly, purging England of those loyal to the kings of Wessex. The turncoat Eadric Streona was murdered on his orders, for how could a man who'd betrayed his former lord be trusted? Heavy taxes were levied to pay off Cnut's army of Vikings, and to maintain a fleet in England – with London singled out for a huge payment of silver. But this Norse king offered something precious in return: security. The Viking raids that had plagued England for a generation could be prevented by a king who controlled the sea routes and who later came to rule the homelands of the Vikings; trade was given a chance to flourish after many years of disruption; and

Cnut became a patron of the Church, making lavish donations and restoring the wealth that had been plundered in Viking raids. When Cnut's older brother Harald died in 1018, Cnut returned to Denmark and swiftly secured his claim to the Danish homeland. Maintaining a kingdom on both sides of the North Sea did not pose the difficulties it might have done to a less adept ruler, and Cnut dealt decisively with a rebellion in Denmark, with English men now fighting in his entourage. When Cnut faced down an alliance of Swedes and Norwegians, he secured his dominance across the whole of Scandinavia, and by 1027 his North Sea Empire was so secure that he even took a trip to Rome to attend the coronation of the Holy Roman Emperor, standing shoulder to shoulder with the great Christian rulers of Europe. Cnut would add Norway to his realm on his return, ousting the unpopular Olaf Haraldsson without a fight, and bringing the northern isles and the sea routes to the west under his control. According to the sagas, Olaf would later die at the Battle of Stiklestad when he returned from the Rus' to reclaim his throne – defeated by an army of Norwegian farmers and given three mortal wounds. Olaf was canonised as a Christian martyr barely a year after his death: under the harsh rule imposed by Cnut's first wife and teenage son, the farmers began to wish they'd stuck with Harald Fairhair's line.

In England, Cnut had married Emma, the widow of Æthelred, to help establish his legitimacy, though he had formerly been married to an English noblewoman in the north named Ælfgifu. Her status does not seem to have been diminished by becoming Cnut's mistress: she was appointed, as Queen Regent, to manage the affairs of Norway along with Cnut's teenage son Svein, and this English queen ruled with all the authority of a Viking warlord: one skald claims that Ælfgifu's rule was so harsh that men were reduced to eating food meant for the ani-mals, and rebellion eventually forced her to flee. In England, the Church had to turn a blind eye to these two marriages, and to the king's fondness for skaldic poetry praising his achievements with reference to Freyr and the Midgard Serpent. Cnut was a major player in eleventh-century Christendom, but the old ways were not completely dead.

Harald Hardrada

We've heard of Harald Hardrada's youth and service in the Byzantine Empire, and of his dramatic escape back north to the kingdom of the Rus'. But Harald Hard-Ruler is most familiar as the leader of the invasion of the north of England in 1066 that so stretched the Anglo-Saxon forces, and played into William the Bastard's hands. Accounts of that momentous year tend to downplay the threat that this invasion posed in and of itself: Harald Hardrada was a serious contender to the English throne in the turmoil after Edward the Confessor's death. Even Tostig, the brother of the Anglo-Saxon claimant Harold Godwinson, was in league with this formidable Norwegian king and self-styled successor to the empire of Cnut.

A great deal had changed in Norway during Harald's fifteen years in exile, and when the former Varangian returned in ships laden down with gold and with the daughter of the Grand Prince of Kiev – Elisiv – as his queen, he had the wealth and status to challenge his nephew Magnus the Good for the Norwegian throne. Magnus was no pushover: he was the only son of the Norwegian king Olaf Haraldsson, and he carried his father's famous battle-axe named after the goddess Hel. He also had the support of the powerful jarls in Norway who'd engineered his return from exile in Novrogod, and during his reign Magnus had routed the Wends, crushed the Jomsvikings and exerted his power over that same Denmark formerly ruled by Cnut. He even had his eye set on the English throne. But wars to seize control of Denmark had taken their toll on Magnus and depleted his reserves of silver; and when his uncle Harald arrived and began raiding the Danish coast, Magnus sued for peace. Harald and Magnus would jointly rule in Norway, and Harald agreed to share the wealth he'd brought home from the east.

After little more than a year of this precarious joint rule, Magnus died in Denmark. Harald inherited Norway, but Magnus had granted the other half of his kingdom to the troublesome jarl of Denmark, Sweyn Estridsson. Harald immediately began a campaign to take Denmark from his former ally. He raided the Danish coast, burned the trading town of Hedeby to the ground, and fought battles on land and sea against Sweyn; however, he couldn't land a decisive blow, and after many costly years of conflict the two kings came to peace. Harald's reputation as a hard ruler comes not from these constant years of war across the sea, but from his tightening grip on Norway itself. His efforts to crush the power of the jarls in the west and to punish those who owed him revenue gave Harald a reputation for ruthlessness, but also strengthened the position of the crown. When Edward the Confessor died in 1066, leaving England without an heir, Harald would be able to draw on a standing army hardened by years of war against the Danes, and on the resources of a unified Norway firmly under his control.

Harald was quick to act. He sailed to the Norse colonies of Shetland and Orkney to gather support and troops, and then took his fleet south to Northumbria, where he was joined by the rebel Tostig Godwinson, sailing with a small fleet from the

south. The Norwegians raided the coast and sailed up the River
Ouse to York, where they were met in battle by the earls of Mercia and Northumbria in a hastily organised defence beside the
marshes of Fulford. The Anglo-Saxons were defeated and the
survivors were forced to retreat behind the walls of York, where
the earls surrendered. Harald accepted hostages from the English, and his army fell back to their ships. With the north secured,
Harald's plan must have been to push southwards building his
support: he certainly wasn't counting on what happened next.

As soon as he had learned of the Norwegians' arrival, Harold
Godwinson had decamped his forces guarding the southern
coast against the Normans, and force-marched them from London to north of the Humber in just four days: an extraordinary
feat that took even the seasoned tactician Harald Hardrada by
surprise. Harald's forces were on the way to Stamford Bridge to
pick up supplies and hostages promised by the defeated earls,
and some sources say they'd left their heavy chainmail back at
the ships. The unexpected arrival of the Anglo-Saxon army
forced the Norwegians to form defensive lines, helped by a single Norse warrior holding the bridge against the Anglo-Saxon
advance with his great long-handed axe: it is said that this giant
of a man was only brought down when one of Harold Godwinson's men floated under the bridge and stabbed him from below.
When the Anglo-Saxon force lined up against the Norwegian
shield-wall the fighting was intense, but in the end the English
pressed their advantage home and broke the Norse lines: Harald
Hardrada was killed with an arrow to the throat, and Tostig cut
down. So many of the fleeing Norse warriors were killed or
drowned trying to reach their ships that, it is said, only twenty-
four ships of the three-hundred-strong fleet were needed to
carry the survivors away. Harold Godwinson had defeated the

great Harald Hardrada – veteran of campaigns as far afield as the Black Sea and North Africa – but this bloody battle would be eclipsed by the one the Son of Godwin would have to fight against the Normans, who were already preparing to sail to Hastings and the English coast. William the Conqueror was the great-great-grandson of the Viking Rollo, and the territory of Normandy carved out by these Norsemen was about to be enlarged.

11

The Final Conflict

It is harsh in the world, adultery everywhere – an axe age, a sword age – shields are sundered – a wind age, a wolf age, before the world plunges. ('The Prophecy of the Seeress', 45)

The Approach of Ragnarok

That's enough about the past, and the petty wars of princes in the world. Now it is time to talk about the future, and to contemplate the conflict that casts a shadow over every story of the Æsir, and every feat of every hero in the world. The final battle, the doom of the gods: Ragnarok.

Ragnarok is the terrible fate that awaits us all. It is as inescapable as the approach of night, and nothing about it will come as a surprise to Odin, who knows he cannot outrun this final confrontation with the giants and the monsters, and that everything built by the gods will be destroyed. But that doesn't mean that the Æsir won't be prepared. The Einherjar – the warriors chosen by the valkyries – have been gathered to Valhalla and to Frejya's realm of Folkvang since the first conflict in the world, and every day they fight and feast in preparation for their final battle. Only those who die heroically have a seat amongst the chosen ones. This is not a place for those who die in peaceful old age, or for warriors cut down as they flee the field. The gods will need the very bravest warriors to face an overwhelming onslaught in the darkness, and to make a last heroic stand.

As well as assembling the Einherjar, Odin has been gathering knowledge about the fate of the gods from every corner of the nine worlds, from the wisest of women and from the knowing dead, in an attempt to delay the victory of the giants and their monstrous allies. He's learned a great deal about what will take place, and almost nothing about how to change its course.

Odin knows that three cockerels will signal the approach of Ragnarok: the red rooster Fjalar will crow in the Gallows Wood of Jotunheim, whilst the herdsman of the giantess Angrboda sits on a mound and plays his harp, happy to receive this omen that the gods will fall. A second cockerel called Golden-Comb will crow to the gods and awaken the Einherjar in Valhalla, and a third rooster, the colour of red ash, will crow in the halls of Hel far beneath the earth and give fair warning to the dead. Garm will bark fiercely outside Gnipa Cavern, and soon Hel's guard-dog will be running free across the world.

As Ragnarok approaches, the bonds that tie people together will unravel, and the failings of the gods – their deceits and infidelities, their war-making and blood-shedding, and the death of shining Baldr – will be mirrored across the worlds. Mercy will be forgotten: brothers will become each other's killers and break all bonds of kinship for the sake of their own greed, and families will be torn apart by incest and betrayal. Nidhog will have a glut of corpses to tear at beneath the roots of Yggdrasil, as oath-breakers and murderers wade through dark waters. For three years in a row, Midgard will be convulsed by armed conflicts that spread throughout the world. It will be an age of axes and swords and shattered shields; an age of wind and wolves, before the world plunges into winter.

Fimbulvetr will be the name given to the winter that heralds the approach of Ragnarok, and it will be colder than anything in the memories of humankind. Snow will come from every direction, blown by biting winds, and the sun will turn black and have no power to warm the land. Three of these winters will come in succession, and there will be no summer between them to bring relief to people shivering and hungry in their homes.

Next, the wolf Skoll, who has been chasing Sol in her chariot since the beginning of the world, will catch up with his prey and swallow the sun. His brother Hatti will devour the moon, and the wolves will spatter the home of the gods with blood. The stars will disappear from the heavens, and the whole earth will tremble with such force that mountains will fall and trees will be uprooted from the ground. The dwarves will groan as they flee their homes amid the crumbling rocks, and even the great World-Tree will creak and bend towards the earth.

The convulsions of the world will cause all chains to break, and the monsters will run free. The wolf Fenrir will be released from the fetter Gleipnir – and after so many years of captivity, he will be mad for revenge. His cavernous mouth will gape so wide that his lower jaw drags along the ground, whilst his snout will reach to the heavens and blot out what little light is left. The wolf's brother, the Midgard Serpent, will uncoil itself from the fathomless depths, and when it does so the waters of the circling seas will no longer keep their place, and will flow over the land. As the Serpent moves towards the home of the gods, it will spit so much venom that a choking fog will float across the world.

The seething waters will also cause the ship Naglfar to slip its moorings and surge forward on the flood. Naglfar is a ship like no other – it is made solely from the toenails and fingernails of corpses, and those who are wise remember to trim the nails of the dead, so that Naglfar takes as long as possible to build. The hosts of Muspelheim will be gathered in this ship of nails, and steering the ship will be Loki himself, freed from his captivity and cursing the gods. Naglfar will sail from the East across the swollen seas towards Asgard, and an eagle will circle in its wake, shrieking as it waits to be fed on the rich blood of fallen gods.

Amidst the turmoil, the sky will split open and the sons of Muspell will ride through the breach – led by Surt himself, brandishing a sword which burns like a sun from the underworld, the curse of all living branches. Everything around him will be consumed by fire, and Surt will leave nothing but smouldering ashes in his wake. The sons of Muspell will storm the rainbow bridge into Asgard, and Bifrost will collapse into flames behind them, whilst the great World-Tree itself will start to smoulder. The cliffs will crack open, and troll-women will be running from the mountains: Hrym will lead the frost-giants as the forces of chaos cross the frozen rivers to the home of the gods. All of Jotunheim will be roaring, and nothing in the giants' path will be left alive.

Heimdall, watchman of the gods, has long since blown the Gjallarhorn to warn of the approaching hosts, and the gods will assemble in their sanctuary to take counsel before the battle. Odin himself will ride on a different path – to Mimir's sacred well – and will question his wise friend one final time about the fate that awaits them. 'Is there nothing to be done, no chance to change what's coming?' he will ask: but there is no escape from the inevitable, and there will be no last-minute turning of the tide. Now Odin places a golden helmet on his head, and prepares the Einherjar for war. Yggdrasil trembles, and there is not a being in the nine worlds who does not feel afraid.

The Final Battle

Vigridr is the name of the plain where the final battle will take place. It stretches for a hundred leagues in every direction, and the forces that will meet in that place are vast beyond measure. Eight hundred Einherjar spill from each of the five hundred and forty doors of Valhalla alone, but their numbers are dwarfed by the forces of chaos converging on the battle from all sides.

Odin stands at the front of the Einherjar, and his golden helmet shines. He wears a coat of polished mail, and carries the spear Gungnir aloft; and he will be the first to advance to meet his fate. The one-eyed god steps up to the wolf Fenrir, a creature he once fed with his own hand: fire flashes from the wolf's eyes in anticipation of his victory. Thor is powerless to help his father, as he is grappling with the Midgard Serpent. The strongest of the gods and the mighty measurer of worlds are well matched, and the plains of Vigridr tremble violently as they fight. Surt, the fire-giant, will pit himself against Freyr, and the struggle will be fierce before Freyr falls. The god of the fields is lacking his precious sword, given to Skirnir to coerce his giant wife, and he will never miss it more than now. Tyr will have his own problems: the Hel-hound Garm, most ferocious of his kind, will leap at the one-handed god, and try to rip his other limbs apart. Heimdall will seek out Loki in the tumult of battle – the two of them have unfinished business to address.

Amongst the slaughter on the blood-red fields, the gods fall one by one. Odin is swallowed by Fenrir's monstrous jaws, a fate he's seen coming many times, and Frigg's grief at Baldr is doubled by her husband's death. Thor will deal a killing blow to the Midgard Serpent, but the poison of the monster has taken its toll: the Son of Odin will take nine steps back from the serpent before he drops down dead. Tyr and Garm will give each other such severe wounds that both will die, and Heimdall and Loki will also die together, locked in the combat that they once began as seals on the shore. Freyr will be overcome by Surt, even as he extinguishes the giant's flames.

Carnage is everywhere, and chaos rules.

Fenrir howls to the darkening sky after defeating Odin, but the wolf does not have long to enjoy his victory. Vidar, son of Odin, will step forward to avenge his father. Vidar is wearing his famous iron-clad shoe, made at the start of time, and reinforced by leather offcuts from the heels and toes of all the shoes in the world. He places his foot in the gaping mouth of Fenrir, and braces himself against the wolf's upper jaw, ripping open the mouth of the ravager with one mighty thrust of his arm. The wolf dies, and Odin is avenged. But this will be small comfort to the gods. The forces of chaos have the field, and fire spreads across the world. The seas are boiling, and water rushes onto the land, drowning everything.

This is what the mighty prophetess or volva sees in her final fateful vision of the world: *The sun turning black, the land slipping into the sea, the bright stars turning away from the sky. Steam seething against the World-Tree; the high flames catching against heaven itself.*

The world sinks. And the world is reborn.

The volva sees a land rising from the waters. It is green with fresh grass: waterfalls plunge, and an eagle soars above, hunting fish in the mountains. Sol is dead, but her daughter escaped the wolf, and now resumes the sun's path across the sky; and the dawn is bright in the world. The plains of Idavoll where Asgard once stood are now a meadow, and some children of the gods have survived and make their way to this place: Vidar and Vali emerge blinking in the brilliant light, and soon Modi and Magni – sons of Thor – will arrive, carrying their father's famous hammer between them. Baldr the bright and his blind brother Hod will be free to walk the road back from the halls of Hel arm in arm, and Hœnir, the old companion of Odin, will join them and bring with him the knowledge of an older generation. The surviving gods will live in a shining hall that escaped the devastation – it is known as Gimle, and it is thatched with gold. They will sit together in the old places of assembly under the renewed sky, speaking of their mothers and their fathers, and recounting the deeds of those who are no more. They will remember the sacred lore, and they will not forget Fenrir or the Midgard Serpent in a hurry. Hœnir will perform the rites: he will carve wooden staves, and fate will be at work in the new world. In time they will spot the sunlight glinting off golden gaming-pieces lying in the grass – the same that the old gods once played with in their days of leisure, when the old world was new – and they will take up the game again.

And what of the men and women of the world? Two people also survived the destruction of Ragnarok by hiding high in the World-Tree. Their names are Lif and Lifthrasir, and they emerge to enjoy this new land where crops grow without sowing and where everything is fresh with dew. Their sons and daughters will repopulate this shining, verdant world, risen from the ashes of the old.

The aftermath of Ragnarok doesn't seem so bad. Yet as the volva's vision fades there's something troubling her sight: a shadow passing over the green fields. Nidhog, the dragon of death, is flying up from the hills as dark as a moonless night – and on his wings he carries corpses. The shadow passes on.

12

Survival and Interpretations

The Sources for Norse Myth

The myths retold in this book come from a range of sources, most of them written down in medieval Iceland. In the year 1000, Iceland adopted Christianity as its official religion, following a dramatic showdown at the annual national assembly, or Althing. Icelanders who had converted to the Christian religion almost came to blows with those who remained loyal to Odin, Freyr and Thor, and to avoid a descent into civil war, the decision about which religion to follow was given over to a man named Thorgeir Thorkelsson. Thorgeir held the position of lawspeaker at the assembly, and he was a powerful chieftain and a pagan priest: both sides agreed to accept his judgement. After a day and night sitting in contemplation beneath a cloak, Thorgeir emerged and told the assembled Icelanders that their future lay with Christianity, and that there must be one law and one religion for everyone: 'for if the law breaks down, so will the peace.' For the time being, pagans could still practise their religion in their own homes, eat horse-meat, and expose unwanted children, but these privileges would not last long; and if, after that, people continued to worship the old gods, they did so quietly. Thorgeir later threw his own idols – carvings of the Norse gods – into a waterfall near to his home, and since then it has been known as Godafoss: the waterfall of the gods.

With Christianity came the Church, with its rituals and riches, and its long tradition of book-writing. The first texts to be written in Iceland were intended for the use of the clergy and to spread the Christian message, but before long the Icelanders began to recognise the value of book-writing for recording different literary traditions. By the year 1200, Icelanders had started to write down the stories of their ancestors who settled the country and explored the North Atlantic, and they would also begin to record the myths and legends that were still circulating by word of mouth. The extraordinary literary culture that developed was unlike anything seen before or since: it not only gave the world the realist prose narratives known as the Sagas of Icelanders, but also intricate skaldic verse preserved from a much earlier time, colourful accounts of kings in Scandinavia, and the collection of mythological and legendary poems known as the Poetic Edda. Some of these poems had been passed down for generations, and some of them were reworked to express the changing world-view of medieval Icelanders: but together they speak of a collective memory of the Norse gods, even after centuries of Christian influence. *Voluspa*, 'The Prophecy of the Seeress' begins this collection of poems: it is delivered to Odin, and follows the whole sweep of mythical history, from the creation of the world to its destruction. 'Do you understand yet, or what?' is the seeress' provocative refrain (and of course, Odin *always* wants to learn more). *Havamal*, or 'Sayings of the High One', combines practical advice and medieval life-hacks with an account of Odin's sacrifice to gain knowledge of the runes.

Other poems exist in several versions, such as the story of Gudrun and her revenge on Atli, showing that Norse myths and legends were never set in stone, but changed as they spread across the world. There are also hints at how much has been lost along the way. As well as the poems of the Edda, other poems referencing the Norse gods were recorded in the sagas, and often attributed to named poets, or skalds, from the Viking Age who travelled to the halls of warrior kings and composed verse in praise of their exploits.

In medieval Iceland, the Age of Settlement, the audacity of those first pioneers and the poetic tradition they had passed down were a great source of pride for their descendants. Skaldic poetry in particular is a very complex form, full of obscure allusions to mythology. Even as the stories of the Norse gods began to fade from memory, traditional poetry relied on references to this vanishing world: to 'Sif's hair' or 'Freya's tears', meaning gold, to the 'storm-happy daughters of Ægir' for the waves, and 'Odin's lip-streams' in reference to poetry itself. Around the year 1220, an Icelander named Snorri Sturluson, an accomplished poet, politician and law-speaker, took it upon himself to record the poetic forms and the myths that lay behind them. His Prose Edda serves as a handbook to the mythology and as a manual for poets, and it is a masterful account of the traditions that he knew. Snorri is responsible for many of the stories that came down to us, and he is our most comprehensive source for information about the Norse cosmos and the gods. But he also turns the complex allusions in the poetry into something that's easier for a Christian audience to understand, reworks the narratives, and smooths out the edges of the myths.

Snorri's stories, written down in medieval Iceland, also help to make sense of what little evidence survives from the Viking

Age itself, when the Norse gods were still actively worshipped. As well as skaldic poems, many of which are ascribed to the Viking Age, we have brief references in runic inscriptions, figurines and amulets in precious metals, ship burials, carvings on stone and wood: all of these sources help us to reconstruct the complex world of Norse belief, and every year further artefacts are uncovered that add to our understanding of how the Norse gods were viewed by the people who worshipped them. Sometimes these finds are not easy to interpret, and hint at a world of active belief about which we know very little. Stone carvings in Norway and the British Isles are a particularly rich source for representations of Norse myth: episodes such as Thor's fishing trip and Sigurd's slaying of the dragon appear in several different forms, and they may have found a new place amongst the Christian mythology. Scenes from the Sigurd legend feature on the elaborately decorated portals of a stave church from Hylestad in Norway, whilst Loki bound in chains, Vidar stepping into the mouth of the wolf, and Thor's hooking of the Midgard Serpent are all represented on a tenth-century cross from Gosforth in Lincolnshire. This wasn't a Norse repurposing of a Christian monument, but a planned effort to bring the old stories and the new belief system together.

Rediscovery of the Myth

In Iceland, the Norse myths and legends were never completely forgotten, but as far as the rest of Europe was concerned, the sources were rediscovered in the seventeenth century by intrepid antiquarians and collectors who 'rescued' manuscripts from the backwater of Iceland and brought them to cities like Copenhagen for safekeeping. Some of them – including the Codex

Regius manuscript of the Poetic Edda – were returned after Iceland gained its independence. In Denmark and Sweden in particular, there was a thirst for material dealing with the early history of the nation state, and Icelanders who were able to read and translate the sources with ease were in as much demand as the manuscripts themselves. Here was a literature that raised the cultural status of the Scandinavian nations amongst their European neighbours, and it was often forgotten that the tradition belonged to Iceland – if it belonged to anyone.

When the Icelandic sources were translated into Latin, and later into languages such as German and English, they reached an audience outside Scandinavia, and came to the attention of poets and artists in England looking for new sources of inspiration. Some of these early translations were quite far off the mark, and it was suggested that the ancient poems were originally written in runes. This was a body of stories very different to the Classical tradition, and Norse poetry was often described using words such as 'raw' and 'barbarous', even though the rules for its poetic composition could be as rigorous as anything in Latin or Greek.

In the English tradition, Thomas Gray was particularly important in bringing Norse myth to a wide audience through two Norse odes that captured the reading public's imagination. 'The Fatal Sisters' is based on the Old Norse poem *Darraraljod* from *Njals saga*, with its gruesome imagery of valkyries weaving out the outcome of a battle using intestines and severed heads strung on a loom. Gray also wrote 'The Descent of Odin', about the god's visit to the underworld to try to learn about Baldr's death; and Gray's several imitators took their cue from his dramatic imagery which touched on the sublime. The artist and Romantic poet William Blake illustrated Gray's Norse odes, and the late eighteenth century saw a craze for the Gothic imagery of valkyries, fatal runes, and warriors feasting in Valhalla.

For the Victorians, the enterprising Vikings were more appealing than the Norse gods: these overseas adventurers fitted well with the imperialist vision of Britain at the time. But though the excesses of Norse myth may have been somewhat alien to mainstream sensibilities, the legendary material continued to have its Victorian admirers, including William Morris – who joined a long roll-call of Europeans who travelled to the exotic destination of Iceland and became inspired by its dramatic landscape and its saga sites. With the help of an Icelandic scholar, Morris translated several sagas, including *The Story of the Volsungs and the Niblungs*. His long poem *Sigurd the Volsung* was a sympathetic treatment of the Sigurd legend which portrays an egalitarian society in touch with nature: an escape from the industrialised, closeted and class-ridden Britain of the time. Morris used archaic language, and his treatments of the legend must have sounded old-fashioned even to the Victorian ear, but along with the first full translations of the Poetic Edda, they brought Norse myths and legends to a wide public.

Norse Myth and Nationalism

In Iceland, Norse myth and legend was part of a living literary heritage, and the material was naturally of great importance elsewhere in Scandinavia: after all, it gave a glimpse into the cultural world of the medieval Scandinavians, and was part of a shared Norse heritage preserved in Iceland. It's also no surprise that the rediscovery of the Icelandic repository of myth and legend helped to fuel romantic nationalist movements in Denmark and Sweden: in Norway, ideas about a glorious Norse past and the freedom-loving northerners helped make the case for independence from its more dominant neighbours.

But for some, the myth preserved in Iceland came to have a wider and far more problematic meaning: it was the expression not only of the medieval Norse imagination, but of a wider Germanic culture that had elsewhere been lost or actively suppressed. Such pan-Germanic thinking gained particular traction in Germany: the *völkisch* movement that arose in the nineteenth century sought to revive lost Germanic traditions, and alongside a fondness for neo-pagan mysticism, it fostered the idea of an Aryan race bound by common origins, culture, and physical attributes. This became more than just misplaced nostalgia for a golden age depicted in heroic legend, but played into the belief that the Germanic *Volk* could rise again and reclaim their heroic legacy: nationalist mystics such as Guido von List even offered access to the occult world of the Germanic ancestors, apparently hidden in the esoteric lore of the Poetic Edda.

A nineteenth-century reinterpretation of heroic legend that played a supporting role in this rise of Germanic nationalism was Wagner's epic 'Ring Cycle', based on the Sigurd legend and its medieval German retelling, the *Nibelungenlied*. The four operas in the Ring Cycle, *Das Rheingold*, *Die Walküre*, *Siegfried*, and *Götterdämmerung*, were performed across Europe, where they met with critical acclaim and introduced the world to the images of valkyries with winged helmets, a deformed race of dwarves, and the 'noble' death-drive of the hero. Wagner's opera – one of the most enduring reinterpretations of the legendary cycle – is high art and not a statement of political beliefs, but there's no denying that his retelling glorifies racial purity and the pursuit of power, and that it served its role in stoking the fires of resurgent nationalism and murderous anti-Semitism in 1930s Germany.

Norse myth became a tool of cultural warfare in Nazi Germany, twisted to fit a fascist creed. Ignoring the complex nature of the sources and the flaws and contradictions of the gods themselves, the far-right in Germany and elsewhere (including Scandinavia) could draw on what appealed: the valorising of violence, an emphasis on male heroics, and a glorification of individual strength. The great Norse explorers were not only enterprising humans: they were perfect specimens of a northern master race, and their gods were gods of war and self-interest. Runes were co-opted as the insignia of the SS and other German military units, chiselled Vikings featured on propaganda posters, and the study of Norse sources was combined with pseudo-science to 'prove' the superiority of the Nordic race and the supposed degeneration of other peoples, most notably the Jews. The myth of a Germanic golden age and claims of Nordic superiority became key components in the Nazis' repulsive ideology.

In England, a different legacy was being set in motion: a response in part to what was happening in Germany. J. R. R. Tolkien, a professor of medieval literature, wrote in his letters of his 'burning private grudge ... against that ruddy little ignoramus Adolf Hitler ... [for] ruining, perverting, misapplying, and making accursed, that noble northern spirit ...', a heroic ethos that he'd first been introduced to through the utopian translations of Morris. Thankfully, the perversions of the Nazis would not be quite as enduring as Tolkien feared, and though Norse myth still holds a depressing (if predictable) fascination for neo-Nazis today, it is Tolkien's own legacy that has had the greater impact on the way Norse myth has been received in mainstream culture, and the associations it holds in the popular imagination. Tolkien combined his intimate knowledge of Norse mythology and heroic legend with elements of other medieval literatures and a large measure of his own invention to build a new mythology with echoes of the old.

Though Tolkien wouldn't have viewed it as such, nationalism played its role here too: he thought it a great shame that England hadn't preserved any more than fragments of its own myths, and his stories set in Middle Earth (echoing Norse Midgard) are in part an attempt to make up for this loss. But Tolkien also understood the complexity of his sources and the flaws of the gods, and he certainly did not admire the death-drive of the heroic world. In the case of the cursed ring from the Sigurd legend – the coveted symbol of power in Wagner's opera – Tolkien chose a very different approach. His epic *The Lord of the Rings* is all about resisting and destroying the seduction of the ring and the mad lust for power; his heroes are the homely hobbits, trying to make sense of an alien heroic world; and his main character Frodo is named after the legendary Norse king Frodi whose success was to bring peace. Tolkien's stories of dwarves and dragons, magic runes and legendary swords established a new genre of medieval fantasy, and his Middle Earth has inspired many people to an interest in the myths.

Modern Myths and Scandinavian Survivals

In Scandinavia, the Norse Myths have a particular cultural importance – and nowhere more so than in Iceland, where the tradition was preserved. Traditional names such as Guðrún and Freyja, Þorstein and Sigurður remain popular, and the poems and sagas are still widely read in the original Old Norse. In the various Germanic languages, the days of the week preserve the names of the Norse gods, including the English variants Tiw for Tyr, Woden for Odin, Thunor for Thor, and Frige for Frigg. Place-names across Scandinavia speak of the past worship of Norse gods: Odense in Denmark, Freysnes in Iceland, Torshavn (or Thor's Harbour) in the Faroe Islands: the insignia of the municipality of Torshavn has an image of Mjolnir being held aloft as a nod to this inheritance. Some more recent place-names also continue this legacy: an area in Reykjavik is known as the Neighbourhood of the Gods, as all the streets are named after the Æsir and Vanir; and a new development near to Viking Dublin is called Odin's Way. When a volcanic island appeared off the southern coast of Iceland in the 1960s, this fiery eruption from the underworld was named Surtsey (Surt's Island) after the giant with the flaming sword. In Sweden a ship used for transporting nuclear waste was called Sigyn, after Loki's wife who collects the poison dripping into his face.

These clever references to the myths help keep the stories current and alive, but there has also been a movement to revive Old Norse traditions themselves: in Norway, it is possible to take a college course that teaches traditional Viking skills, whilst temples allowing worship of the neo-pagan Ásatrú faith have been built in Denmark and Iceland. Often an interest in reviving old beliefs is a statement of identity and heritage (particularly in Scandinavia), but neo-paganism is still sometimes aligned with white nationalism, much to the annoyance of those whose interest in practising a pre-Christian faith is not exclusionary or political. The fact that the far-right Norwegian terrorist who massacred teenagers at a youth-camp describes himself as an Odinist and named his handgun after Mjolnir is one tragic example of how Norse heritage is always in danger of being yoked to violent white supremacist ideas, and why racist misappropriations must always be countered and resisted.

Myths have developed around Norse and Viking heritage itself: in Shetland, the annual fire-festival Up Helly Aa, with its burning of a replica longship, is a Victorian tradition which pays homage to the real Norse history of these islands; whilst a loyal group of supporters still maintain the authenticity of the Kensington rune-stone – an inscription that came to light in Minnesota in 1898, and which was soon recognised as a forgery by scholars. In an area of the United States settled by many Scandinavian immigrants, and with a football team called the Minnesota Vikings, the desire for a Norse foundation myth is strong. So far, the only clear evidence of a Norse settlement in North America is L'Anse aux Meadows in Newfoundland, Canada, though this may change in the future.

Other responses to Norse myth continue to play with this heritage in creative ways: Viking heavy metal music, which originated in Scandinavia, is full of references to the Norse gods and to Ragnarok; and there are healthy re-enactment scenes in many countries, as well as festivals and markets which see the myths performed as living history, and meticulously reconstructed Viking ships which recreate the voyages of the Viking Age. There are many ways that the Norse past can be engaged with, but for most of us, the experience comes through the many ways the myths have been retold in popular culture.

The twenty-first century has seen many high-profile literary engagements with Norse myth, from Neil Gaiman's much-loved novel *American Gods* and his lively reworking of the myths themselves, to A.S. Byatt's personal take on the stories in her *Ragnarok*. Norse myth has been introduced to a generation of children (and adult readers) through Kevin Crossley-Holland's masterful retellings, and encoded in young adult fiction by Melvin Burgess in his dystopian *Bloodtide*. The extremely successful *A Song of Ice and Fire* novels by George R. R. Martin and the TV series *Game of Thrones* owe a great deal to Tolkien's plundering of medieval literature, and the books incorporate elements of Norse mythology and culture, including the threat of chaotic forces advancing on the settled world from a land beyond the wall. Another recent series to draw heavily on Norse myth is the History channel's *Vikings*, whose main characters are the legendary Ragnar Lodbrok and his sons. Stories of the gods and snatches of poetry are retold throughout this popular series, which emphasises the rich and complex culture of the Vikings as well as their legendary raids.

The gods themselves are the inspiration for Marvel's Thor franchise, which repackaged the myths for a twentieth-century American audience. In this comic-book vision of the Norse cosmos, the gods live on the planetoid of Asgard which is connected to Earth via an interstellar bridge called Bifrost. The Mighty Thor is sent to Earth to learn humility, and becomes a superhero and champion of humankind, joining the Avengers and battling his brother, the master-villain Loki. This re-imagining of Thor and the Norse cosmos has reached an even greater audience on screen. An ever-expanding range of video games incorporate elements of Norse myth, including the immersive *Skyrim* and the hugely popular *World of Warcraft*. Norse myth has been reinterpreted in Japanese manga and in Korean online role-playing games: from high-art to high-school anime, the Norse cosmos and its colourful characters continue to influence many aspects of our cultural world.

For most recent appropriators of Norse myth, it's the richly textured stories that appeal, rather than that 'northern spirit' so admired by Tolkien and so distorted by those who politicise Norse heritage. But perhaps the enduring popularity of Norse myth in the twenty-first century also has something to do with the fact that in the flawed gods and their race towards annihilation we can see more than a little something of ourselves.

FURTHER READING

Translations of Primary Sources

Egil's Saga, trans. Bernard Scudder with Introduction and Notes by Svanhildur Óskarsdóttir (Penguin, 2005)

The Elder Edda: Myths, Gods and Heroes from the Viking World, trans. Andy Orchard (Penguin, 2011)

The Poetic Edda, trans. Carolyne Larrington (Oxford World Classics, 2014)

The Saga of Grettir the Strong, trans. Bernard Scudder with Introduction and Notes by Ornolfur Thorsson (Penguin, 2005)

The Saga of King Heidrek the Wise, trans. Christopher Tolkien (Thomas Nelson & Sons, 1960)

The Saga of the Volsungs, trans. Jesse L. Byock (Penguin, 1990)

The Saga of the Volsungs: With the Saga of Ragnar Lothbrok, trans. Jackson Crawford (Hackett, 2017)

Saxo Grammaticus, *Gesta Danorum: The History of the Danes*, ed. Karsten Friis-Jensen, trans. Peter Fisher (OUP, 2015)

Snorri Sturluson, *Edda*, trans. Anthony Faulkes (Everyman, 1987)

Snorri Sturluson, *The Prose Edda: Norse Mythology*, trans. Jesse L. Byock (Penguin, 2006)

Snorri Sturlusson, *Heimskringla*, trans. Alison Finlay and Anthony Faulkes, 3 volumes (Viking Society for Northern Research, 2011–16)

The Viking Age: A Reader, ed. Angus A. Somerville and R. Andrew McDonald (University of Toronto Press, 2010)

The Vinland Sagas, trans. Keneva Kunz with Introduction and Notes by Gisli Sigurdsson (Penguin, 2008)

Introductions to Norse Mythology and Old Norse Literature

Clunies Ross, Margaret, *A History of Old Norse Poetry and Poetics* (D. S. Brewer, 2005)

Crossley-Holland, Kevin, *The Penguin Book of Norse Myths: Gods of the Vikings* (Penguin, 1980)

Larrington, Carolyne, *The Norse Myths: A Guide to the Gods and Heroes* (Thames & Hudson, 2017)

Lindow, John, *Norse Mythology: A Guide to the Gods, Heroes, Rituals and Beliefs* (OUP, 2001)

McTurk, Rory, ed., *A Companion to Old Norse-Icelandic Literature and Culture* (Blackwell, 2005)

O'Donoghue, Heather, *From Asgard to Valhalla: The Remarkable History of the Norse Myths* (I. B. Tauris, 2007)

O'Donoghue, Heather, *Old Norse-Icelandic Literature: A Short Introduction* (Blackwell, 2004)

Orchard, Andy, *Cassell's Dictionary of Norse Myth & Legend* (Cassell, 1997)

Simek, Rudolf, *Dictionary of Northern Mythology* (D. S. Brewer, 1993)

Turville-Petre, E. O. G., *Myth and Religion of the North: The Religion of Ancient Scandinavia* (Greenwood Press, 1975)

ACKNOWLEDGEMENTS

I am grateful to Anne Schoerner, both for her interpretation of the Norse cosmos and for her assistance throughout the writing process.

PICTURE CREDITS

All pictures are courtesy of Wikimedia/Public Domain except as follows, in order of appearance: 2 – Anne Schoerner: 4 – Creative Commons/Arnold Mikkelsen/National Museum of Denmark: 7 – Ivy Close Images/Alamy Stock Photo: 8 – Heritage Image Partnership Ltd/Alamy Stock Photo: 10 – The History Collection/Alamy Stock Photo: 14 – Creative Commons/Colin Smith: 15 – Creative Commons/Micha L. Rieser: 17 – Everett Collection Inc/Alamy Stock Photo

INDEX OF NAMES AND PLACES